A NEED TO TESTIFY

A Need to Testify

*Portraits of
Lauro de Bosis,
Ruth Draper,
Gaetano Salvemini,
Ignazio Silone
and an Essay
on Biography*

*Foreword by
Ted Morgan*

IRIS ORIGO

Books & Co. / Helen Marx Books
New York

First published in 1984 by Harcourt Brace Jovanovich

© 2001 by Books & Co./Helen Marx Books
Foreword © 2001 by Ted Morgan

LCCN 2001-131231
ISBN 1-885586-51-5

Design and composition by
Wilsted & Taylor Publishing Services

Printed in Canada by Transcontinental Printing

in memory of

EDOARDO RUFFINI

who also felt

'a need to testify'

CONTENTS

ILLUSTRATIONS

FOREWORD

Iris Origo's long attachment to Italy was the happy byproduct of a series of accidents, including the accident of marriage. Her American father, William Bayard Cutting, left Harvard in his senior year to take the job, offered via family connections, of private secretary to the U.S. ambassador in London, Joseph Choate. This was in 1901. Thanks to the embassy social life, young Cutting was introduced to the upper strata of London society, and met the exquisite and overbred Lady Sybil Cuffe, whom he quickly married.

But a lethal cloud floated over the young couple. William Cutting was tubercular, and spent the remaining years of his life moving from sanatorium to sanatorium in vain pursuit of healthy lungs. Thus it was that Margaret Cutting (later to bloom into Iris) was born in August 1902 in the village of Birdlip, the site of a sanatorium in the Cotswolds.

When William Cutting died in 1910, Sybil moved to Florence with her eight-year-old daughter, who spent the rest of her life in Tuscany. Her father, looking askance at parochialism, had stipulated on his deathbed that she should grow up "somewhere where she does not belong."

Iris' mother bought the Villa Medici, a majestic pile in the hills of Fiesole, above Florence, with long rows of cypresses framing the formal gardens. Her neighbor Bernard Berenson, who presided over the villa I Tatti (which Iris found unremarkable), helped Sybil choose the right furniture among the antiquarians of Florence. Sybil eventually married Berenson's secretary, Geoffrey Scott, an erratically brilliant writer on architectural topics, but the marriage did not last. Geoffrey fell prey to dark moods, and might today be diagnosed as manic-depressive. After the divorce, Sybil in 1927 married the critic Percy Lubbock, author of *The Craft of Fiction*.

One can picture a certain splendid isolation during the 14 years that Iris spent in the landscaped cloister of the Villa Medici, surrounded by nannies, maids, chauffeurs, and gardeners. Her only escape was to Florence, an hour on the rickety tram, to plunge into studies of medieval history. In 1924 she married Antonio Origo, a *marchese* of the minor Italian nobility, with good manners and looks to match. Perhaps she was deeply in love, or perhaps she also wanted to get away from her increasingly fussy mother and move into smaller quarters.

But Antonio Origo, although he had gone into banking to please his father, was one of those Italian aristocrats in whom there co-exists a reformist bent with nostalgia for the feudal fragmentation of the Italian city-state. Remnants of the feudal order still prevailed, such as the *mezzadria* share-cropping system, which had remained largely unchanged since the 13th century. Under the *mezzadria*, the landowner built and repaired the farmhouse, supplied half the capital to cultivate the land and buy the livestock, and shared in the harvest.

Such was the landed life, a throwback to medieval times except for updated agricultural machinery, to which the Marchese Origo aspired. He bought 7000 acres in the hardscrabble Val d'Orcia near Siena and proceeded to transform it into a fertile valley that sprouted olive trees, wheat fields, and vineyards, with 57 farms and a population of 600, over which Antonio and Iris Origo benevolently ruled.

As it happened, the time of their marriage and the purchase of the property of La Foce, with its large and terraced house facing the rust colored hills known as the *Crete Senesi*, and its surrounding farms, was also the time that Mussolini came to power. In its early years, the fascist regime, hoping to curtail the flight from the countryside to the cities, assisted landowners with loans for irrigation projects to reclaim wasteland. Iris Origo saw the positive side of the Duce, and it was only later that she became aware of the graft, the bluff, the mismanagement, and the lawless brutality.

As co-manager of the estate, she saw herself as responsible for the care and well-being of 57 tenant farmers and their large families. In an area with 80 per cent illiteracy, she built a school. At a time when the peasants still relied on witch doctors to cure them, she opened a clinic.

But managing the estate was not enough. Having made this corner of Tuscany her home, she needed a larger life —not geographically, but intellectually. With her deep knowledge of Italian history, she began to explore Florentine archives, drawn at first to medieval figures with whom she may have felt a kinship, thanks to her peculiarly anachronistic life at La Foce.

She felt the urge to write, and since she was not a certified historian, she took up the genre of biography, to which anyone may aspire. Among her subjects was Cola De Rienzo, the 14th century man of the people who challenged the Roman nobility and was eventually killed by the mob he had once courted. She also wrote about the Merchant of Prato, Francesco Datini, a 16th century venture capitalist with offices as far as Avignon. His papers, consisting of thousands of letters and hundreds of ledgers, were found in 1870 in a recess under the stairs of his house, which had remained in the family. After 300 years of neglect, they were scalloped with mice nibbles but still legible. Each page of the ledgers was stamped with the company logo, "In the Name of God and Profit."

Finding the Datini papers in the Florence archives, the Marchesa Origo hit upon one of the seldom admitted truths of biography: it is not a special affinity with his subject that guides the author, so much as stumbling on marvelous material. She had another stroke of luck when she advanced to the 19th century and wrote of Byron's "Last Attachment" to Countess Teresa Gucciolo, the married daughter of Count Ruggiero Gamba. She went to see Teresa's nephew, old Count Gamba, and asked about the letters from Byron. Count Gamba told a servant, "Fetch Countess Teresa's chest," and out tumbled the bundles of letters, tied with ribbons. For a biographer, a moment like that is as thrilling as an explorer's discovery of a landscape feature that will someday bear his name.

Iris Origo became known as "the best writer in English about things Italian." Her books were thorough in their research and elegant in their prose. Her theory of biography was untainted by postmodern concerns with "the nature of the text." "The biographer's real business," she wrote, "is to bring the dead to life." In other words, biography is the literary form of resuscitation. Though bound by conventions of reticence and taste, she grumbled about those writers devoted to smoothing out and touching up. "Warts and all" was not her style, but neither was cosmetic embellishment. Above all, she believed, the biographer must neither suppress nor invent. He (or she) must go where the evidence takes him (or her). Iris shared Virginia Woolf's distrust of Lytton Strachey. Woolf wrote of Strachey's *Elizabeth and Essex*: "Very little was known—he was urged to invent; yet something was known—his invention was checked. There is a sense of vacancy and effort."

The warnings of Origo and Woolf against invention in biography seem more pertinent than ever today. Edmund Morris, a disciple of Strachey, provides a recent example of extensive invention in his book on Ronald Reagan. Iris Origo added that Strachey in *Eminent Victorians* had committed the cardinal biographical sin of condescending to his subjects; in looking through them instead of at them. Again his disciple took the cue and condescended to Reagan.

The only book in which Iris Origo did not write about the dead (except for her autobiography, *Images and Shadows*) was this one, *A Need to Testify*. It was her last book, published in 1984 (she died in 1988), and it is in the nature of a memoir about four friends who shared an anti-fascist commitment. The four were not only her friends, they knew one another. Their paths had crossed. They had a common goal, the end of the Mussolini regime, though they went at it in different ways. Two of them, Lauro de Bosis and Ruth Draper, were lovers. The other two, Salvemini and Silone, lived in exile, as Origo herself did, though her exile was voluntary. Iris Origo loved and admired all four, though she herself, as has been previously noted, came late to militant anti-fascism. Immersed in her latifundium and her research, she did not pay strict attention to the day-to-day actions of the Mussolini government.

Only when the war brought chaos to her quiet valley did she really come to grips with political reality. Generous as always, she took in 20 refugee children who fled the bombing of Genoa. When British airmen were imprisoned in an old castle on her property, she helped them escape. By June 1944, all the major belligerents seemed to have invaded the Val d'Orcia. The Germans were going in one direction, the Americans in another, and in the hills the partisan bands were forming. Everyone wanted food and the partisans wanted money. On occasion, the Nazis were knocking at one door while the partisans were marching by on the other side of the house. It was pandemonium, but they survived. And it may have been the memory of those times, with Mussolini's endgame and the fall of fascism, that prompted her in her eighties to look back on those who had fought the regime from the start.

Lauro de Bosis, whom Iris Origo calls Icarus, was a poet who on October 3, 1931, flew over Rome and dropped anti-fascist leaflets. His plane was presumed to have then crashed into the Mediterranean, for it was never found. This footnote to history might seem futile and a bit silly, but Iris Origo gives it meaning by filling in the context. In Rome, Lauro de Bosis had formed an anti-fascist cell that circulated pamphlets. The pamphlets were printed in the home of his 66-year-old mother, who was arrested and jailed. A deal was struck, under which she would be let off if she wrote a humiliating letter to Mussolini. And so, Lauro de Bosis' political opposition was compounded with the shame and anger at what his mother had been forced to do, which inspired him to act.

He fled to France to avoid arrest, learned to pilot a plane, and bought one in Germany. Two German pilots who served as his instructors brought the plane to Marseilles. He told them he was flying to Nice and back, a mere hop, and so they did not fill up the extra gas tank. Nor did they ask what was in the packages they helped him load onto the plane. Just before takeoff, they told him to be sure and pump the gas from the wing tank to the main tank in a timely way.

Lauro de Bosis flew for five hours at 12,000 feet over Corsica to Rome, dropped to 1000 feet and began throwing out leaflets. It must have been a glorious moment, circling the Eternal City, so close that he could see nannies pushing baby carriages down the Spanish steps, and the balcony on the Piazza Venezia from which the Duce harangued the crowds. He then flew out to sea, ran out of gas, and crashed.

One comes away from Iris Origo's account with the sense that his neglect was deliberate. Why else would he have prepared a letter entitled "The Story of My Death," to be distributed to newspapers if he did not return to Marseilles? In this letter he wrote, "if I had come back alive it would have been only a beau geste . . . In this way, it is much more . . ." By backing up his gesture with his life, he made it memorable.

Lauro de Bosis was 30 when he performed his self-immolation. Three years earlier, when he was in America lecturing, he met the 43-year-old Ruth Draper and pheromones flared. He took her to Italy, where they were happy together, as in a parenthesis, outside their respective activities. The pattern of Lauro's passion combined the carnal and the maternal, for while he addressed Ruth as *Caramadre* in his letters, their recipient said she had never known such ardent love-making. When he flew to Rome, Ruth Draper waited in Paris, already mourning him, for she had sensed that he wanted to die.

Iris Origo's portrait of Ruth Draper is the most fully realized of the four in this book. The other three seem a bit perfunctory, like the work of those between-the-wars society portraitists, in which a hand or an arm, or a diamond necklace, is sketched in rather than fully painted—Boldini and Laszlo come to mind. But with Ruth Draper, the world-famous monologuist of the twenties and thirties, Iris Origo was able to solve what to me has always been like the Riddle of the Sphinx—how did she do it? How did this matronly woman, without props or costume, without any other actor on stage, mesmerize her audiences?

She had about 30 monologues, and in giving us detailed descriptions, Iris Origo makes the "Company of Characters" come to life. Just to give one rather over-simple example, in "Railway Accident on the Western Plains," she is cutting an imaginary pie to send out to the men on the snow plough, and before giving the imaginary pie slices to an imaginary boy, she picks from the imaginary plate some imaginary crumbs with her fingers. One begins to understand why Shaw and Henry James were among her admirers. They knew that art is in the details.

It was Ruth Draper's grand passion that brought her into the anti-fascist circle. As a tribute to her beloved Lauro, she funded a chair of Italian literature at Harvard, which was filled for a time by the next figure in Iris Origo's quartet, Gaetano Salvemini, who, born in 1873, straddled two centuries. A teacher and historian, he became the leading anti-Mussolini figure in Florence, to the point that his university classes were broken up by blackshirts.

Arrested in 1925, Salvemini spent a few weeks in jail but was able to slip away to France before he came to trial. The rest of his life was spent in exile, as the self-described "Wandering Jew of anti-fascism." When he taught at Harvard, the Italian consul in Boston tried to get him fired. Salvemini was an Italian Mr. Chips, beloved of his students, but his life was relatively uneventful when compared with those of his bookmates. He produced no important work and performed no dramatic acts. There is however one incident worth noting as an illustration of the way politics tears up families, like those American families in the Civil War where one brother fought with the blues and another with the greys. Salvemini married a French woman, Fernande Luchaire, and helped raise her two children, a boy and a girl. He left his family behind when he came to the United States. His stepson, Jean Luchaire, became during World War II a prominent collaborator with the Germans, the editor of a pro-Nazi and anti-Semitic newspaper, *Les Nouveaux Temps*. It was tragic for Salvemini when Jean Luchaire was shot on Feb. 22, 1947.

Of Iris Origo's four friends, Ignazio Silone was the only one who experienced and repudiated both Fascism and Communism. As a child of the Abruzzi, he knew the unalterable misery of southern Italian village life. An earthquake killed his mother and two of his brothers. Another brother was beaten to death in a fascist prison by blackshirts. Silone had reasons both personal and political to loathe the Mussolini regime. From Socialism he transited to Communism, and traveled to Spain and Russia as an underground organizer. But in the late 20s, when he saw how Stalin had framed Trotsky and sent him into exile, he realized that Soviet Communism was merely another form of dictatorship, with a Utopian façade. He left the party, but could not return to Italy, so he moved to Switzerland and began to write.

His real name was Secondo Tranquilli, but he used a pen name in order to protect what remained of his family from fascist reprisal. For the theme of his first novel, *Fontamara*, was the exploitation of the peasants in a southern Italian village, and their attempts to obtain justice, brutally crushed by the fascists.

Fontamara was a worldwide sensation, published in 27 countries, but suppressed in Silone's native land. Oddly enough, his old friend Salvemini did not like it, writing Silone that his Fontamara peasants were cartoonish and stupid. Silone replied that they displayed the mental and moral deterioration among all classes that was a byproduct of fascism. Iris Origo greatly admired *Fontamara* and its successor, *Bread and Wine*, for she too knew something about Italian peasant life. She and Silone became friends, and he often came to visit at La Foce after the war, when he was welcomed back to Italy. She admired also his independence of mind—he was not a man to be swayed by doctrine and orthodoxy, not a man of "isms." Indeed, he told her, "a man must always be ready to change sides." He had seen through Stalin as he had seen through Mussolini—all their positions were tactical, their only principle being the urge to stay in power.

The need to testify, which Iris Origo invokes in her title, led these three Italian men and one American woman to make various sacrifices to achieve the aim of a non-fascist Italy. It led one of them to give up his life, another to give up the appointments and university titles that Italians are so fond of, and the third to write powerful novels that shed all party lines; it led Ruth Draper to adopt the views of her lover and keep his memory alive. These were people who did not necessarily do the smart thing, or the convenient thing, but they were not self-serving and they had great heart.

Ted Morgan

Preface

The lives of the four people whose portraits are included in this volume were pervaded by an irresistible, a desperate need to tell—in so far as they were able—the truth that is the crux of all human experience; the need to understand, and then to tell what we have understood. This has been the motive underlying all sincere biography. 'What the devil am I?', cried Carlyle in his old age. 'After all these eighty years, I know nothing at all about it!' Yet this same man, as I have related in my essay on Biography, devoted the last years of his maturity to trying to find out what it was.

The link that bound together the subjects of my four portraits was of a somewhat different nature. They are linked to each other not only by their unswerving devotion to a common cause—the defeat of fascism—but by the conviction that their main purpose should be to bear witness to the reasons for this faith. All of them (except perhaps Ruth Draper) shared this motive. Silone, during his long years of exile in Switzerland, after his deliberate defection from the Communist Party, expressed it most clearly: 'If my literary work has any value,' he wrote, 'it consists just in this: at a certain moment, writing has meant for me an absolute need to bear witness.' His novels, his essays about dictatorship—first published abroad and, only after Mussolini's fall, in Italy—all have this purpose. He felt bound to explain to the young what had happened to him (however painful) so that they might be warned not to follow a similar path. What, he asked, should these young people be told? 'Simply the truth.'

Salvemini felt a similar compulsion. During his years of exile in England and America, when friends urged him to devote all his energies to his great gifts as an historian, he felt that it would be a betrayal to steal a single hour from his political activities, while in Italy his friends were fighting fascism at the risk of their lives. All his life this conflict tormented him—on the one hand, his inner conviction that his true métier was to be a historian; on the other, the feeling that he must continue abroad the activities from which he was cut off at home.

Lauro de Bosis, who came from a very different, aristocratic, background, at first had hoped that Mussolini might provide some solutions to the problems of post-war Italy. He was soon disillusioned, and joined the fight against fascism by publishing and distributing clandestine leaflets. His final appeal to his countrymen, to recognise and resist the evil in their midst, cost him his life. Through her love for him, Ruth Draper was drawn into the circle of anti-fascists, and after his death she continued to support those who worked for Italy's freedom.

For those of my readers to whom the history of Italy between the wars is unfamiliar, I should explain that Mussolini came to power from a position of comparative obscurity in 1922. Since the end of the war in 1918, law and order in Italy had increasingly broken down. Giolitti, the prime minister, could not muster enough support to deal effectively with the situation and, while the politicians wrangled, the nationalist poet and war hero, d'Annunzio, led a group of adventurers to occupy Fiume, in Croatia, which had been ceded to Yugoslavia at the end of the war. This blatant defiance of the rule of law by a private army encouraged rival political factions to adopt strong-arm methods, and savage clashes between bands of armed thugs ('squadristi') terrorised the country. Many moderates supported Mussolini because they believed he was the only man who could crush the Communists and control fascist extremism; indeed he at first appeared to be both alarmed and astonished by the violence of the fascist 'squadristi,' and when the socialist deputy, Giacomo Matteotti, was murdered by them as late as 1924, he denounced the crime with apparent sincerity. Soon after this, however, the authority of the totalitarian dictatorship began to tighten its grip; opposition to the State became a crime, all anti-fascists were branded un-Italian, and there was even a new word to describe a new political objective: 'smatteottizzare,' meaning 'to eradicate Matteotti-ism.' Mussolini's opponents had to make the choice between prison (and possibly execution or murder), or exile.

I have the advantage—if it is one—of still being able to steep myself in that climate almost too vividly. For all four of these people were also close personal friends. Ruth Draper had been a family friend since my childhood, and it was in her house in New York that I first met Lauro de Bosis. On the day on which he was dropping his leaflets over Rome, I listened on a clandestine radio to the report that an 'unidentified plane' had flown over Rome and been shot down by the fascist airforce. (This was not true, but it was only too easy to imagine Ruth's despair as, in frantic anxiety, she waited for the same news in Paris.) It was Ruth whom I continued to see after Lauro's death, witnessing her courageous efforts, for the rest of her life, to fulfil Lauro's last request to her—to carry on her work and be happy ('Stai allegra').

As for my friendship with Salvemini, it began when I was only eight years old, after the tragedy of the Messina earthquake, when he was still hoping that one at least of his children had survived the disaster, and it continued during the years of his American exile, when I brought him news of the friends whom he so sorely missed, and about whom he was so desperately anxious. I saw his correspondence with Silone, a friend of later years, knew about the friendship that united them, and heard Silone's commemoration of Salvemini in the Teatro Eliseo of Rome, in which he declared his belief (which the future has confirmed) that the socialist doctrines expressed by a man as disinterested as Salvemini would never die out.

It was in 1944, while living and collaborating with the partisans of the Val d'Orcia, that I brought my diary of the war years to an end with this reflection: 'The Fascist and German menace is receding. The day will come when at last the boys will return to their ploughs, and the dusty clay hills of the Val d'Orcia will again "blossom like a rose." Death and destruction have visited us, but now—there is hope in the air.'

Those who bore witness to the truth during those years of oppression had triumphantly achieved their purpose.

⌒

I am deeply grateful to many friends for help in writing this book and particularly to Charis de Bosis Cortese, Lauro de Bosis' sister; to Neilla Warren and William Carter; to Signora Ada Rossi of the Archivio Salvemini and Dott. Sergio Bucchi and to Darina Silone for permissions to quote that have made this book possible.

A Need to Testify

I
Biography
True and False

We are like the relict garments of a Saint:
the same and not the same: for the careful
Monks patch it and patch it: till there's
not a thread of the original garment left,
and still they show it for St Antony's shirt.
—KEATS, Letter to George and
Georgiana Keats, 17–29 September 1819

One day in his eightieth year, Carlyle told William Alling-ham that earlier that morning, as he was drying his old bones after his bath, he had been stirred into a kind of frenzy about the mystery of his own existence. 'What the devil then am I?' he exclaimed. 'After all these eighty years I know nothing at all about it!'[1] And some years earlier he had noted in his Journal: 'The world has no business with my life. The world will never know my life, if it should write and read a hundred biographies of me. The main facts of it are known, and are likely to be known, to myself alone of all created men.'[2]

These words are disconcerting reading, because instinc-tively we feel them to be true. We know little about other people, and it is gradually borne in on us how little more we know about ourselves.

What fraction of even that part of us of which we are aware, do we succeed in communicating to others? Novelists have been much concerned with this private person— the man who remains before the glass when the bedroom door is shut, and picks his nose, alone. The novelist has his own licence. But you, my friends, you—if all your letters (even your love-letters and that unpleasant note to Uncle George about his Will) and all your portraits were handed over to a biographer, and he could hear you talk to your children and friends, how much would he be able to perceive of what is yourself, to *you*?

How can we then presume to write biographies? I have quoted Carlyle's own words, 'The world will never know my life'—but very soon after writing them, he demonstrated the second virtue essential to a great biographer: enthusiasm. I say the second virtue, because there is one that is even more important, and equally recognisable in all its possessors: veracity—the capacity, or at least the attempt, to produce an unvarnished picture. Let us consider this quality first.

According to Geoffrey Scott, in one of his brilliant introductions to the *Malahide Papers*—that inexhaustible fountain of information about both Boswell and Dr Johnson— Boswell had a very clear image in his mind. He thought that 'a "life" should be like a flawless print struck off from the engraved plate that is bitten in our memory.' It should be 'a *duplication* of an image in the mind.' Scott comments that this was 'an aim beyond human reach,' but adds, 'The knowledge that his arrow pointed to that impossible mark was Boswell's source of confidence. Other biographers might *forestall* his book, that they could rival it he never, in his most sombre moments, conceived. Those others did not even know that biography is impossible.'[3]

Boswell was constantly aware of 'that fixed and remote aim.' On 19 October 1775, he drove into Edinburgh in a chaise with his uncle, Commissioner Cochrane, and perhaps intended to set down a portrait of him. But in his diary he noted, 'The great lines of character may be set down. But I doubt much if it be possible to preserve in words the peculiar features of mind which distinguish individuals as certainly as the features of different countenances . . . I cannot portray Commissioner Cochrane as he exists in my mind.'[4]

Yet perhaps it is precisely this—with Dr Johnson, and to a lesser extent, with Rousseau and Voltaire—that Boswell did achieve. 'In how small a speck does the painter give life to an Eye!' he observed. He stored the authentic word, the strange gesture, 'in the Flemish picture which I give of my friend.'[5]

This is why Boswell as a biographer remains unrivalled, and all others who, like him, desire in widely different ways to tell the truth or 'a speck' of it—whether with the broad splashes of the brush of a Carlyle or the restrained pencil of a Quentin Bell—remain, in a sense, his pupils. They all try 'to depict Commissioner Cochrane as he exists in my mind'—and when they are most successful, they portray not only an individual, but a whole society. How can such works be resisted?

It is not necessary that the subject of such Lives should be giants themselves. The first instance that comes to mind is Dr Johnson's own *Life of William Savage,* whom he admitted to have been not only a failure and a scoundrel, but a very commonplace man. He firmly denied that a biography need necessarily hold exciting adventures or events. The whole of human life was what interested him. 'A blade of grass,' he said to Mrs Thrale, 'is always a blade of grass. Men and women are *my* subject of inquiry.'[6] He wished 'to pass slightly over those performances and incidents which produce vulgar greatness, to lead the thoughts into domestic privacies, and to display the minutest details of daily life.'[7]

These precepts he fully carried out in his *Lives of the Poets* in which his passion for candour and truth appear on every page. 'The value of every story,' he said to Boswell, 'depends upon its being true. If it is false, it is a picture of nothing.'[8] The only kind of biography, he declared, worth writing was that written by those who had 'eaten and drunk and lived in social intercourse' with their subject. Failing personal acquaintance, he considered that a biographer must be able to talk to the friends of his characters—even though he acknowledged that these reports were often unsatisfactory. And he related that when, in his youth, he had wanted to write a Life of Dryden and had applied to two old men, Sweeney and Cibber, Sweeney's information was no more than this, 'that at Will's coffee-house Dryden's chair was settled by the fire in winter and in the summer was placed on the balcony and that he called the two places his winter and summer seat.'[9]

So long as Boswell wrote about Dr Johnson, he had of course precisely the advantages that Dr Johnson required: he was writing about a world he knew, and talking to a man he could see every day. But let us see what happened to him when he found himself in an entirely new world—one which he had always longed to enter, that of Rousseau and Voltaire. Geoffrey Scott, the first editor of the *Malahide Papers*, comments: 'No man could be less French than Boswell, and the distance between Auchinleck and Ferney is immeasurable.' Yet, up to a point, Boswell succeeded here, too—within his limitations. 'To all that is within his grasp, the visitor is minutely and skilfully attentive; of what lies beyond, he is heroically unaware. Insensibility clothes and shelters him like a magic garment.'[10]

Yet in their way Boswell's accounts of these visits, at the age of twenty-four, are as convincing—and as entertaining—as anything he wrote. 'They are equally remarkable,' Scott writes, 'for the dramatic portraits of the two great figures, for the contrasted backgrounds of Voltaire's court at Ferney and Rousseau's "wild retreat," and for the unfailing comedy of Boswell's own character as he enters the lists . . .'[11]

At Moutiers, where Rousseau was rewriting the laws of Corsica, Boswell subjected him to a veritable five days' siege. 'To prepare myself for the great interview I walked out alone . . . The fresh, healthful air and the romantic Prospect around me gave me a vigorous and solemn tone.' Then he went to Rousseau's house, having been warned that the visit must be short. 'I talked to him with undisguised confidence. I gave him a written sketch of my life. He studied it and he loved me with all my failings . . . He is to correspond with me when I leave. When I took leave of him, he embraced me with an elegant cordiality and said *"Souvenez-vous toujours de moi. Il y a des points où nos âmes sont liées."*'[12]

Then came Boswell's visit to Ferney. This—partly no doubt because of Voltaire's weakness for any oddity in his guests—seemed to Boswell an even greater success. Dressed in green and silver, and later in flowered velvet, he persuaded Voltaire's niece Denise ('Since M. de Voltaire, in opposition to our Sun, rises in the evening') to let him spend a whole night in the house, 'even upon two chairs in the bedchamber of your maid.'

At first all went well:

> The Magician appeared a little before dinner . . . I placed myself by him. I touched the keys in unison with his Imagination. I wish you had heard the Music. He was all Brilliance. He gave me continued flashes of Wit . . . When he talked our language he was animated with the Soul of a Briton. He had bold flights.

He had humour, he had an extravagance . . . He swore bloodily as was the fashion when he was in England . . . At last we came upon Religion. Then did he rage. The Company went to supper. M. de Voltaire and I remained in the drawing-room with a great Bible before us, and if ever two men disputed with vehemence, he was one indeed and I another. For a certain portion of time there was a fair opposition between Voltaire and Boswell.

But then what happened? 'His [Voltaire's] great frame trembled beneath him. He cried, "O, I am very sick; my head turns round," and he let himself gently fall upon an easy chair. He recovered. I resumed our Conversation . . .'[13]

The next day Boswell wished to make his farewells, but enough is enough, and Voltaire had now fully appreciated the peculiarities of his recent guest. He sent him instead a delightful letter of farewell in which courtesy only thinly veils his determination to bring their conversations to an end.

My distempers and my bad eyes do not permit me to answer with that celerity and exactness that my duty and my heart require. You seem solicitous about that pretty thing called Soul . . . I do protest you, I know nothing of it: nor whether it is, nor what is it, nor what it shall be. Young scholars and priests know all that perfectly, for my part I am but a very ignorant fellow . . . Let it be what it will, I assure you that my soul has a great regard for your own . . .'[14]

'Temple,' wrote Boswell, in sending his friend this account, 'is this not an interesting scene? Would a journey from Scotland to Ferney have been too much to obtain such a remarkable interview?'[15]

Then Boswell returned to the British Isles and here, in a

setting that was his own, devoted himself entirely again to Dr Johnson. And it is now that, once again, the *Malahide Papers* enable us to follow each step of Boswell's method. How did he procure all the details he needed? One conversation may throw some light. On 21 March 1773, Johnson was 'expatiating on the different requisites of conversational excellence' and, wrote Boswell, 'while he was talking triumphantly, I was fixed in admiration and said to Mrs Thrale, "O, for shorthand to take this down!" "You'll carry it all in your head," (said she); "a long head is as good as shorthand."' Five years later, however, in April 1778, Boswell wrote in the *Life*, 'I this evening boasted that, although I did not write what is called stenography, I had a method of my own of writing half-words . . . so as to keep the substance of the discourse which I had heard so much in view that I could give it very completely after I had set it down.'[16]

Nevertheless any picture of Boswell always sitting in a corner with a notebook putting down all Johnson's remarks, would be a falsification. Two things rendered it impossible: 18th-century good manners (because, said Mrs Thrale, 'wherever it was adopted, all confidence would soon be exiled from society') and Boswell's own natural conviviality. Boswell certainly *listened* intently, as Dr Burney has described, to 'the smallest sound from that voice to which he paid such exclusive, though merited, homage . . . His eyes goggled with eagerness; he leant his ear almost on the shoulder of the Doctor, and his mouth dropt open to catch every syllable of what might be uttered.'[17] But he only wrote it down afterwards: the Notes among the *Malahide Papers* (written on small, torn scraps of paper) confirm this.

Moreover we must remember Boswell's pride in steering the talk, and bringing Dr Johnson out. How hard he worked to achieve this, his *Life* assuredly shows. He was so overwhelmed by the mass of his material that he would sit in London cafés with tears pouring down his cheeks—yet he went on gathering still more. He arranged interviews, he planned encounters, he set a stage, in the hope that Dr Johnson would consider these happenings to have occurred without any preparation. He even questioned Johnson so persistently that at least once—it is Boswell himself who records it—the great man turned upon him. 'You have but two subjects,' he boomed, 'yourself and me. I am sick of both.'[18] The words have the unmistakable ring of truth—almost photographic truth. Harold Nicolson has compared biography before and after Boswell to the difference between a series of studio portraits and a film. Boswell, he says, invented actuality. 'He was able, by sheer constructive force, to project his detached photographs, with such certainty and speed that the effect produced is that of motion and of life.'[19] It is thus that we come to feel that we, too, have entered into Dr Johnson's intimacy. We become aware of his arrogance and his humility, of his intolerance and his kindness, of his hours of despair—and also 'of his brown stockings, his disordered buttons, of the dust settling on his wig as he bangs two folios together, the way he cuts his nails, of his servants and his cat.'[20]

So there the great doctor stands before us.

> The *djinn* in the Arabian tale [I am again quoting Geoffrey Scott, who more than anyone was qualified to express these opinions] once liberated from the confining vessel, forms and expands his astonishing shape, until at last the whole chamber is full, and men look at his vast and unpredicted motions. So, since 1791, when the world first opened Boswell's book, the figure of Johnson is enlarged, has filtered through the air and yet is still palpable, has achieved not mere pale immortality but an increase of demonic life . . .

No biography was ever so free from generality: there is no attempt to explain the secret, to forestall the shape that will form itself upon the air; scarcely any propounding or summing; all is particular . . . In his [Boswell's] letters and diaries we overhear the groans of authorship; but we are witnessing the contrition of an idler or the perplexities of a scholar, never the doubts, still less the despairs, of an artist . . . He will run half over the city to verify a date. But once at work, never does he question how to give life to this or that element of humour or poignancy . . . Of his power to give life to that vast pile he never hints one doubt.[21]

In the *Malahide Papers*, Boswell's method can be traced in every phase, 'from his first jottings of Johnson's talk to his last touches upon the revised draft of this life.' But when, in 1791—seven years after the Doctor's death—the great *Life* was at last given to the public,

Boswell found no exultant vision of his achieved task . . . The zest and eager humanity which permeates it, he had experienced long ago . . . it seldom lit his own darkened mind . . . Unlike Gibbon on the shore of Lausanne, he indulged no luxury of retrospective regret at the closing of the long panorama. Very simply, he turned to his accounts and learned that the clear produce of the first edition had brought in £1555.12.2 which, after paying his debts, left him £608.

Then he allowed himself, at last, a hospitable gesture, giving 'a dinner, a kind of feast' to a few faithful old friends—his adviser and supporter Malone, his printer, his brother and three of his children.

The toasts were, 'Church and King,' the pious memory of Dr Johnson and 'Health and long life to the Life of Dr Johnson.'[22]

A wish which has surely come true.

And now I must turn to what I have called the second virtue of a good biographer—enthusiasm. Its most celebrated possessor Carlyle was the very man whom, in the first paragraph of this essay, I quote as saying that the real truth about a man can never be known, and who yet dedicated the best years of his maturity to defeating this impossibility. 'Had I but two potatoes in the world,' he wrote, 'and one true idea, I should hold it my duty to part with one potato for pen and ink, and live upon the other until I had got it written.'

His enthusiasm was not restricted to a character of his own choice; it was based on a conviction of the value of human life itself, of the actual process of living. 'How inexpressibly comfortable,' he wrote, 'to know one's fellow-creature, to see into him, understand his going forth, decipher the whole heart of his mystery, nay, not only to see with him but even out of him, to view the world altogether as he views it.' But this work was done in a state of constant ferment, a burning blaze of effort and 'bewildered wrestlings,' of which his family received their full share. Jane once wrote grimly about how Miss Martineau used to talk about writing being such a *pleasure* to her, 'In this house we should as soon dream of calling the bearing of children "such a pleasure."'

His unflagging enthusiasm not only caused Carlyle to spend nearly six years in writing about Cromwell and thirteen more about Frederick the Great, but to express a great many things that for a long time had needed saying.

> The English biographer [he wrote], has long felt that if in writing a man's biography anything appears that could possibly offend any man, he had written wrong. The plain consequence was that, properly speaking,

no biography whatever could be produced. No man lives without jostling and being jostled; in all ways, he has to elbow himself through the world, giving and receiving offence. The very oyster, we presume, comes into collision with other oysters . . . To paint life is to paint these things. It can be presented fitly, with dignity and measure, but above all it can be represented. The tragedy of Hamlet, the part of Hamlet omitted by particular request! . . . Once taken up, the rule before all rules is to *do* it, not to do a ghost of it . . . having, we may say, the fear of God before our eyes, and no other fear whatever . . . To produce not things, but ghosts of things, can never be the duty of man.[23]

No bilious attacks, no dyspepsia, no lack of money, no infuriating disturbances from a neighbour's cocks, could hold him back, though they could thoroughly upset him.[24] 'We move up and down the house,' wrote Jane. 'A sort of domestic wandering Jew he is become.'[25]

In vain did Jane build for him, in despair—during his temporary absence—a 'sound-proof room' at the top of the house.[26] When he returned, he found that the stove would not burn, and that the skylight let in a new sort of noises—river hootings, church bells and railway whistles. He discovered that a neighbour kept bantams, and on the other side a young lady played the piano. And Cheyne Row itself had become a busy street: organ-grinders had to be bribed to go away, street vendors shouted their wares and on summer nights there were fireworks at Crome. 'The sound-proof room,' wrote Jane, 'is the noisiest room in the house. Mr C. is very out of sorts.'[27]

But Carlyle's gloom had deeper roots: he could not come to terms with his subject. When the first idea of writing about Cromwell had taken shape in his mind, in September 1840, he wrote: 'It is the one use of living for me.'[28] But during the course of the winter he became appalled by the dreariness of his material, 'of a dullness to threaten lockjaw.'[29] 'Yet I say to myself, "a great man does lie buried under this waste continent of cinders . . . Cans't thou not unbury him?"'[30] In December he was writing, 'I don't know where to begin. I have not yet got through the veil, got into genuine sympathy with the thing . . . Yet I am loth to quit it. In our whole English history there is surely nothing as great.'[31] Two years later, he was still in the same quagmire. 'Oliver . . . is an *impossibility*.' But still he persevered. On the last day of 1843 he wrote to his mother, 'I must get in upon it, and drive it before me.'[32] But in the following May he was admitting to himself, 'My heart was never *rightly* in it, my conscience rather was what drove me on. Yet Oliver Cromwell is an actually pious, praying, God-fearing, Bible-reading man, and struggles in the high place of the world before God and man, to do what he finds written in his Bible—an astonishing spectacle . . .'[33]

It was only in August 1845, that at last the work was finished. 'I have at last finished Oliver . . . He is ended, thrums* and all.'[34]

Froude comments, 'It was not a whitewashing. It was the recovery of a true human figure of immense consequence . . . Cromwell stands actually before us . . . We shall love or hate the man himself, not a shadow or caricature any more.'[35]

For several years Carlyle abstained from biography, devoting his energies instead to Cassandra-like warnings evoked in him by the European revolutions of 1848. But in 1851, when he was fifty-six, a new plan began to form in his mind: he would write a book about Frederick the Great, the man who had made Prussia what it was. Frederick was not

---

*Thrums are short ends of thread—a weaver's term. Carlyle must have meant wrapping up all the odds and ends in his book.

really akin to Carlyle, as Cromwell had been. Frederick had no 'piety,' no fierce convictions; his was a different age. But he was a man of great stature, and Carlyle at once plunged into research about him, even forming a plan of going to Germany with Jane, to tread in Frederick's footsteps.[36] Fortunately the plan was given up and Carlyle went to Germany alone, and, on his return, at once set to work. Thus began the 'dark years of Frederick.' 'The problem is to burn away the immense dung-heap of the eighteenth century with its ghastly cant, foul black sensualities, cruelties and inanity now fully petrified, to destroy and extinguish all that, having got to know it . . . after which the perennial portion, pretty much Friedrich and Voltaire, may remain conspicuous and capable of being delineated.'[37]

After six years of toil the first two volumes were finished. He brought to life Frederick and Voltaire and Frederick's family and generals and court. But still Carlyle could not rest. In 1858 he set forth on a second tour to Germany to Frederick's battlefields, mastering the details of every battle and returning home worn out, to find that the first two volumes had met with great success, 'much babbled of by newspapers.' It was not until 1864 that the whole book was at last finished, 'a long stiff journey.' 'It nearly killed me, it and my poor Jane's dreadful illness.' He was left with 'a kind of solemn thankfulness . . . I had done with it for ever.'[38]

What remains to us now, after this long struggle? Not quite what Carlyle himself had in mind. He saw himself, first of all, as a searcher for truth, and then as a moralist and a prophet, whose stern duty it was to deliver a great message to the world. It was nothing less than the riddle of the Universe with which he wrestled. 'The idea of the Universe,' he wrote, 'struggles dark and painful in me which I must deliver out of me or be wretched.' But later generations have seen a different picture. To Henry James, Carlyle seemed far less a moralist than an unconscious artist; according to Leslie Stephen, he was a painter who depicted 'those little islands of light in the midst of the darkening gloom of the past in which you distinguish the actions of some old drama actually alive and moving.' To Logan Pearsall-Smith, he was 'the Rembrandt of English prose.' 'From his great canvasses, as from Rembrandt's, strange old faces look at us with all the sadness and mystery of existence in their disdainful, weary eyes.' The taste for him, as Pearsall-Smith remarked, is 'a special taste,' but those who have acquired it will return to it. They gaze at 'the volumes of this outrageous old Enchanter, which they know they are fated to read again.'[39]

One last outstanding example of Carlyle's passion for setting down the truth must also be given: his decision to hand over to his closest friend James Froude the most detailed information about his and Jane's married life, so that, if Froude thought fit, the whole story could be told. Subsequently misgivings overtook him: on one day he would forbid Froude ever to repeat what he had told him the day before. But he did provide him with all the material—and when, after Carlyle's death, Froude did make use of it in a brilliant but not impartial biography, a hornet's nest was stirred up, dividing all of literary London into two camps. But Carlyle had once again, in his own manner, borne witness to the truth.

I have dwelled so long on Carlyle's struggles and achievements—which are both on the scale of 'a sick Giant'—because I know no other writer who has approached biography with such a mixture of persistent enthusiasm and despair. But now I must go back to more general observations, and to an earlier phase of English biography.

∽

Three insidious temptations assail a biographer: to suppress, to invent, and to sit in judgement—and of these the earliest and most tempting is suppression. In what it is convenient to call the Middle Ages, this was rendered inevitable by the purpose which biography was intended to fulfill—to draw a noble example. The medieval view of history was that of a drama enacted within an established pattern—God's pattern for mankind. Bede, writing in 755, insisted that we must say 'good things of good men' and 'evil ones of evil persons,' and subsequent chroniclers followed his lead. The lives of men who came nearest to conforming with God's pattern were related as an example to other, lesser men, and consequently these chroniclers were mostly concerned with the lives of saints, while others were about rulers and leaders rather more than life-size. The emphasis was on the saint's virtues or the prince's exploits. All that was unedifying was omitted.

Moreover in many early chroniclers we become conscious of another kind of suppression, caused merely by incomplete knowledge. There is, for instance, the chronicle of Asser, Bishop of Sherborne, who wrote in the 9th century a life of King Alfred, in whose household he had been a monk. It is, as far as we know, accurate regarding the life of the king's household (though we are not sure about the cakes), but its account of the King as his country's defender against the invading Danes was gathered by hearsay and in some points can be proved inaccurate.

In the 12th century another monk, Eadmer, wrote a life of Saint Anselm which had similar weaknesses. He stressed the monastic aspect, even attributing to the saint the inconvenient faculty of being able to see through the monastery walls and thus discover what his monks were doing, but of Saint Anselm the statesman and pilgrim he tells us practically nothing.[40]

It is not until Tudor England that a real change takes place. Harold Nicolson, in writing about the two most celebrated English biographies of the 16th century—William

Roper's *Life of Sir Thomas More*, and George Cavendish's *Life of Cardinal Wolsey*—has described it well. The biographer's emphasis, he says, has shifted: these biographers are primarily interested in human beings as individuals. They care less about what their subjects do, than about who they are.

William Roper's life of his father-in-law, Thomas More, does precisely what Dr Johnson recommended later on. He leads his reader 'into domestic privacies' and displays 'the minutest details of daily life.' His biography has the defects of his own limitations: a less clever man than his father-in-law, he tells us nothing about Erasmus, Holbein or More's *Utopia*; he has a strong Catholic bias, and he is sometimes inaccurate; he does not explain how More was able to reconcile his conscience with his position as Henry VIII's Chancellor. But he is a most devoted son-in-law and secretary, and his recollections—vivid, humorous and entirely convincing—take us into the very heart of More's family life. Here is his description of Sir Thomas More's daughter's last attempt to receive her father's farewell blessing:

> When Sir Thomas More came from Westminster to the Tower again, his daughter, desirous to see her father . . . and also to have his final blessing . . . and without consideration or care for herself, hastily ran to him openly, in the sight of them all . . . took him about the neck and kissed him . . . And whereas he ever was used before, at his departure from his wife and children, whom he tenderly loved, to have them bring him to his boat and bid them farewell, then would he suffer none forth of the gate to go with him, but pulled the wicket after him, and shut them all from him. Thus after four days he was committed to the Tower.[41]

The other great biography of the 16th century, George Cavendish's *Life of Cardinal Wolsey*,[42] is in a different vein. The writer was the Cardinal's 'gentleman-usher,' who was present at the most important scenes in his master's life, and he describes them very vividly. We see the great Cardinal riding forth in all his scarlet panoply, attended by 'such a number of black velvet coats as hath not been seen with an ambassador.' We watch his power grow 'until it cast a shadow over the throne itself'; we see his arrogance and ostentation, his craving for money and for power.

We are shown the innumerable members of the Cardinal's household, including those in his 'private kitchen' (he had three), with 'a master cook, who went daily in damask, satin or velvet, with a chain of gold about his neck'; his choir of 'twelve singing children' and 'sixteen singing men,' with a 'Gospeller' and a 'Pisteller' (readers of the Gospel and the Epistle), his doctors and chaplains, his clerks and his footmen, his apothecary, his armourer and five minstrels. In all about 500 persons.[43]

We see the growth of the King's infatuation with Anne Boleyn, his 'pernicious and inordinate carnal love.' We see the Court held in Black Friars, where two Cardinals sat as judges, when the King and Queen Katharine were brought before them, 'like common persons,' and she knelt at the King's feet, to utter her plea for mercy. 'Sir, now that you intend to put me from you, I take God and all the world to witness that I have been to you a true, humble and obedient wife, ever comfortable to your will and pleasure.' We hear the King putting up his defence: 'All such issue males as I have received from the Queen have died immediately after they were born ... [and this] drove me at last to consider the state of the realm and the danger it stood from lack of issue made to succeed me.'[44]

We see the Cardinal being arrested for high treason in

Cawood Castle by the Earl of Northumberland, 'with a very faint and soft voice' . . . We see 'a crowd of three thousand persons' running after the Cardinal through the town, crying 'God save Your Grace!'[45]

And what this faithful servant thought about all these happenings, he set down, after his master's death, in the Epilogue to his book. 'Who likes to read and consider, with an impartial eye, this history, may behold the wondrous mutability of vain honours; the brittle assurance of abundance; the uncertainty of dignities; the flattering of feigned friends; and the fickle trust of worldly princes . . . O madness! foolish desire! O fond hope!'

A new sort of biography has begun. Yet it is not until 1662 that we find an English writer, Thomas Fuller, daring to state in so many words that a biography should also aim at what he calls 'lawful delight.' In his introduction to his *Worthies*, he admits that this is the *fourth* of his purposes: 'First, to gain some glory to God. Secondly, to preserve from the manoeuvres of the Devil. Thirdly to present examples to the living.' And only fourthly, 'To entertain the reader with delight.'

Certainly, we are now upon new ground, and it has become difficult to agree with Harold Nicolson's pronouncement that 'the seventeenth century, to the student of English biography, is a great disappointment.' Nicolson defends his assertion by saying that 'the seventeenth century grafted upon our healthy native stock a further element extraneous to pure biography.'[46] He deplores the importation, by English exiles in France, of French character-sketches, such as those composed by Mlle de Montpensier's guests in her salon—vivid, subtle and entertaining— but he admits that those composed in England were more often drawn from older models: imitations of Tacitus or Theophrastus or especially of Suetonius and Plutarch. Dryden, indeed, affirmed that he admired Plutarch precisely because he had dared to show his heroes in undress. 'You may behold,' he said, 'Scipio and Laelius gathering cockle-shells on the shore, Augustus playing at bounding-stones, and Agesilaus riding on a hobby-horse among his children. The pageantry of life is taken away: you see the poor reasonable animal as naked as ever nature made him; are acquainted with his passions and his follies, and find the demi-god, a man.'[47]

Here, surely, is the beginning of modern biography. Who else was writing it in the 17th century? John Aubrey, of course, but also Izaak Walton. It is true that there are still traces of an earlier age in Walton's *Lives*, and that they lead, as with the old chroniclers, to the danger of suppression. The virtues which Walton admired were piety, earnestness, charity, humility, and he endowed all his subjects with them, whether they were John Donne, Sir Henry Wotton, George Herbert or a country parson called Mr Hooker. He took as his text, 'These were honorable men in their generation,'[48] and he ignored any such inconvenient traits as Donne's tortured sensuality or Wotton's worldliness. But his transparent sincerity and his tranquil style—a moonlight landscape—have a perennial value. He describes how, shortly before his death, Donne caused to be drawn a figure of Christ, not lying on a Cross, but on 'an Anchor—the emblem of hope.'[49] He tells how George Herbert presented *The Temple* 'to my dear brother Ferrer, who said, "there is in it the picture of a divine soul on every page ... as would enrich the world with pleasure and piety."'[50] He tells how the same poet, on the day before his death, 'rose suddenly from his bed, called for one of his instruments, and said:

My God, my God,
Music shall find Thee
And every string
Shall have his attribute to sing.'[51]

To all his characters he attributed, in life, the 'grave be-haviour' which he called 'a divine charm,' and he prayed that his death might resemble theirs.

And then there was John Aubrey. In the *Introduction to the Minutes of Brief Lives*, Oliver Lawson Dick says: 'Not long after Aubrey's death, a wise man warned us against treating books like members of the nobility: that is, against learning their titles and bragging afterwards of acquaintance with them.'[52] In so far as this has also been Aubrey's fate, Dick attributes it to the fact that Aubrey's love of life 'was so intense, his curiosity so promiscuous and so insatiable, that he proved quite incapable of completing any work he undertook.' And that this was true is acknowledged by Aubrey himself, who suggested that after his death there might be 'some Ingenious and publick-spirited young man to polish and compleat what I have delivered rough hewn.' Completed, his *Lives* have never been, but Aubrey's delight in his pursuit gives life to every page. He undertook it to oblige a friend, but (in his own words) 'did it playingly . . . It is a pretty thing and I am glad you put me onto it.' 'I fancy myself closely discoursing with you,' he writes—and indeed we can still hear his voice, and see what he saw.

Here are the members of his University: Isaac Barrow, 'pale as the candle he studied by' who said 'in the agonie of death, "I have seen the Glories of the world."' And William Harvey, discoverer of the circulation of the blood, who 'kept a pretty wench to wayte on him, which I guess he made use of for warmeth-sake, as King David did.' Here is Sir John Birkenhead, who was 'exceedingly bold, confident, witty, not very grateful to his benefactors, would lye damnably . . . great gogglie eyes, not of sweet aspect.' There is Francis Bacon, who 'had a delicate lively hazel Eie; Dr Harvey told me it was like the Eie of a viper.'

Here too are the great ladies of his day. First among them, the Countess of Warwick, who 'needed neither borrowed Shades nor reflective Lights to set her off, being personally great in all naturall Endowments and accomplishments of Soul and Body.' And Venetia Digby ... 'a most beautiful and desirable creature ... The colour of her Cheekes was just that of the Damaske rose, which is neither too hot nor too pale.'

And then come the poets—John Milton, whose 'harmonicall and ingenious Soul did lodge in a beautiful and well-proportioned body,' and Sir Philip Sidney, Knight, 'whose fame will never dye while Poetrie lives . . . The most accomplished Cavalier of his time . . . not only of an excellent Witt, but extremely beautifull.' And to rival him, 'Mr William Shakespeare.' 'His father was a Butcher and I have been told ... that when he was a boy he exercised his father's trade, but when he killed a Calfe, he would do it in a high style and make a Speech ... This William, being inclined naturally to Poetry and acting, came to London, I guess about eighteen, and was an Actor at one of the Playhouses and did act exceedingly well ... He began early to make essays at Dramatique Poetry, which at that time was very low: and his Playes took well. He was a handsome, well-shap't man, very good company and of a very readie and pleasant smooth witt . . . His comedies will remain with us as long as the English tongue is understood, for that he handles *mores hominum*.'

This is a book very easy to open, and very difficult to close.

Very soon after John Aubrey's death, at the beginning of the 18th century, he had a successor, Roger North. 'I fancy myself,' North wrote, 'as a picture-drawer, aiming to give the same picture to a spectator as I have of the thing itself.' He wrote biographies of his three brothers—Francis North, a successful lawyer, Sir Dudley North, a merchant-adventurer, and finally Dr John North, Master of Trinity —ugly and effeminate, and so easily frightened that on a moonlit night he imagined that a ghost was standing before him in a white sheet, only to discover that it was his own towel. All this is very much in Aubrey's tradition and takes us (since North's books, though written earlier, were not published until the 1740s) onto the doorstep of Dr Johnson.

About him and Boswell we have already said enough— or never enough, but as much as this essay can hold. Instead we must turn over yet another page, to the beginning of the 19th century, when a reaction had set in. Biography was then accused of not being 'instructive' but merely 'the instrument of an impertinent curiosity.' The earnestness of what was to become Victorian biography had begun. All unedifying or inconvenient facts, once more, were to be suppressed, in case they might damage either the subject of a biography, or its author. 'Too long and too idolatrous!' was the comment of Leslie Stephen on one of the great Victorian Lives in three volumes. 'The two fat volumes,' wrote Lytton Strachey, 'with which it is our custom to commemorate the dead ... as familiar as the *cortège* of the undertaker.'[53] In the eyes of the supporters of the Evangelical movement every word in a book had to be improving. Mudie's circulating library and W. H. Smith's chain of bookshops were founded to meet this demand. Indeed towards the end of the 19th century an Evangelical bishop used his influence with W. H. Smith to condemn every work by Thomas Hardy and it transpired in a trial that the telephone code message 'W. H. Smith' meant 'The police are coming —display only decent books in your window.'[54]

An outstanding example of suppression appears in what is nevertheless one of the great biographies of the 19th century: Mrs Gaskell's life of Charlotte Brontë. Mrs Gaskell knew precisely what she was doing. 'I weighed every line,' she wrote, 'with my whole power and heart, so that every line should go to its great purpose of making her known and valued as one who had gone through such a terrible life with a brave and faithful heart.'

In order, however, to achieve this admirable purpose, she did not hesitate to omit whatever revealed the banked-down fires in Charlotte's nature which burst into flame when she fell in love with the head of her school in Brussels, Constantin Heger—a Catholic and a married man. Without such passion we should not have had *Villette* or *Jane Eyre*. But four of Charlotte's letters to M. Heger, though Mrs Gaskell undoubtedly read them, were deliberately omitted, and never does she suggest that Heger was anything more to Charlotte than a kind and stimulating teacher. However, in the last few years, no less than four detailed, accurate and humane accounts of the Brontë sisters and of Branwell have been written by Winifred Gerin, who quotes in detail all that Mrs Gaskell had suppressed. Miss Gerin not only visited the school where Charlotte watched the sufferings and deaths of her elder sisters Mary and Elizabeth, but she studied in detail Charlotte's early writings, as the key to her later masterpieces. She saw the various schools and private houses where they were employed as governesses or tutors. ('What! love the governess, my dear!' was the spontaneous exclamation of one employer). She lived for many months in Brussels and became well acquainted with the characters of both Monsieur and Madame Heger. And above all she spent no less than ten years in Haworth, to become familiar with 'the tremendous skies and illimitable moors' that to Charlotte, Emily and Anne spelled joy and freedom. One can ask no more of a biographer than this—and indeed Miss Gerin has produced four most remarkable books.

Yet, nearly half a century after the publication of her book, Mrs Gaskell wrote to a friend: 'I did so long to tell the truth, and I believe *now* that I hit as near to the truth as anyone *could*.'[55] And the strange thing is that, even now that we are aware of her suppressions and inaccuracies, we still feel that it *was* the truth that Mrs Gaskell was seeking. 'All biography is, in effect,' says Leon Edel 'a re-projection into words of material re-assembled through the mind of the historian or the biographer.'[56] Here Mrs Gaskell, 'laying bare the facts as she had understood them,' was the informing mind.

A painful instance of suppression—for now it is a writer who is blaming himself—appears in a series of poems written by Thomas Hardy after his wife's death. The poems are loaded with guilt, which is accounted for only after one has learned all the facts. According to Hardy himself, he was inconsiderate to his wife in many minor ways. He did not listen to her playing, he did not take her to places she liked visiting,

> We might have said,
> In the bright Spring weather
> We'll visit together
> Those places that once we visited.

This would seem fairly harmless, but when a little more knowledge of the facts is added, the poems come to have a tragic significance. Though Hardy went on insisting that his wife was perfectly well up to the day of her death, a letter attested by the family doctor has revealed that she suffered from infected gallstones, a condition which causes intense pain over a long period, as well as weakness and an inability to walk. For years her husband ignored this knowledge—perhaps even deceiving himself. The remorse of the poems is now only too easily explained, and also throws a new light upon Hardy.

We must also mention a suppression of an entirely different kind. It is to be found in Henry James's letters, and it is himself that he is defending. He wrote thousands of letters for over fifty years—to relations, friends, acquaintances—

but he was extremely anxious, as old age drew on, as to what could be deduced from them. Even in a letter to his sister Alice he insisted, 'Burn this, please, burn, burn.' After having heaped his correspondence upon a roaring fire in his garden at Lamb House, he could boast, like his own character in *The Aspern Papers*, 'I have done the great thing!'[57]

But he was still tormented about what had happened to his *own* letters. He was acutely conscious of having lived into a new age of journalism, which is too curious about the great. With his meticulous need for putting everything in order—the house of fiction as the house of life—he suggested that the writer's defence should be carefully planned.

> There are secrets for privacy and silence: let them only be cultivated on the part of the hunted creature with even half the method with which the love of sport—or call it the historic sense—is cultivated on the part of the investigator . . . Then at last the game will be fair and the two forces face to face; it will be 'pull devil, pull tailor' . . . Then the cunning of the inquirer, envenomed with resistance, will exceed in subtlety and ferocity anything we today conceive, and the pale forewarned victim, with every tract covered, every paper burnt and every letter unanswered, will, in the tower of art, the invulnerable granite, stand, without a sally, the siege of all the years.[58]

This was Henry James's challenge to his biographer: every track covered, every paper burnt, and every letter unanswered . . . But not all papers do get burned; not every track can remain covered.

There exists, for instance, a monograph on angina pectoris by the late Sir James Mackenzie . . . His little book is the last place in the world where we would look for biographical material concerning an American novelist. Yet it contains the following passage:

I was once consulted by a distinguished novelist. Just before he came to see me I had read one of his short stories, in which an account was given of an extraordinary occurrence that happened to two children. Several scenes were recounted in which these children seemed to hold converse with invisible people, after which they were greatly upset. After one such occasion one of them turned and fled, screaming with terror, and died in the arms of the narrator of the story. After my examination of the novelist I referred to this story and said to him 'You did not explain the nature of the mysterious interviews.' He at once expounded to me the principles on which to create a mystery. So long as the events are veiled, the imagination will run riot and depict all sorts of horrors . . .

I tapped him on the chest and said 'It is the same with you, it is mystery that is making you ill . . .'

Now this passage sounds uncommonly like *The Turn of the Screw*—and, discreet as Sir James Mackenzie had been, his case did eventually come into the open. When asked by another doctor, he admitted that he had been referring to that little masterpiece.[59]

Lytton Strachey—who considered biography 'the most delicate and humane of all branches of the art of writing'[60]—affirmed that a biographer's equipment consists in three qualities—'a capacity for absorbing facts, a capacity for stating them, and a point of view.' The definition is a good one, for without a point of view no history can be written, but there is also a danger that it may not only shape but distort the facts. And here we come to the third of the biographer's temptations: to sit in judgement. The biographer who puts his wit above his subject will end by writing about one person only—himself. My personal complaint about *Eminent Victorians* would not be that it is inaccurate, but that it is *thin*, and that its thinness springs from condescension. If you wish to see a person, you must not start by seeing *through* him. Another instance of this occurs in the first sentence of Harold Nicolson's *Tennyson*. 'We smile today at our Victorians,' it begins, 'not confidently, as of old, but with a shade of hesitation. A note of perplexity, a note of anger, sometimes a note of wistfulness, has come to mingle with our laughter.'

The fatal words are, of course, the first ones: 'We smile today.' The biographer has started by putting up a barrier —and even if, in the next few words, he suggests that it is beginning to crumble, he is still writing from the other side.

'To penetrate,' wrote the great French historian, Marc Bloch, 'into the foreign awareness of a man separated from us by a long stretch of generations, one must almost cast off one's own self. To tell him what one thinks of him, one need only remain oneself. The effort is undeniably less strenuous.'[61]

Every work of art implies a previous process of assessment, and this process still remains the central problem of biography. But in so far as a biographer is also an historian, he should be very careful not to drown his subject's voice with his own. One function of biography is to show history as it was to the participant, to observe, for a moment, 'das Gewordene als Werdendes'—what has come to pass, while it is occurring. Through the individual peephole of the man whose life we are describing, we can see history in the course of being lived. In one sense, all organised histories are unsatisfactory, because they are written with what in Italy is called *il senno del poi*, wisdom after the event. But in individual lives we can seize, if nothing else, a vivid sense of actuality: it is a pity to blur it.

Besides, our own evaluations are surely not immune

from change. We do not, at the age of sixty, regard a man in the same way as we did at thirty. Ten days before his death, Dr Johnson asserted that he was 'ready now to call a man a *good* man, in much easier terms than formerly.' With the passing of the years, the muscles of moral indignation sometimes begin to sag, and the voice becomes less sharp— and this is true even in the field of abstract thought. I remember asking George Santayana in his old age—when he was preparing an abridged edition of the great work of his youth, *The Life of Reason*—whether there were many things he would now like to change. 'No,' he gently replied, 'I feel I have much the same things to say, but I wish to say them in a different tone of voice.'

Moreover, when we are writing a biography, we are not only drawing upon the documents before our eyes, but on deeper sources within ourselves.

> A single word [wrote Marc Bloch], dominates and illuminates our studies: understanding . . . We always judge too much; we do not understand enough. The man who does not agree with us—a foreigner or a political adversary—must necessarily be evil. History, provided it renounces its false superhuman airs, should aid us to overcome this error. It contains a vast experience of different varieties of men, of a long meeting between them. Life, as well as science, has much to gain from rendering this meeting fraternal.[62]

Just as, in a conversation, there is sometimes a secondary silent conversation going on in which the real exchange of feelings takes place, so in writing there should be a rich background of unstated knowledge, a tapestry which is never unrolled. We must know more, a great deal more, than what we tell. When Lytton Strachey said that 'a biographer's business is to lay bare the facts of the case, *as he understands them* . . .'[63] he was setting forth the only answer to the problem of omniscience. A biographer can only put down what he has gathered in the light of his own understanding and the book that he will produce will be *his* vision, and *his* picture. Two biographies, though extremely dissimilar, occur to me as instances: David Cecil's *Lord M.* and Carl Sandburg's *Abraham Lincoln*. Both are good books, because both writers were well acquainted, long before they began to write, with the worlds that they describe: that of the families of 'the great Whiggery,' and that of the prairies of Knox County in Illinois. No amount of painstaking research can take the place of the sixth sense which is granted, even after a long lapse of time, to writers who have been at home in precisely the same world as their subject; it is only they who can distinguish a phrase subsequently invented from one really spoken, a likely gesture from an unlikely one. They know, long before being told, how their subject moved, spoke, ate; what his neighbours spoke about, and what he saw, on looking out of the window in the morning.

A lack of this kind of familiarity may produce unexpected pitfalls. I am thinking of one into which John Heath-Stubbs fell, in a single sentence of his excellent translation of Leopardi's poem 'Il Sabato del Villaggio.' He described the 'fascio dell'erba,' the bundle of grass, which the girl in the poem is carrying, as 'a truss of hay.' The image brought to mind is one of green hayfields and pitchforks and buxom country girls—an Austrian scene, or an English. But there are no hayfields near Recanati; there are only steep, dun-coloured hills on which olive trees grow, with wheat beneath them and perhaps a few vines, and by the edge of the road there are sometimes tufts of grass, of which town-dwellers bring an armful home to feed their rabbits. This was the bundle of grass brought back by Leopardi's *donzelletta*. A single misleading sentence—written not because the translator did not know Italian, but because he did not know Leopardi's birthplace—conjured up a whole non-existent world.

This reminds me of a similar mistake that I once made myself, caused by insufficient knowledge of both my subjects and their period. I described, as an instance of Jane Carlyle's touchiness, the disastrous Christmas party at the Grange, at which Lady Ashburton presented to Jane, from the Christmas tree, a silk dress, after which Jane retired to her bedroom in tears. I said that she had made a lot of unnecessary fuss. Rebecca West, however, in a kind letter, pointed out my mistake. Her great-aunt, Isabella Campbell, had often spoken of the episode, and had considered it 'a most extraordinary thing for Lady Ashburton to have done, as a silk dress was the recognised present for a housekeeper, and a friend of the family would have felt bewildered at receiving it.' To be given such a gift was a sign of social inferiority. Plainly, therefore, on this occasion Jane was right to be offended, and I did not know what I was writing about. I still think, however, that Mrs Carlyle was glad of so good an excuse to resent the behaviour of the woman whom her husband described as having 'the soul of a princess and a captainess,' and whom he considered, which was worse, as witty as herself.

It is always prudent, besides, to assure ourselves that the aids we call upon in our picture of a life are being approached with due caution. Are we really seeing what was being seen at the time? When Strachey, for instance, wrote about Queen Victoria, he had no need to feel any doubts about his information. He not only had an abundance of precise and authenticated material, but he stuck to it, 'keeping strictly to the world of fact.' When the Prince Consort died, he said quite firmly, 'a veil descends.' We must be content with a brief and summary relation. In consequence, in future it is probable that just as Boswell's Johnson is our Dr Johnson, so perhaps Strachey's Queen Victoria will remain our Queen Victoria.[64] This at least was Virginia Woolf's opinion, but she also pointed out that when, in writing about *Elizabeth and Essex*, Strachey tried to 'worm his way into a world that was composed half of speculation'—in short, began to invent—Elizabeth 'never became real in the sense that Queen Victoria had been real, yet she never became fictitious in the sense that Falstaff or Cleopatra are fictitious. The reason seems to be that very little was known —he was urged to invent; yet *something* was known—his invention was checked. There is a sense of vacancy and effort.'[65] 'Let there be fact,' she wrote firmly some years later, 'or let there be fiction; the imagination will not serve under two masters simultaneously.'

But, for all that, Strachey's kind of invention rather appealed to Virginia; she thought it 'a daring experiment' which might herald a new kind of biography. She thought this with the adventurous part of her mind which caused her to write the words 'A biography' on the first page of *Orlando*—though it is rather a dazzling fantasy, a Midsummer Night's Dream. But she went on worrying at the problem, like a dog at a bone. 'On the one hand there is truth,' she wrote, 'on the other there is personality. And if we think of truth as something of granite-like solidity, and of personality of rainbow-like intangibility, then reflect that the aim of biography is to weld these two into one seamless whole, we shall admit the problem is a stiff one.'[66]

Yet still she thought that the biographer should be 'like the miner's canary, testing the atmosphere, detecting falsity, unreality and the presence of obsolete conventions.' So what should the writer do? In the end she comes back to Dr Johnson's starting-point, the need for truth. 'For there is a virtue in truth. It has an almost mystic power. Like radio, it seems able to give off for ever and ever grains of energy, atoms of light.'[67]

And then, see what pitfalls we fall into, if we replace

truth by invention! They are well described by Professor Trevor-Roper in a somewhat merciless attack on Lytton Strachey: the length of Dr Arnold's legs. Strachey had formed a very clear image of Dr Arnold in his mind: he saw him as a noble, pompous figure, and—to introduce just the right additional touch of absurdity, of debunking—it was necessary that his legs should have been too short. However, as Strachey himself once admitted to a friend, there is absolutely no evidence to show that Dr Arnold's legs were shorter in proportion to his body than any other man's.

Now the danger of all kinds of invention is that they shake our belief in *anything* that their creator has said. 'Suppose we believe one half of what he tells,' suggested Lord Mansfield to Dr Johnson, about an acquaintance whose stories, he said, 'we unhappily found to be very fabulous.' 'Yes,' Dr Johnson replied, 'but we don't know *which* half to believe. By his lying we lose not only our reverence for him, but all the comfort in his conversation.'

Every biography, then, whether one admits it or not, is based on a process of selection—and here at once new problems arise. Is it possible to choose without becoming biased, to reject without falsifying? Most writers are familiar with the seductive tricks of the trade: the slight juggling with dates, the suppression of letters or remarks that are out of character or merely flat, the placing of a telling conversation or document where it is most effective, the smoothing out and the touching up. In the end a portrait is built up: slick, vivid, convincing—and false. Moreover, with the admission that heroes, too, may be shown as naked and fallible, the problem arises as to whether this true picture is likely to dismay or corrupt the reader. If this danger exists, has the biographer the right to speak the truth? The problem had been set by Boswell to Dr Johnson. Was it right to relate that Addison, having lent a hundred pounds to Steele, recovered his loan by sending an officer to remove his friend's furniture? Dr Johnson charitably suggested that perhaps Addison had done this with the intention of reforming Steele, but he also maintained that, whatever the interpretation, the facts should be told. 'If we owe regard to the memory of the dead, there is yet more respect to be paid to knowledge, to virtue, and to truth.'[68] And he added that another reason for complete honesty was that 'if nothing but the bright side of characters should be shown, we should sit in despondency and think it utterly impossible to imitate them in anything.' He believed, in short, in telling the unadorned truth for a highly characteristic reason: 'It keeps mankind from despair.'

Then there is the question of evidence. There is a parlour-game in which each player in turn is required to give his version of a scene—perhaps a bank-robbery or an accident—which he has witnessed or been told. No two versions are likely to be identical. A similar problem confronts the biographer. Kenneth Clark has supplied us with an entertaining instance, in describing the first encounter of that formidable Victorian, Sir Edmund Gosse, with Walt Whitman at Camden—a story so entertaining, indeed, that it is hardly possible to believe. Mary Berenson claimed that she first introduced Gosse to Walt Whitman at Camden—indeed, asked Gosse to push her through the open larder window, in order to be able to get in. 'I shall never forget Gosse's face,' says Kenneth Clark. 'It turned white with rage . . . and he said in icy tones: "Dear Lady, your picturesque narration is entirely untrue. I remember my visit to Whitman perfectly. I rang the doorbell; it was answered by a smart parlour-maid [most improbable Lord Clark comments] and facing me, at the head of the stairs, was your great poet, who raised his hand and said 'Is this my friend?'" "[69]

The biographer, like the historian, must make his choice.

Finally, there are some subtle forms of distortion, perhaps only open to writers who are also artists. For such writers a few days' interval, during which recollection turns into composition, may bring about a falsification. In Virginia Woolf's *A Writer's Diary* there is a detailed description of the day in which she and her husband went to tea with the Hardys in their country cottage—'a good tea, with a chocolate roll'—Hardy 'a little puffy cheeked cheerful old man' talking about *Far From the Madding Crowd*, putting his head down 'like some old pouter pigeon'; 'fresh and yet sarcastic a little, anyhow shrewd.' 'What impressed me was his freedom, ease and vitality.' Mrs Hardy talking about the dog and how he bit people, leaning over the teacups, saying about Lawrence, 'I hope he won't commit suicide'—all of them going out to see the lights of Weymouth. A few days later, in the same diary, Virginia asked: 'If art is based on thought, what is the transmuting process? I was telling myself the story of our visit to the Hardys, and I began to compose it; that is to say, to dwell on Mrs Hardy leaning on the table, looking out apathetically, vaguely, and so would soon bring everything into harmony with that as the dominant theme. *But the real event was different.*'[70]

That is very honest. The real event is always different. We may hang up looking-glasses, as Virginia advised, at odd corners—we may look at our subject's face at every angle and in every light. We can discover curious pieces of information: that Dr Johnson liked to carry orange peel in his pocket, that Aristotle had a hot water bottle made of leather, filled with hot oil, and that Leopardi, in the winter in Bologna, spent his days in a bag lined with feathers, from which he emerged looking like Papageno. But never, never do we see enough. 'In every fat man,' wrote Cyril Connolly, 'there is a thin man crying to get out.' How often are we aware of him? There is surely no better evidence of a biographer's sensitivity than his willingness to remind himself constantly of all that he cannot see. Here is Howells' description of Mark Twain in his old age: 'He was apt to smile into your face with a subtle but amiable perception, and yet with a sort of remote absence: you were all there for him, *but he was not all there for you.'*

For when indeed—except perhaps for brief moments between lovers—is the whole of another human being ever there for us? Though, as we have said, Virginia Woolf considered the central and unsolvable problem of biography to be the welding 'into one seemless whole' the 'granite-like solidity' of truth and 'the rainbow-like intangibility' of personality, it continued to fascinate her—not only in literature, but in daily life. 'Go on, this is enthralling,' she would say, when her friends brought her an exciting piece of gossip. 'I feel as if a buried statue were being dug up piece by piece.' One of her friends once told me that he came upon Virginia Woolf standing in the fog beside an apple-barrow, asking the old apple-woman, in her deep, throaty compelling voice: 'Tell me, what does it *feel* like to stand here in the fog on a dark evening selling apples?' I cannot vouch for the truth of this story, but certainly the question was one she often asked.

I vividly remember my first meeting with Virginia. I had gone to Bedford Square, with considerable trepidation, to take to Leonard, downstairs, the typescript of my second book, *Allegra*—which, to my surprise, he accepted. Flushed with pleasure, I was about to go away when Virginia's voice came floating down the stairs, 'Bring her up, Leonard,' and I found myself sitting at a tea-table, before a large brown teapot. But before a cup had been drunk, 'Tell me,' said Virginia, 'what does it *feel* like to wake up in the morning on a Tuscan farm?' I was unable to tell her, but suggested that they should come to see for themselves. And so, in the following autumn, Virginia did, with Vita Sackville-West, and Vita found inspiration in our white oxen for some of the best lines in her English Georgic, *The Land*.[71]

This intense interest in other people always remained

with Virginia—but often as if she were gazing, armed with a microscope, through a pane of glass. And when, later on, she came to write a *Life of Roger Fry*, who had been one of her closest friends and her sister's lover, the book was less vivid, more conventional, than the characters in her novels. She found, indeed, the sheer effort of putting together the material for a full biography almost unbearably tedious. 'Donkey work,' she recorded in her *Writer's Diary*, 'sober drudgery, appalling grind.' And when at last the book was finished: 'What a curious relation is mine with Roger at this moment—I who have given him a kind of shape after his death. Was he like that? I feel very much in his presence at the moment, as if I were intimately connected with him: as if we together have given birth to this vision of him; a child born of us. Yet he had no power to alter it. And yet for some years it will represent him.'

And that the portrait was a true likeness is surely shown by Vanessa's letter to her sister, 'It made me cry, but you have given him back to me.'

Is biography, then, worth attempting at all? Where there are so many snares, would we do better to be silent? I do not think so. Many critics would deny to any biography the truth that is truer than truth, of poetry and fiction: 'It is,' Virginia affirms, 'a life lived at a lesser degree of tension . . . The artist's imagination at its most intense fires out what is perishable in fact . . . but the biographer must accept the perishable, build with it, embed it in his very fabric.'[72]

His is a craft, not an art. Is this really true? and if true, is it relevant? The biographer has, of course, a fixed pattern; he is, as Desmond MacCarthy once said, 'An artist upon oath.' But the calls upon his imagination and intuition are hardly less exacting. The novelist and dramatist do not create their characters in a void, but out of their experience or intuition. Shakespeare himself invented hardly any of his plots, but—having accepted a ready-made pattern for his characters' actions—was then free to give his whole attention to bringing them to life. And so, surely, the biographer's true function—the transmission of personality—may also be an act of creation.

> By telling us the true facts, by sifting the little from the big . . . the biographer does more to stimulate the imagination than any poet or novelist except the very greatest . . . Almost any biographer, if he respects facts, can give us much more than another fact to add to our collection. He can give us the creative fact; the fertile fact; the fact that suggests and engenders.[73]

It is of course possible to wonder whether there will soon be any demand for biography at all. Reading is a private pleasure and people's curiosity about other people's lives can now be satisfied in more dramatic ways: every housewife in America is able to watch the debates in Congress or to follow the attempt on the Pope's life while she does her cooking.

But I do not really believe in these substitutes. The story of public exploits may become the field of the radio and of television; but the slow development of character, the processes of thought of the writer and the artist, and above all, the relation of human beings to each other—these are things that fortunately cannot be simplified, and that will always have to be told, however imperfectly, in words.

Leon Edel has set down for us an illuminating passage of Henry James's about his dead friend James Russell Lowell, describing:

> the change that takes place when a man is alive, holding the unusual connecting threads that bind him to the world and his fellow-men, and the moment when the threads are suddenly snapped, for all time . . .
>
> After a man's long work is over, and the sound of

his voice is still, those in whose regard he has held a high place find his image strangely simplified and summarized. The hand of death, in passing over it, has smoothed the folds, made it more typical and general. The figure retained by memory is compressed and intensified ... It stands, sharply, for a few estimated and cherished things.[74]

These 'estimated and cherished things' are of the stuff that does not fade. As long as human beings go on feeling affection for each other, such memories will be renewed—and some of them may become material for biographies. In this sense biography is, or should be, a completion of life, finding, in the routine and triviality of daily experience, the universal pattern that gives them harmony and meaning. Every individual life is also the story of *Everyman*, and while it is the biographer's task to describe the passions, foibles and idiosyncracies that made his subject a *person*, his work will be very incomplete if these traits are not also seen as a part of a universal drama. 'A man's life of any worth,' said Keats, 'is a continual allegory, and very few eyes can see the Mystery.'

In Pasternak's great novel, *Dr Zhivago*, there is a moving image. A candle has melted a little patch in the icy crust of a window-pane, through which the candle's light is seen by Yuri from the street below. 'It's light seemed to fall into the street as deliberately as a glance, as if the flame were keeping a watch on the passing carriages, and waiting for someone.'

Perhaps this is the most that a biographer can ever hope to do, to clear, in the icy crust of each man's incomprehension of other men, a little patch, through which a faint, intermittent light can shine. But at best it will only be a very little light, in a great sea of darkness, and it is surely very arrogant to attempt more than this. All that needs to be said about this was said by Sir William Temple in a single perfect sentence: 'When all is done, Human Life is, at the best, but like a froward Child, that must be played with and humoured a little to keep it quiet until it falls asleep, and then the Care is over.'[75]

I do not think of truth as being made of granite, but rather as a note in music—a note which we instantly recognise as the right one, as soon as it is struck. Proust describes in a famous passage how in later life he was sometimes able to hear again certain sounds which, he wrote, 'in reality had never stopped'; the sobs which had shaken him at a crucial moment of his childhood—'like convent bells which one might believe were not rung nowadays, because during the day they are drowned by the city hubbub, but which may be heard clearly enough in the stillness of the evening.'

The biographer who has acquired a similar sensitiveness to the continuity of emotion may realise, when life is silent about him, that he has become aware of something about his subject for which he could not give chapter and verse, but which he knows to be true. But certainly even its faintest echo can only be heard by temporarily casting aside, as Bloch advised, one's own self and one's own opinions. Therefore the young biographer who has upon his desk his first intriguing file of papers, will do well to arm himself with humility, and let them speak for themselves. Later on the time will come to sift, to compare and to bring to life again; but first he should listen without interrupting. Then, as he deciphers the faded ink, a phrase may stand out which reveals the hand that wrote it. He may see—as suddenly as, at the turn of a passage, one comes upon one's image in a mirror—a living face. He may hear, like John Aubrey, 'a most melodious twang.' In that fleeting moment, he may perhaps reach a faint apprehension—as near to the truth as we are ever likely to get—of what another man was like.

Lauro de Bosis photographed beside his
aeroplane before the flight over Rome

II

Lauro de Bosis

Icarus

He has outsoared the shadow of our night;
Envy and calumny and hate and pain,
And that unrest which men miscall delight,
Can touch him not and torture not again; . . .
—SHELLEY, Adonais: An Elegy
on the Death of John Keats

At about eight o'clock on the evening of 3 October 1931, the Romans who were sitting at outdoor cafés in the Villa Borghese or the Pincio, or strolling in Piazza di Spagna, suddenly saw falling from the sky a snowdrift of small white leaflets. They whitened, too, the green lawns and hedges of the Quirinal gardens. The plane that dropped them circled low over the centre of the town and Piazza Venezia, where the Duce was sitting in council—so low that, when it reached the Piazza di Spagna, it almost seemed to be climbing up the Spanish Steps. For about half an hour, it continued to hover over the city, also dropping its leaflets over the spectators at an open-air cinema. Then it rose rapidly and disappeared into the Western sky.

The next day, only one Roman fascist paper mentioned

the exploit, in a short article entitled 'Una carogna,'* without mentioning the pilot's name, or saying whether the plane had been pursued and shot down. But on 14 October a remarkable document, entitled *'The Story of my Death'*— the pilot's own testament, which he had posted to a friend in Brussels, Francesco Luigi Ferrari, on the day of his flight, with a request to publish it if he did not return—appeared in *Le Soir* of Brussels, the London *Sunday Times*, the *New York Times*, and in most of the chief European papers. It was signed Lauro de Bosis. This is the first time that his story has been fully told, together with Ruth Draper's. From the time of their first meeting, his story also became hers.

What makes it somewhat difficult to talk about Lauro in contemporary terms is not a change in ideology—for indeed, the concept of sacrificing a man's life in a single gesture of protest is very much of our time—but that the idiom in which Lauro expressed his opinions and ideals has now changed. This has caused him to be described on various occasions as a new Shelley or a figure of the Risorgimento. But in reality Lauro de Bosis was very much a man of his own time and to understand this fully it is necessary to know something about the background of his childhood and youth—the soil in which his ideas first took root.

Lauro had a singularly happy, Arcadian childhood. The youngest of his family, he grew up in an atmosphere of closely-knit affection, with much laughter, many books, and a great deal of beauty around him—living in Rome, at first in the grassy park of Villa Diana, where a small boy might play among great trees and rushing streams and catch a glimpse of a timid deer, while the family summers were spent at Portonovo in the Marches, in a lonely tower on the Adriatic, so close to the sea that the children felt as if they were living on a ship.

*A skunk.

Born in Rome on 6 December 1901, Lauro was a son of the well-known poet and man of letters, Adolfo de Bosis, the author of *Amori ac Silentio* and a translator of Homer, Shelley and Walt Whitman. These were the poets whom he read to his children, and moreover he was the founder of the most interesting periodical of the time, *Il Convito*, which published such works as Carducci's *La Canzone di Legnano*, D'Annunzio's *Le Vergini delle Rocce* and some of Pascoli's *Poemi Conviviali*. These writers were among the family friends; Lauro listened to their talk, caught fire from their ideas. His mother, Lillian Vernon, who had first come to Rome as a girl of sixteen with her father—a New England clergyman who founded the first Methodist church in Rome—shared both his enthusiasm and his tastes. Her grandson, Arturo Vivante, has described her very vividly, as she was in later life:

> A tall, upright, silver-haired woman with large boney hands . . . simple and gracious, quite beautiful in her mauve or grey long dresses and shawls. Forty years after her arrival in Italy she still looked like a girl, a tall Puritan girl, full of good will. She was so optimistic that one of her daughters could not take it. 'But, my dear Mother,' she would say, and try to explain the hopelessness of a situation—but in vain. [This was not naïveté, but a deep strength of character.] 'Goodness, she doesn't see it,' her daughter would say to us afterwards, 'but how can she not see it?'[1]

The same indomitable hopefulness she passed on to her youngest son. 'Caramadre' ('Motherdear' in one word) all her eight children always called her. 'It was an odd form of address, I never heard it used by others, but it did show the affection and respect they had for her.'[2]

Lauro's mother also passed on to her youngest son a profound and serene *joie de vivre* and above all a warm generosity, which is shown in the wording of his ex-libris: 'Lauro de Bosis et amicorum liber.' His enthusiasm for classical studies was part of his inheritance from his father, and by the age of twenty he had translated three Greek tragedies—*Antigone, Prometheus in Chains* and *Oedipus Rex*.* But there was also an entirely different side to his intellectual development—an intense interest in the evolution of modern science which caused him to take his degree in the University of Rome in chemistry, in philosophy and in anthropology—in subjects, in short, that would help him to understand the nature of the universe and of man, and, in Gilbert Murray's phrase, 'to know the superstitions and voodoos in which the human soul is stifled and from which it must, gradually and painfully, be set free.'[3] An old friend has described Lauro while working for his degree in chemistry, using a test tube and chanting to himself a verse of Euripides.

It was at this time that Lauro also translated into Italian the shorter version of Frazer's *Golden Bough*. In 1927 he wrote his own poetic drama, *Icaro*, which in 1929 was awarded the Olympic prize for poetry in Amsterdam.

The theme of the play—which had been suggested by Lauro's mother—was inspired by a sonnet by Philippe Desportes:

> Icare est cheut icy le jeune audacieux
> > Qui pour voler au ciel eust assez de courage;
> > Icy tomba son corps dégarni de plumage,
> > Laissant tous braves coeurs de sa chute envieux.
>
> O bienheureux travail d'un esprit glorieux
> > Qui tire un si grand bien d'un si petit dommage
> > Qu'il rend le vaincu des ans victorieux!

---

*The latter was performed in the Greek Theatre on the Palatine.

Un chemin si nouveau n'estonna sa jeunesse,
 Le pouvoir lui faillit mais non la hardiesse,
 Il eust pour le bruler des astres le plus beau.

Il mourut poursuivant une haute aventure.
 Le ciel fut son désir, la mer sa sépulture,
 Est-il plus beau dessein, ou plus riche tombeau?

This poem probably owed its inspiration to one by Jacopo Sannazzaro which Lauro included in his *Golden Book of Italian Poetry*.

Icaro cadde qui: queste onde il sanno
 che in grembo accolser quelle audaci penne;
 qui finì il corso e qui il gran caso avvenne
 che darà invidia agli altri che verranno.

Avventuroso e ben gradito affanno
 poi che morendo eterna fama ottenne;
 felice chi in tal fato a morte venne
 chè si bel pregio ricompensa il danno.

Ben può di sua ruina esser contento,
 se al ciel colando a guisa di colomba
 per troppo ardir fu esanimato e spento.

Ed or, del nome suo, tutto rimbomba
 un mare si spacioso, un elemento,
 chi ebbe mai al mondo sì larga tomba?*

*He fell here, Icarus; these waves received
 in their soft lap his bright audacious wings . . .

Happy the man who meets with such a fate
 And by his death obtains so great a prize! . . .

And now his name re-echoes far and wide.
 Across the sea, thro' a vast element
 Who else has ever had so wide a tomb?

For Icarus, the two conflicting forces of the world, Power (Minos, the tyrant) and Science (Daedalus), could only be reconciled in a poet's vision. The pure scientist, Daedalus, is indifferent to the Tyranny of Minos, provided he is able to pursue his own quest for knowledge.

> Tiranni e libertà passano entrambi
> Crollano i regni e crollano i dei
> Solo il pensiero vigile avanza . . .*

Daedalus makes his great discovery, and furnishes Man with wings, but Minos forbids him to make use of them. Only Daedalus's son, Icarus, the poet, succeeds in translating his vision into reality.

> E quel che oggi è sogno
> per virtu del poeta si fa viva
> forza operante, una terrena cosa.†

As Lauro wrote these lines in the tower by the sea at Portonovo, did no presage of his own destiny brush him with its wings?

Professor Gilbert Murray says, in his introduction to Ruth's translation of *Icaro*:

> He left, for publication in case of his death, a most remarkable letter, which appeared in *The Times* of October 14. When I read it, I recollected that, some three or four years before, a young Italian poet had sent me some very striking translations of Sophocles, and, later on, a drama in verse about Icarus: Icarus, who flew from the despotism of Minos towards Athens

---

*'Tyrants and liberty both pass away; kingdoms decay and gods are overthrown. Thought alone advances, vigilant . . .'
†'And what today is a dream, through the poet's vision becomes a living, working force, an earthly thing.'

and freedom, but flew too near the sun and fell to his death in the Icarian sea. I looked up the book, and found the name 'Lauro de Bosis.' He had fulfilled the destiny of his own hero!

It was a strange heroic act, and I was eager to know more about the man who had done it. Was he a mere seeker after fame? Was he an unstable romantic, a poet of morbid fancies? Inquiry gave a clear result. He was certainly nothing of the kind. He was a man of vigorous health and intellect, with a sense of humour and no affectation; a fine swimmer; a high-spirited companion and beloved of children. 'All in all,' said a distinguished scientist about him, 'he was one of the best and clearest minds we had.'

Like Shelley, with whom he had such close ties, he was a poet in love with philosophy. His poetry he could not help, it came spontaneously. It was his natural language, and, for that reason, he rather undervalued it. He thought of it chiefly as a means of reaching and understanding philosophic truth and practical wisdom. Philosophy was what he industriously worked at and pursued. He was engaged on a study of 'The philosophic implication of scientific thought from Galileo to the present day.' And one can sometimes see in his verse a prose-like, or at least unconventional, phrase due simply to his determination to seek truth of statement rather than grace of expression. The same feeling inspired his interest in anthropology, and led him to translate Frazer's 'Golden Bough.' He wanted to know what the creature Man, was really like . . . As to his actual flight over Rome, he must have known, or friends must have pointed out to him, that it involved almost certain death. The government war-planes had more than double the speed of his. It would certainly not, in the existing conditions of Italy, bring a good name to him or ease and safety to his family. He counted the disadvantages; and then 'followed the light'; for though, as we have seen above, he was emphatically not the kind of man to commit suicide, he was the man to face death for a cause. As I look through his *Icaro*, his translations of Sophocles, still more perhaps some of his unpublished essays on philosophical subjects, the general nature of that cause reveals itself. Allowing for Lauro de Bosis's knowledge of science and his modern outlook, it is the old cause of Mazzini and Condorcet, of Shelley and the young Browning; the ideal of those who think little of the conventional side of life and much of the spiritual, who love justice as they love beauty, and who claim freedom as a necessity without which the soul cannot live . . .[4]

During the years in which these thoughts were taking shape, Lauro compiled for the Oxford University Press *The Golden Book of Italian Poetry* which is still, to my mind, the best anthology in existence of Italian poetry. The foreword by G. M. Trevelyan reveals (as does Gilbert Murray's preface to *Icaro*) the many-sided aspects of this remarkable young man.

> The ardours of his soul; his strong love of life and its joys, of earth and its beauty; his claim to individual freedom as the birthright of man; his classical scholarship and his intense devotion to the poetry of Greece, Italy and England, all seem to spring from an older tradition and to reincarnate an ancient faith. But in some respects he was most modern. His great interest in the discoveries of modern science and the speculation and science brought him round to the ancient faith in man's destiny, in the presence of which he felt his own to be of small account.[5]

Cosa t'importa se a soffrir sei tu?
Trionfa altrove un'altra gioventù.*

Certainly the first spark that kindled the boy's enthusiasm lay in the talk which he heard during d'Annunzio's visits to his father's house. At that moment many enthusiastic and patriotic young men like him, who feared the mismanagement and chaos which had overtaken their country after World War I, and the rising strength of communist power, saw in the early days of fascism a hope for a regeneration of their country, a second Risorgimento. And when in 1924 and 1926, Lauro spent some months in America (giving a summer course at Harvard in 1926) his convictions were strengthened by the prestige which he saw his country had gained abroad.

There were at that time about five million Italians in the United States, and of these a large number had come there as uneducated, bitterly poor emigrants, who suffered great humiliation and hardship before carving a place for themselves and their families in this new world.

> They had felt themselves despised by everyone because they were Italians—and now they heard everyone say, even Americans, that Mussolini had turned Italy into a great country, that there were no unemployed, that everyone had a bathroom in his house, that trains ran on time, and that Italy was now respected and feared. Whoever contradicted all this, not only destroyed their ideal country, but insulted their personal dignity.[6]

These words were written by Gaetano Salvemini, the most vehement anti-fascist propagandist in the United

* 'What if today yours be the pain, the strife?
Another Youth, tomorrow shall have life.'
—Translated by Prof. Neville Rogers, *Ohio Review* XII.

States, but whose propaganda was seldom addressed to his immigrant fellow-countrymen; it was the educated American public whom he intended to convince. Moreover one cannot deny to Mussolini a remarkable talent for the presentation to foreign public opinion of the reassuring and conservative aspects of his régime: the reestablishment of law and order, the repression of communism, the abolition of the right to strike, the agricultural projects for draining and reclaiming wastelands, the Crucifix again placed in the public schools, the trains which ran on time. (At one moment it was hardly possible to pronounce the words 'on time' in Salvemini's presence, without his rising to his feet in a rage.) All these fascist measures, well calculated to impress a Republican administration, were presented with care and courtesy to a small group of journalists considered worthy of attention (Anne O'Hare McCormick, the well-known American journalist, for instance, was received by the Duce himself, according to Salvemini, 'as if she were the Queen of Sheba!') and above all were interpreted by Prince Gelasio Caetani, who arrived in Washington on a 'special mission' only a month after the 'March on Rome,' with all the prestige attached to his personal standing and charm, his political skill, and his expert knowledge of America, where he had worked for several years in his youth. He himself was much too intelligent not to realise that however great an admiration of fascist achievements might be professed by such men as the President of Columbia University and his friends, there was behind their enthusiasm an ulterior economic motive, and that, while they verbally deplored the rhetoric of the Duce's speeches and the violence of his militia, they privately considered that such behaviour was in harmony with their preconceived conviction (shared by many Anglo-Saxons), that democracy was really unnecessary for the Latin races: dictatorship was good enough for them.

In *Problemi di storia nei rapporti tra Italia e Stati Uniti* Gian Giacomo Migone quotes some examples of the manner in which the new Ambassador presented to the American public the differences between the 'new' and the 'old' Italy. 'Italy is now divided into only two parties—a large one made up of those who love their country and a very small one represented by those men who are always prepared to subordinate its supreme good to their personal interests or those of their class.'[7]

Caetani was, however, experienced enough to oppose firmly the formation of fascist groups in the U.S.A.—not only to avoid offending American susceptibilities, but from the realisation that, on the contrary, one of the chief objects of Italian policy should be the incorporation of their emigrants into the American political body. 'As American citizens duly organized they will come to enjoy all the benefits of the law, exercise an important political influence where electors are people who matter and succeed in protecting their own interests, instead of having to invoke the protection of the Italian government.'[8]

Such remarks show a shrewd awareness of the realities of the situation, and also of the financial plans underlying much of the American pro-fascist propaganda. The Italian Ambassador's position, indeed, was not an easy one, for already by 1926 doubts were beginning to arise, especially in financial circles, in both England and America, in consequence of what Montagu Norman called Mussolini's incendiary speeches.

> Sentiment in this country towards Italy is very much less favourable, [wrote Thomas Lamont to his representative in Rome, Giovanni Fummi, on 4 March 1926] than what it was when you and Count Volpi were here. There is no use in mincing words about it. I must talk with you just as I would with one of my

partners and I must say to you that the chief disturbing factor as to sentiment has been the disturbing utterances from time to time of your Premier. I don't know how accurately the newspapers have reported these, and it is not my function in any event either to praise or criticize what Mussolini says, but the effect created on the public here has been that Mussolini was preparing for a fresh war.

He added, however, 'This I regard as perfectly absurd.'[9] And indeed he and his firm continued to support the stabilisation of the lira.

This letter was written soon after the period in which Lauro had given his first course of lectures at Harvard, but since his arrival in America much had happened to make him, too, change his mind. The news brought over by Italian exiles—the assassination of Matteotti, the muzzling of the press, the ever-increasing restrictions of every form of intellectual freedom, all these were a deep shock to him, and gradually his enthusiasm for fascism was transformed into a firm determination to do anything he could to free his country from its tyranny. It was at this point, in the early summer of 1928—on the warm recommendation of Irene de Robilant—that he was offered the post of Executive Secretary of the Italy-America Society of New York, a cultural offspring, founded in 1920, at Casa Italiana, for the nominal purpose of promoting cultural good will between the two countries, but increasingly dominated by the Republican pro-fascist President of Columbia, Nicholas Murray Butler, by Thomas Lamont and by the great banking house of J. P. Morgan. It is not surprising that (badly as Lauro needed the job) he felt considerable hesitation over accepting it.

However in the end he did agree, chiefly owing to his belief in the integrity of the President of the Italy-America Society, Chester Aldrich, a staunch Liberal and lover of

Italy who, with his sister Amey, had done much to alleviate the hardships of the newly arrived Italian emigrants, and who genuinely believed that the duties asked of Lauro would be merely in the field of Italian culture. On this understanding, de Bosis took the job, but not without a certain uneasiness which the next two years fully justified. His intention had been to limit his activities to making Americans more aware of 'the Italy that belongs to the civilisation of the whole world, which existed before Mussolini and will continue to exist when Mussolini has disappeared from the scene.'[10] Gradually, however, Lauro realised that it was almost impossible to confine his work to cultural lectures and meetings, while in the same office (though he did not yet realise to what an extent) a strong fascist element was opposed to him. Moreover he soon came to realise that, like all his collaborators in the Italy-America Society, he was now regarded with deep suspicion by the anti-fascists of New York. The most important and sympathetic of these was the historian Gaetano Salvemini, who was about to leave for a journey to England. Though Lauro knew about Salvemini's mistrust of him, he decided to take the bull by the horns and asked for an interview, to explain his situation and his opinions. At first Salvemini was reluctant to receive him, but afterwards wrote how glad he was to have done so, since he was 'at once conquered by Lauro's simplicity and frankness.' Salvemini wrote:

> He told me that he had at first followed the fascist movement with sympathy . . . believing it to represent, after the preceding years of confusion and conflict, a true re-awakening of national feeling. But his main interests did not lie in politics, but in study and poetry. He was, he said, a 'Liberal' like Croce, in the sense that that word still had in Italy—that is, a conservative who desired the return of the Italy of the

Risorgimento. But gradually, as he became better informed, he had turned against fascism in all its forms, and had been especially disgusted by the propaganda that described the Italian people as a pack of barbaric idiots who after sixty years of free government had not yet learned to read, to write nor to wash; who had let themselves be governed by the *mafia* and the *camorra*, until Mussolini had performed the miracle of civilizing the population by means of the stick and of castor oil.[11]

De Bosis told Salvemini that after he was offered the post of secretary to the Italy-America Society, he had 'eliminated fascist propaganda from the society's activities.' This was not entirely accurate, since it merely meant that Lauro had passed on that part of the work to some of his collaborators, but Salvemini was already convinced, and even at this first meeting received a hint of what was gradually taking shape in the young man's mind. Lauro asked him what he would think if a plane flew over Rome, inciting Italians to put an end to their present state of shame. Salvemini commented:

> I have never instigated other people to perform actions I would not undertake myself. But I have never said a single word to discourage a project which seemed to me useful, even if dangerous. I have drawn attention to difficulties; I have discussed the possible consequences; I have given advice—and if I have been able to lend a hand, I have done my best. I behaved in the same manner with Lauro. I said to him that if it was technically possible I would applaud the venture with my whole heart. 'It is possible,' he replied.[12]

Soon he and Salvemini became fast friends—though their political opinions could hardly have been more diverse. All Salvemini's followers were of the Left, Lauro de Bosis was a strong conservative. Lauro's ambition was to defeat fascism by gathering together all the conservative forces of Italy (monarchists, liberals and Catholics) 'to rally round the King, the Pope, the Army and the Senate.' He hoped to awaken and crystallise public opinion in Italy by the clandestine circulation of anti-fascist propaganda, to inform Italians about the true state of things in their country, and to publish any important anti-fascist news.

Meanwhile in the Italy-America Society Lauro was finding the idealistic detachment he described to Salvemini increasingly difficult to maintain. He had found there a strong fascist group which began sending malicious reports about him to the Italian Ambassador in Washington.[13] And though the liking that Salvemini felt for him was immediate and strong, it was not shared by other anti-fascists in New York.

It was during this lonely and disturbed period that Lauro found solace in the house of the person who had become the most important figure in his life and remained so until its end. This was Ruth Draper, whose international fame as a monologuist was already fully established, and whom he had met in Rome on 14 March 1928, at a lunch party of the gifted painter Katherine Presbitero. The attraction that sprung up between them—even though Ruth was already forty-three, seventeen years older than Lauro, swiftly ripened into love. Both were vital, idealistic and romantic; both also had a similar Puritanical streak, in contrast with their intense love of natural beauty and the arts, their child-like capacity for laughter and for the enjoyment of each fleeting minute. In addition, Ruth brought with her the glamour of her success on the stage; Lauro, his poetry, his ambitions—and his youth.

His nephew, Arturo Vivante, has written about him as he was at this time: 'I remember him walking in the garden with my parents, his step much lighter and gayer than theirs . . . something about him winged . . . He was a great entertainer, both of children and grown-ups—handsome, cheerful, high-spirited.'[14]

But after his death Ruth wrote that the quality in him that first struck her was:

> the extraordinary honesty and maturity of his mind . . . He was full of a strange prescience and wisdom beyond his years that continually amazed me. Life never puzzled him—he felt himself a part of the Cosmic 'order' and accepted and rejoiced in life as it was—with all its conflicts . . . He would have lived out his life with the same impulse of integrity and force if destiny had not brought him this tragic and proud end to his ambition: to work for the cause of freedom.[15]

In what setting could their mutual attraction have found fuller expression than in a Roman spring? There are two pages in Ruth's writing, dated 20 April (1928) and headed: 'Lauro—here is the record of our happy days.' They drove to Frascati, Arcinazzo, Villa d'Este and Ninfa; they walked on the Pincio and the Palatine and down the Appian Way; they attended a concert of Segovia's and a Pirandello play. Then there were two evenings of Ruth's own performances at the Teatro Odescalchi, with Lauro looking in between the acts. They did some sightseeing—in the Sistine Chapel, in S. Gregorio and in the little Romanesque cloister of Santi Quattro Coronati. In the following week, they spent three days in Florence together visiting San Miniato, the Badia Fiesolana and the Bargello; there was a day in Pistoia and Prato and another one at San Gimignano, and a drive to Castel Trebbio. But even before then—only thirteen days after their first meeting—Lauro had taken Ruth to see his mother, who had accepted her so completely that, after

Lauro's death, she signed her letters to Ruth as she did those to her own children, 'Caramadre.'

Then Ruth had to leave Italy to give a series of performances in London, to be presented at Court at Buckingham Palace on 28 May, and then to return to New York. In his first letter after their parting Lauro wrote to his 'beloved Archangel' (his favourite name for her), 'I don't love anything any more that is not in some way connected with you . . . What a miracle to have such a touchstone! . . . How shall I ever mould my life to make it show what you have put into it of light, of strength, of inspiration, of faith?'[16]

After another most successful season in England, Ruth had to return to work in New York, and by October Lauro was there too, to take up his new job as the Executive Secretary of the Italy-America Society. It was then that Lauro became Ruth's frequent guest in her charming new apartment at 66 East 79th Street, and found there some hours of forgetfulness of the difficulties he was meeting in his new post and his anxieties for the future.

During the summer of 1929, Lauro asked for a period of leave in Italy, and then, after a brief period of separation and a few days together in Venice, both Ruth and Lauro spent some happy weeks at Portonovo, in his family's tower on the Adriatic coast. It was here that Lauro had written *Icaro*, and here that Ruth now rehearsed, in a little deserted 18th-century church on the beach, one of her 'dramas,' 'Three Women and Mr. Clifford.' They talked, walked, read aloud, planned Lauro's anthology of Italian poetry—and laughed. 'My cheeks are quite stiff with laughing,' Ruth wrote. It was perhaps the last time they had together of complete serenity, unalloyed by any shadow of anxiety or fear, though in that summer Lauro may have begun to plan his Alleanza Nazionale. But at this point Ruth was still only very partially aware of the hardening of Lauro's political opinions and he himself was still trying to shield her from their consequences as long as possible.

And when, in the autumn, Ruth sailed back to New York, Lauro accompanied her. She was engaged for most of the autumn on a tour in the Middle West, but Lauro spent a week with her in Connecticut (staying with Corinne Alsop) and was with her when she opened a long and successful season on the day after Christmas at the Comedy Theatre in New York.

But all this time, his anti-fascist plans were taking shape. In 1930 he asked for leave, and his first visit was to London, to the founder and former leader of the Partito Popolare (the Catholic Popular Party). Don Luigi Sturzo, whom he described to Ruth as 'the most serious of the exiles,' was a man who intended to start a very serious periodical in French in Brussels, which would be a 'constructive, critical and political forum, aiming not so much at fighting fascism as at clarifying ideas and preparing the Italy of tomorrow.' Lauro added that Don Sturzo had asked him for his collaboration, and that he had agreed to change the review's title, *Res Publica*, 'because, though it only means "The Commonwealth" in Latin, it has to modern ears the suggestion of a republic that we must avoid.'[17]

He went on to Italy and here he set up, with a handful of men with similar opinions, the embryo of an organisation which he called Alleanza Nazionale. The first of his confidants, whom he called his lieutenants, were Mario Vinciguerra, a distinguished Liberal historian and essayist, and a journalist, Renzo Rendi. Benedetto Croce, the anti-fascist historian, signified his approval from a distance.

Lauro then set to writing and circulating six hundred bi-monthly chain-letters, in order to awaken in Italians of the most various political views an awareness of what fascism was really doing in their country. These pamphlets were prepared anonymously by Lauro, cyclostyled by his mother, and then posted to as many people as possible, exhorting each one of the recipients to type at least six more copies and to forward them to their acquaintances (two of them to be fascists)—taking care never to break the chain.[18]

During the whole summer Lauro toiled away writing and posting his pamphlets. Eight of them were written then and were cyclostyled, and sent by him and his friends from different cities in Italy. Lauro was firmly convinced that many people who were still nominally fascists were already disgusted with the régime, and only needed a little more information and some support, to be galvanised into action. What he considered most urgent was 'to prepare a programme of political entente to unite all anti-fascist forces and prepare them for action,' but what he really meant by this was all *conservative* anti-fascist forces. In short, this was 'an appeal to all men of order, to unite in solving the country's problems.'

The first pamphlet defined the purpose of the National Alliance: to fight against the inertia which had overtaken the Italian people by informing them of the real state of their affairs, through news from the foreign press. The second urged all anti-fascists to unite in supporting the Crown, the Vatican and the Army, so that anti-fascists should not all be communists. The third and fourth described, with some humour, various forms of fascist bluff, from the march to Rome to its financial policy; the fifth dealt with fascism and communism. The sixth was an excellent 'anthology' of Mussolini's own pronouncements and promises in the past—all now proved false. The seventh and eighth were statements of the disastrous financial situation. The ninth was concerned with Mussolini's speech of 'fear and hatred' at the opening of the ninth year of fascism. The tenth was a further 'Mussolini anthology.'

The pamphets concluded with an appeal to action: 'It is only our inertia that makes possible the existence of the present régime. Woe to Italy if we let anti-fascist opposition be monopolised by the Reds! The problem of fascism must be solved by those who stand for ordered government.'[19]

How much impression these pamphlets really made, how many reached their destination and were handed on, or how many were confiscated or thrown away, it is very difficult to assess. Certainly Lauro himself was convinced that they had struck a blow for freedom, and when in October 1930, he returned to the United States, he left behind him his two 'lieutenants'—Vinciguerra and Rendi—to publish the newsletters in his absence. A third associate was supposed to take the place of Lauro's mother, but failed to keep his promise.

The reason for Lauro's return to New York was that he had to hand in his resignation to the Italy-America Society, and also obtain from the Italian Ambassador Giacomo De Martino, an approval of two posts which had been offered him when he returned to Italy: one as the representative for Italy of the Institute of International Education and one as the trustee of what was called the 'Westinghouse Foundation.' These plans were already known by De Martino, since, in the previous autumn, Lauro had triumphantly announced to him that he had succeeded in extracting 7,500 dollars from Columbia University for the annual balance sheet of the Italy-America Society, and also 1,000,000 lire from 'an old lady of Chicago, Mrs. Celeste McVoy,' who appears to have been susceptible to Lauro's charm, to form a foundation—the 'Westinghouse'—on the slopes of Monte Mario, north of Rome, as well as the endowment of four scholarships 'to support four writers who wish to dedicate themselves completely to a work of high culture (literary, political, historical).'[20] Mrs McVoy had that day paid out the first 50,000 dollars and appointed Lauro as trustee, and this information had been transmitted with satisfaction by the Ambassador to the Foreign Minister in Rome with the comment, 'I consider it my duty to draw your Excellency's attention once more to the most useful and totally disinterested work that he [de Bosis] is doing to improve and consolidate the cultural relations between Italy and America. In this case he has obtained for us considerable financial benefits.'[21]

De Bosis, therefore, on his return to New York, had every reason to believe that he was on good terms with the Ambassador and would easily obtain what he wanted. At this point, however, he made a great mistake. While he was anxiously waiting for an answer to his requests, he received, to his considerable surprise, a telephone call from Ambassador De Martino himself, saying that he presumed that the report about the reorganisation of the Italy-America Society which he was expecting, would include, as a farewell gesture, a clear statement of de Bosis's fascist solidarity. It was implied—though not said in so many words—that this was a necessity, but how much Lauro hesitated before writing the required letter, we shall never know. He may have been reminded of Salvemini's repeated assertions that one can only fight dictatorships with their own weapons, but he certainly soon had reason to regret bitterly an act so incongruous to his nature.

He started by confirming to the Ambassador the two appointments that had been offered him and by outlining his views about the reorganisation of the Casa Italian after his departure, and went on to remind De Martino (as was true) that he himself had told him that his lectures should preserve 'an unpolitical attitude and that for this reason it was not even advisable for him to wear the fascist badge,' and finally he added the sentence expressing loyalty to the régime which the Ambassador had required. Lauro added that on leaving his post, 'to which I have given the whole of myself,' he wished the Ambassador to grant him only one more request: 'That I may still be used in Italy to serve my country and Fascism . . . The engagements I have accepted for the Institute of International Education will not permit me to undertake any steady or continuous work, and I for my part do not desire any kind of compensation. I only wish to be useful in one way or another to Italy and Fascism.'[22]

This letter—or part of it—was precisely what the Ambassador required and explains the cordial and flattering tone of his reply: 'Your enthusiastic and intelligent work will not cease after your return to Italy, to intensify cultural relations between Italy and the U.S.A. Your activity in this field here is the best guarantee of your success in the same field in Italy, according to your noble desire to be useful to your country and the Régime.'[23]

What however the Ambassador's letter omitted to say was that de Bosis's letter had not been (in his own words) 'wholly spontaneous,' but had been forced upon him.

For indeed the Italian Ambassador's position at that moment with regard to the Italy-America Society was a very complicated one. On the one hand the President of the Italy-America Society, Chester Aldrich, was a staunch liberal and intellectual, whose persuasions, given in all good faith, de Bosis had accepted as a guarantee that his work would be entirely unpolitical. On the other hand the real powers on the throne were the President of Columbia University and his friends, all ardent Republicans and pro-fascists, and the whole complicated matter of the stabilisation of the lira was at stake. It was therefore vital to Ambassador De Martino to seem to have been following the affairs of the Italy-America Society very closely, and in a subsequent long letter to his Foreign Minister, Dino Grandi, he explained how it was that de Bosis came to be appointed to the Italy-America Society at all.[24] He admitted that it was easy to presume that Lauro 'belonged to the category of so-called sympathisers rather than real militants' but pointed out that he had been warmly recommended by the Contessina de Robilant. Moreover he stated that certainly 'no militant fascist would have had a chance of being chosen by the Board of Directors of the Italy-America Society, an American organisation of an essentially unpolitical character.' In addition he added that 'to be honest, it would have occurred to no-one that de Bosis was nourishing anti-fascist sentiments.'

He himself has publicly confessed that his anti-fascist activity had begun in the preceding summer in Italy. One must remember that in this country de Bosis had many opportunities of speaking in public before his nomination to the Italy-America Society, and even afterwards. From all sides I have heard that de Bosis, without being aggressive, always spoke with tact and good effects about the fascist régime. (He) was away on leave during the whole summer, and only returned to New York on October 15 [1930].

On my return I had a vague impression that the set-up of the Italy-America Society should be followed closely. *The well-known letter of November 15 to me by de Bosis* (see my report N. 2258 of the 22nd of the month) *was not really spontaneous.* As if I had a presentiment, when I telephoned to de Bosis to send me an account, before his departure, of the new organisation of the Society, I said that I hoped that this farewell report would also contain a frank declaration of fascist solidarity. And it was lucky that, in his ingenuousness, de Bosis should have accepted my suggestion, for he has thus practically destroyed his own personality.

As I have said, we should follow the activities of the Italy-America Society closely. It is an American society, made up of Americans who are friends of Italy, and it must keep this character so as not to lose its effect on public opinion here . . . But if the Society cannot and should not have a fascist label, we must protect ourselves as far as possible against falling into the opposite extreme. It is not an easy matter![25]

Both de Bosis and De Martino, in short, were taking part in a purely political manoeuvre. But to Lauro, who had inherited both his father's idealism and his mother's sincerity, the expression of sentiments so contrary to his real convictions must have gone deeply against the grain—and indeed, later on, caused him such constant mental distress as to become one of the causes that led to his tragic end. He wrote shortly before his last flight to his friend Francesco Luigi Ferrari, 'that the most convenient road to me to find my peace of mind again is the road to Rome.'[26]

It is plain from the whole of this correspondence that Lauro's protestations of loyalty to fascism were taken by the Ambassador with a grain of salt—indeed had been required by him for the main purpose of detaching de Bosis from the Italy-America Society, without injuring its reputation. In this he was successful. Lauro's American friends (or those who came to hear of the letter) were puzzled and dismayed, but the Italy-America Society continued to function.

Whether or not Lauro was surprised by the Ambassador's cordial assent to his request, we do not know, but certainly he lost no time in taking advantage of it. Only a few days later, after saying goodbye to only a very few friends, and telling no-one of his plans, he set sail for Europe on 27 November 1930, on the *Mauretania*, to visit Don Sturzo on his way home.

It was not until after his voyage that Lauro was able to express his real views, in a letter to the Consul General in New York, Emanuele Grazzi:

I am sure that your indignation will render the reading of this letter odious to you. It is, nevertheless, my duty to make some plain statements which I would have no reason to make unless they were true. I have always thought that the precise duty of an Italian abroad is to keep secret in his own conscience the convictions he may feel about his Government, and to occupy himself only with the prestige of his own country, even if it turns to the advantage of a party which in his heart he detests. It was for this reason that for two years I was able to serve the Italy-America Society in America, even with the adjective 'fascist,' without offending my own conscience, just as after handing in my resignation and returning to Italy, I have been able to give myself up to serving Italy as my conscience ordered me. Needless to say, in view of the fascist and pro-fascist atmosphere in which I was working in New York, I could not confide my ideas to anyone . . . and so I feel I have fully deserved the confidence that you have had the kindness to show towards my work in America. I can assure you, I never betrayed that trust, even in private conversations. [This was true.] I think with regret, Mr. Consul, that your duties with regard to the Italy-America Society will become every day more difficult and more unpleasant. With the institution of the reign of terror, with the arrest of old ladies accused of spreading sedition (I allow myself to send you copies as proof) it will become more and more difficult to defend the good name of fascism in America. Contributing in my own small way to the coming of a better Italy . . . I am also preparing a better task for you. One day you will agree with me that it is better to be the Consul or the Minister of a liberal Italy than the Consul of fascist Italy.'[27]

This letter (though this was hardly a wise moment to make a new enemy) bears the stamp of truth, but it also implies the receipt of bad news. Indeed, on the day before he landed in Southampton, Lauro had received a cable (possibly from Ruth) telling him that his mother and friends had been arrested.

Lauro's first letters to Ruth after receiving this news were remarkably euphoric, even if one must allow for his wish to calm her anxiety. His first instinct on hearing of the arrest of his mother and his friends was naturally to hurry back to Italy and to share their situation, but all his anti-fascist friends implored him not to be so foolish. To get himself arrested, tried and condemned, they pointed out, would save neither his mother nor his friends and would put himself out of the running. His duty, they said, was to show his solidarity with his mother and his friends by going on with the battle and not by getting himself walled up in some jail.

With regard to his mother, Lauro wrote that he felt quite confident, because:

> assurances have been given to the American Foreign Office that she will be released ... As for my two friends, they were ready to [face] this as well as I, and I am only sorry not to share the full glory with them. If I were not sure that I can wage a good war from here, I would take the first train and join them. You know that this is not bluff. They feel too, I am sure, that to receive two or thirty years is the same, since the régime cannot possibly last for more than two years. For my part, I pray with all my heart that I may receive a condemnation of death. It would be such a feather in my cap! I hardly dare hope for such an honour.
>
> Fascists send the news that I have 'run away,' but

all the French papers added a note saying that it was a lie, and that I was on the contrary on my way back to Italy . . . I have seen Nitti and Sforza and will tomorrow see Salvemini, but no other . . . One text I have sent to my successor (whoever he may be) is written with lemon juice in the pages of an English novel entrusted to an English girl who was taught the procedure, to find and elect my successor. Happy man! . . . I have seen a report written by a serious young man in Rome belonging to the movement rival to ours (*Giustizia e Libertà*) in which he says that the King realizes that he must do something—and he is only waiting for the right instant.[28]

There was, of course, a great deal of wishful thinking in these early letters, but after the details of the trial reached him, his tone changes:

I am awfully disappointed at not having received a death punishment (sic) not even a tiny bit of condemnation. I don't understand why, if my two lieutenants get 15 years, then I should get 25 . . . Perhaps they hope that this suspended sentence may induce me to be quiet, if so, they are certainly mistaken . . . still it is a terrible anti-climax and I am deeply humiliated at the too secondary role that I am going to have for years. Up to yesterday I lived in the thrill of the fight, but now it is a bit sad and this evening, in my bourgeois and peaceful, comfortable room, I feel very *embusqué*.[29]

At the same time an urgent telegram was sent by Ambassador De Martino to his Foreign Minister asking for authorisation on his own behalf and on that of the Consul General Grazzi in New York 'to separate the case of Lauro de Bosis from that of the Italy-America Society,' adding that 'it is very urgent to define our attitude with regard to the Italy-America Society.'[30]

The immediate causes of this urgency on the Ambassador's part were three: first Lauro's letter to Grazzi, secondly an interview which he gave soon after his arrival to the correspondent in Geneva of the *New York Times,* Clarence Streit, stating that he had recently resigned from the Italy-America Society, as he considered that anti-fascist propaganda should be carried out in Italy and not abroad, and thirdly a copy of the American paper *The Sun,* sent by Grazzi to the Ambassador, stating that a warrant for arrest had been issued against de Bosis and that his mother had been arrested in Turin. (At that moment both were inaccurate.) Grazzi added that he had received a telephone call from Mr Egon, the head of the Press Office of Morgan's Bank, showing acute anxiety for the repercussions that a threat against de Bosis might have upon the future of the Italy-America Society.

The Ambassador's reply was the following statement in the American press:

> Dr Lauro de Bosis has for the last years been associated with the Italy-America Society as its Executive Secretary. He resigned from this position . . . in November, 1930. The reason given for his resignation was a desire on his part to study in Italy and to represent the Institute of International Education in Rome . . . The Italy-America Society is a cultural organisation in no way concerned with Italian politics. The Society has no information concerning Doctor de Bosis's activities in Italy.[31]

And so Lauro de Bosis passed out of the Italy-America Society.

We owe a sober and honest account of exactly what had meanwhile occurred in Rome to a little periodical published in England by a group of Salvemini's friends, supporters of Giustizia e Libertà, who called themselves 'Italy Today: Friends of Italian Freedom.' One double number, dated November-December 1931, was dedicated to de Bosis, another, dated 31 May 1931, to 'The Case of Vinciguerra and Rendi.' The two booklets—for which the information was largely supplied by Salvemini—are one more proof of the strength of Salvemini's anti-fascist feeling, and of his willingness to collaborate with anyone who shared it, however much they might differ on other points. 'I was convinced,' he wrote, 'that whoever intends to fight Mussolini's dictatorship—Monarchist, Catholic, Republican, Socialist, Communist or Anarchist—should be welcomed as a collaborator. Let everyone fight,' he added, 'under his own flag and with his own methods. When the common enemy has fallen, each one will take his own road in the new climate of liberty for all!'[32]

What actually happened in Rome was this. For some time the fascist police had been aware of the pamphlets of the National Alliance, and even of the area in which most of them were posted, but did not know who was responsible for them. The last two pamphlets sent from abroad by Lauro were being cyclostyled by Lauro's mother in her own house, while his friends saw to the addressing and posting, but one of them—Vinciguerra—was caught in the act of posting a whole batch. He was at once arrested and beaten up (receiving so severe a blow on one side of his head that he remained permanently deaf in that ear), and was left naked for a whole December night on a roof top.

Neither he nor Rendi, who was caught soon after, gave any information, but it was easy to follow the tracks of such close family friends, and under the bed of Signora de Bosis the police found what they were looking for—the mimeograph which had copied the letters.

As five strangers entered her house without taking their

hats off, Lillian de Bosis behaved with her customary dignity. 'But why did you do it, Signora?' one of them asked. A famous phrase of Mussolini's passed through Lillian de Bosis's mind: 'The Italian people are forty million sheep ready to give their wool to their régime'—and she swiftly retorted, 'because I am not a sheep.' But it is doubtful whether her interlocutor understood what Signora de Bosis was talking about.[33]

She was not able, however, to keep up this tone. After spending the night in the Police Station with one of her daughters, she was taken to prison and cut off from contact with anyone but her advocate, whom her daughter persuaded that a woman of her age and state of health could not possibly stand a period of imprisonment. (She was sixty-six and had had a recent operation). Signora de Bosis's lawyer under persuasion from her daughter, told her that both Vinciguerra and Rendi had been set free, but that her own children were in prison, and that their future careers would undoubtedly suffer. If she would write a letter of submission to the Duce she would save both them and herself. 'Much as I loved Italy,' said her daughter Charis in justification of the pressure she had put upon the lawyer, 'I loved my mother more.' In the end Signora de Bosis—far more for her children's sake than for her own—gave way and the letter was written, thanking the Duce for his 'great kindness' in transferring her to the prison hospital, and enabling the fascist Tribunal to show (as was intended) their magnanimity.

The trial, conducted by a Special Tribunal composed entirely of fascists, was held unusually quickly, on 22 December 1930, and every facility was given to foreign journalists to be present. It is easy to imagine the surprise and dismay of Signora de Bosis, as soon as she entered the Court, and realised that she had been deceived. Her children were at liberty, while Vinciguerra and Rendi were both in the

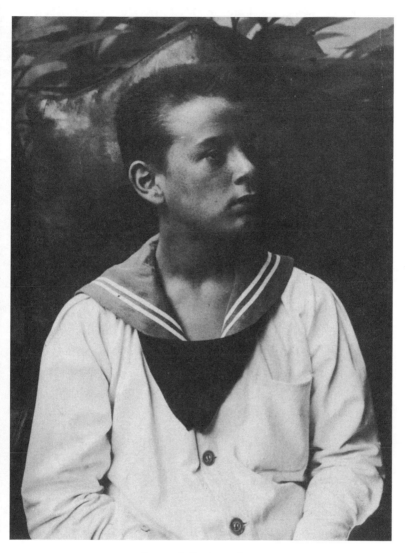

Lauro de Bosis as a boy

prisoner's cage and received sentences of fifteen years imprisonment. Moreover, her own letter to Mussolini, and, afterwards, Lauro's letter to De Martino, were read aloud. The sentences of Vinciguerra, who was sent to the prison of Fossombrone, and Rendi, who was sent to that of San Gimignano, were unusually severe. The first two and a half years of their sentences were to be served in solitary confinement, which meant living in a cell of ten by six and a half feet, and in Vinciguerra's case, without even a table and chair. The bed was padlocked against the wall at 7:30 every morning; exercise was confined to forty minutes a day in the prison yard, and visitors were limited to one a month, in the presence of two carabinieri. The prisoners were allowed to receive books, but no writing materials, and were forbidden to speak to their warders.[34]

The whole trial was deliberately and skilfully conducted in a manner calculated to produce as poor an impression as possible of the Alleanza Nazionale on the foreign journalists who were warmly invited to be present. In addition to Vinciguerra and Rendi, four other men were brought to trial, of whom three were only guilty of having received leaflets of the Alleanza, and the fourth of having made some copies of them. All four expressed their regret and disclaimed their responsibility, and three of them were at once acquitted, while the fourth (who had copied out the leaflets) received a three years' sentence—the object clearly being to impress the foreign press both with fascist leniency and with the unimportance of the movement. They were timid, half-educated men, included in the trial merely to show the 'leniency' of the fascist authorities.[35]

This device was entirely successful. The correspondent of the *New York Times*, for instance, Cortesi—a notorious fascist—while forced to admit that 'Vinciguerra and Rendi maintained a dignified bearing throughout,' added:

It must be admitted that this first group of intellectuals did not cut a particularly good figure in its appearance before the Special Tribunal. Although several of their number were caught red-handed in the act of either writing, printing or circulating the pamphlets of anti-fascist propaganda, not one had the courage to make a clean breast of his political opinions against the present Italian régime. The majority protested that they were keen admirers of Mussolini and the fascist movement and tried to ingratiate themselves with the Tribunal by making fascist salutes to the right and left and loudly proclaiming their repentance. Even Mario Vinciguerra and Renzo Rendi, who were convicted as the ringleaders of the plot, tried to shift the greater part of the blame on their absent companion, Lauro de Bosis, and on various occasions accused each other of having played a leading part in the compilation of the incriminating circulars. [Both statements were untrue.] Indeed, looking back on the trial, one cannot but agree with one of the counsel for the defense, who exclaimed: 'These are not conspirators! They are idiots!'[36]

The foreign correspondents, however, were obviously not provided with copies of the courageous statement of Vinciguerra, a greatly respected historian and journalist, who—after pointing out that his summons to the trial had not included any explanation of the cause of his arrest—'except for a rumour of being dangerous to the order of the State,' proceeded to say:

> Though my political views are no mystery, no special accusation has been formulated against me ... It is probable that a recent episode had formed the pretext for suspicions of this kind, but all that the competent

authorities have been able to investigate about any aspect of my life excludes . . . not only that I should be habitually guilty but should even occasionally or unaware, have been guilty of *crimes* . . . or even of attempts against 'the personality of the State' . . . What is ascertained with regard to myself is as follows: that I have never heard anyone speak of secret societies, and that any such suggestion would at once have ended my relationship with whoever had done so . . . May I be permitted to lay claim to the consistency and inflexibility with which, in all my career as a historian and writer, I have served my country as a conservative liberal under a Constitutional Monarchy, strengthened by the studies I am making of our Risorgimento . . . I have served this ideal within the limits of my capacity, but openly and with complete independence of judgement, without any incoherence or ambiguity, and also, in the difficult times after the War without intolerance or intemperance . . . To sum up everything in a few words, moved by a filial sentiment of love for my country . . . even the most restrictive of the current laws cannot establish that the profession of liberal is a crime or an attempted crime . . .

It is a pity, though under the circumstances inevitable, that this courageous and sincere speech—with which Rendi (though himself no orator) agreed—did not reach the foreign press. But of course this was not the Court's purpose. The only comment made was in *Italy Today*:

We are convinced that every impartial reader will admit that they [the pamphlets] contain not a single word which 'instigates to insurrection against the powers of the State.' It is not to 'instigate to insurrection' to urge citizens to rally round the King, the

Army and the Pope, in order to free a country from a dictatorship that has abolished the Constitution, and to forestall the triumph of the communist party on the day when the dictatorship falls.[37]

But the sentence was nevertheless served by both men, in its full rigour. None of Vinciguerra's statement was printed anywhere abroad, and our only knowledge of it comes from *Italy Today* which necessarily had a very small circulation.

All this was bad enough, but what most deeply upset Lauro was that his mother's letter had been read aloud in Court, and also his own letter to the Italian Ambassador. 'Now many believe,' he wrote to Ruth Draper, 'that I am an "agent provocateur" and Mother a traitor.'[38] For his mother he was prepared to make every excuse:

> [She] has been fooled by people around [her] and by the lawyer. I feel perfectly sure that if she had con-tinued in her heroic attitude of the first day, not only would she not have run any risk, but she would not have been tried . . . I cannot blame her because, apart from the rest, she has been fooled by everybody, but I regret even more that I left Italy in October . . . [39] [And a few days later] I have passed days of deep bit-terness, realizing every day more completely what a terrible blow to the credit of the movement and to the cause in general Mother's weakness has been.[40]

To his mother herself, however, when at last he suc-ceeded in telephoning to her from a friend's house in Paris, he spoke with his usual warm affection, which became her chief comfort in the terrible remorse from which she suf-fered later on.

Lauro soon found himself a job as a concierge in the Hotel Emanuel III, in Rue Ponthieu, near the Champs Elysées, and between carrying out his duties of calling cabs and sending up breakfasts, he was composing two more pamphlets, which were posted to Italy by friends from various European cities, and also compiling for the Oxford University Press an excellent anthology of Italian poetry. He was even able to send a small contribution to Vinciguerra's and Rendi's families—500 francs out of his monthly wage of 800. 'You cannot imagine what a joy it is to send even so small a sum, but earned by *me*.'[41]

To Salvemini he wrote, after seeing the account of the trial in the *Evening Post* and the *New York Times*:

> I have heard that in a single day after the arrest [of his mother and friends] our Embassy received more than 500 telegrams of protest from all over America. I have been assured that I wasn't tried owing to the recommendation of De Martino and the Morgan Bank, who feared the impression that would be made in America where I have so many friends. The Ambassador does everything possible to give the impression that I was not the originator [of the movement] but a good, rather unbalanced young man led by bad companions. P. S. I think it would be very important to write in your publication that the Special Tribunal refused to listen to the witnesses for the defence, and the extraordinary fact that a Foreign Minister and an Academic [Fedele and Volpi] were willing to testify in our favour.[42]

In February Lauro sent to Salvemini the draft of one of the pamphlets he had written in Paris, which friends were posting for him to Italy from various cities abroad, and for which he had apparently asked H. G. Wells to write a preface.

Wells has replied that he cannot write the preface on a point of principle. He does not approve that we should desire to reconstruct Italy together with the King and the Vatican. Evidently he has not read the last paragraph in which it is clearly stated that the Alleanza does not wish to impose a programme for the future . . . We believe that the three plagues of Italy (fascism, monarchism and the Vatican) must be eliminated one by one, but that to attempt to resolve all three with one blow would only lead to their conservation. Neither Vinciguerra nor any of us are more monarchist by a hair's breadth than our friends of Giustizia e Libertà. We only believe in the necessity of manoeuvring with forces which do exist and not with ideas (which we share) but behind which there is not today in Italy the strength to fall back upon. That this opinion is right seems to me to be shown by the attitude of fascism towards the Alleanza. It seems to me clear that no formula has so much preoccupied fascism as that of the A.N., as is shown by the sentences inflicted.[43]

At this time Lauro was leading a very lonely life. Apart from Salvemini and sometimes the Nitti family or Sforza on his way through Paris, he saw scarcely anyone since most of the anti-fascists in Paris disagreed with his opinions and did not wholly trust him, and there were few other people whom it was safe to see. He did have occasional visits, however, from his faithful friend Ferrari, a monarchist Catholic living in Brussels, and was introduced by him to another great admirer of the National Alliance, the monarchist Auguste d'Arsac, a rich newspaper proprietor who, later on, helped Lauro to raise most of the funds needed to buy his first plane.

Salvemini, in their friendly but often vehement discussions, did not hesitate to say to Lauro how little he believed in his getting any serious help from either the Church, the Army or the King:

> Pope Pius Eleventh forbids the clergy to participate in politics because 'the kingdom of Heaven is not of this world'; and so the anti-fascist little parish priests are obliged to stay shut up in their churches, confining themselves to administering the Sacraments. But if some Cardinal, Bishop or Jesuit wished to make a public demonstration in favour of Mussolini and his government, you may be sure that no superior authority will ever remind him that 'the kingdom of Heaven is not of this world' . . . As for the army, the soldiers—almost all workmen or peasants—are strongly anti-fascist. But the higher officers are almost all pro-fascist . . . If the King decided to abandon his passive attitude the situation would change . . . but it is useless to hope for this. The first stand with which one resists is strength of character, and that is just what he lacks . . . Victor Emanuel III . . . is not a man but a machine for signing decrees. He is the *roi fainéant* in the highest degree—the last of the Merovingians.[44]

But none of these arguments convinced Lauro. He and Salvemini argued interminably, never agreed, and remained on as good terms as before.

> The more I go on [Lauro wrote to Ruth from Paris] the more I realize how little foreign opinion weighs in the balance. We must work out our problems ourselves. If Freedom wins, it is right; while it is still engaged in the fight it cannot but represent for the average foreigner anything but a disturbing force. It is not right that gives success, but success that enables people to see

where the right was. If the American Revolution had failed, Washington and Jefferson would be considered as seditious Bolsheviks; if the Civil War had been lost, Lincoln would be considered a kind of George III . . . But I promise you we will win. And, if I am not mistaken, I can still give a hand to it.[45]

To Salvemini, in a letter explaining the sequence of events, he wrote:

> You can imagine how I feel about Vinci [guerra] and Rendi. It is a bitter irony that I should be free instead of them and I shall have no peace of mind until the fight is over . . . I had arranged for other people to do the mailing and especially emphasized that Vinci should not do it because he was too suspect . . . While waiting for some other man to be found to carry on the A.N. in Italy, I will continue the mailing of circulars from abroad. Even if one tenth arrives, it will start the chain in the interior again.[46]

And later on: 'Fascism is not going to fall by itself, suddenly leaving a hole that must be filled by somebody; it will be overthrown by a group of people or interests. It will make a tremendous difference in the general situation whether these forces come from the right or from the left.'[47]

In his letters to Ruth, Lauro's strongest wish was to make her feel not only that he was in no danger, but was always close to her in spirit. But certainly, as Salvemini wrote, the following months were for him 'a time of silent, tragic grief.' How could he defend himself against the reproach that he was enjoying freedom while his friends were buried alive? How explain and justify the bewilderment of his poor mother? What saved him from utter despair was the crystallisation in his mind of what had been there for a long time: the conviction that he could only testify to his own moral rectitude by recklessly facing the mortal danger of flying over the city of Rome, dropping leaflets exhorting the King and the Italian people to listen to the call of honour and duty.[48]

Lauro had indeed already taken the first steps to realise this dream. He had turned to an old Harvard friend, Eric Wilmer Wood, a retired pilot who had distinguished himself in World War I in the Pacific and who seems to have been a man of much experience and common sense. In a letter dated 12 November 1930, Lauro told Wood about the foundation of the Alleanza Nazionale, adding that he had a scheme for which he needed Wood's advice:

> I don't know whether you read about it in the papers, but last August a young Italian called Bassanesi learned to fly and after only ten hours of flight, flew from Switzerland over Milan, throwing down anti-fascist manifestos. On his way back, being so inexperienced, he crashed in the Swiss Alps and broke a leg (nothing serious). Unfortunately, the manifestos were not good, because he was a socialist, but anyhow they made a tremendous hit in Italy and his gesture has become a great spur and symbol. Now I must absolutely do the same thing for the National Alliance and . . . if I succeed it will make a far greater impression. Because instead of appealing to the lower classes and socialists and preaching insurrection as the other man did, our movement appeals to the higher classes and preaches organisation and political manoeuvres rallying round the King, the Pope, the Army and the Senate.
>
> Now what do you advise me to do? I can probably raise several thousand dollars. How much do you think the flight would cost? Do you know anybody in France or England that might be willing to do it with

me? or is it better that I should learn to fly and do it alone? Would it be too difficult or too expensive to reach Rome instead of Milan? I suppose it might be better to do it by night to avoid anti-aircraft guns. Would you advise a hydroplane? . . . It would be glorious![49]

Soon after he added that he had now spoken to Bassanesi and learned that his flight had cost 45,000 francs ('I could easily find that sum') and that he was now definitely planning his flight to Rome: 'I could, I think, learn to pilot in three or four months, but of course the ideal would be to find an experienced flyer, who would just take me for the raid. He would not risk anything, because being a [foreigner] he would merely be expelled. Could you find such a man? If you have hopes to find him, send me a cable addressed to Tristram Shandy, Morgan Bank, Paris.'[50]

Wood's sympathetic but discouraging reply came a few weeks later:

> I did not answer you at once for two reasons. I wanted time to think out what advice to give you, for I feel quite a responsibility. You have too many friends and you are too valuable to Italy to be in a position to make any mistakes. Furthermore we know each other's temperaments so well that I took it for granted that I could read between the lines of your letters that you wanted me to come over and do the flying. There is nothing I would rather do than put my plane aboard a liner and sail at once to help you. I cannot leave America at present, but any Cause that is yours is also mine. All I can do is to give you expert advice regarding the plane and the flight . . .
>
> It is easy to learn to fly if all you want to do is to circle over an airport. The flight you mention is extremely difficult, and includes either flying over

water in a landplane or over land in a seaplane. It may also include flying through bad weather, flying after dark, a forced landing in rough country, and escaping from military pursuit planes equipped with machine guns . . . So it is completely out of the question for you to attempt to learn to fly without sufficient skill and experience to undertake the flight without at least two years' of intensive training.

I know no-one in Europe that I can advise for a pilot, but whoever you choose should have the following qualifications:

1) He should have had at *least* 600–800 hours flying experience.

2) He should have had at *least* 200 hours in the air during the past year. (No war-time flyers who have neglected their flying.)

3) He should recently have passed an airplane pilot's physical examination.

4) He must have had a great deal of experience in 'cross-country' flying over routes he does not know, and

5) If the flight is to be made partly or altogether at night, he should be one of the best pilots in Europe and must have had considerable experience in night flying . . . I consider your choice of a pilot the most important decision you must make.

Now, Lauro, here is some advice that you won't like, but which I *know* is right . . . Since you are not going to fly the plane yourself, and anyone can drop pamphlets, there would be no excuse for you to go on the flight at all. You are too valuable on the ground, and your job is to organise the plan, write the pamphlets, and stay on the ground . . .

I gather from your letters you wish to drop the pamphlets on Rome and Milan, and to leave from

Corsica. I do not know whether there is a suitable flying field for landplanes that you could use in Corsica, nor whether one could level off a field there without arousing suspicion. If so, you can use a landplane; if not, you must use a seaplane. Whatever plane you use probably would not have a cruising range of over 500–600 miles. Therefore I suggest that you fly from Corsica to Rome and then return to Corsica for fuel. In case you use a seaplane it *might* be possible to refuel at sea from a boat, but this is doubtful . . .

Should the flight be made by day or by night? Here are two answers. It would be better to make the flight by day because a) it would be more spectacular, since the people would actually see the plane, and would see the pamphlets fluttering down . . . b) there would not be the risk of night flying over an unlighted route . . . c) it would show the [pilot's conviction] that his pamphlets would be sympathetically received by many people. It would be better to make the flight by night (if you can find a pilot of sufficient nightflying experience) because a) you would stand less chance of being shot; b) it would be less likely that anyone would find out where the plane came from; c) it would add mystery to the pamphlets.

If the flight is made by day, the weather should be heavy broken clouds 1,000–2,500 ft. in altitude, for it would be possible to disappear rapidly if pursued. If by night, the route is without beacons and over open water, the weather must be excellent, with clear sky and a moon . . .

I suggest you first obtain your pilot, and have him help you to decide what type of plane to use . . . If the flight was to be made in this country, I would advise your using either a Lockheed Vega on pontoons or a Consolidated Fleetstater on pontoons. A type of high performance biplane such as the 500 H.P. Boeing or Stearman mailplane would also do . . . I think your best chance for success would be to fly with a very fast plane on pontoons in cloudy weather, and to arrive at your destination just as the sun goes down, approaching from at 12,000 or 15,000 feet . . .

I will await eagerly any further news from you.[51]

It is hardly necessary to say, given Lauro's temperament and the circumstances which led him to make this venture, that the advice to stay on the ground himself was ill-received:

Pardon me if I only tell you that my blood curdled seeing that you could seriously suggest that I should not go on the trip! But probably you don't realise: that the whole object is to acquire the right to speak to the Roman people and to the King through some daring and gallant enterprise like that one. The fact that my lieutenants are in prison for 15 years and that I am free, is such a shame that unless I justify to my own conscience my freedom with the hope of doing something of that kind, I would cross the frontier just to give an example of gallant behaviour at a trial. People do not realise that my mother is 66 and nervously prostrated, and her behaviour at the trial has been a terrible blow that I can counteract only with something sensational like the flight to Rome . . .

I went Sunday to London on purpose to speak to a distinguished aviator. He at first jumped at the idea and seemed quite enthusiastic and ready. Today he telephoned that he had thought it over and that one should not try before May on account of the weather . . . I am trying now to persuade another man with more experience to try it with me now . . . [52]

A few days later Lauro's news was more definite:

> I have found the plane, the money and *all* the other
> paraphernalia. I had found also a man (an Italian), but
> afterward he withdrew because, being a staunch anti-
> monarchist, he did not approve of the leaflets. So I am
> going to England again to look for another man. The
> idea now is to go by motor boat to the Eastern beach
> of Corsica, where we would meet the plane (coming
> from Nice), load the cargo of leaflets (250 lbs, equal-
> ling 300,000 leaflets) and proceed. Corsica-Rome-
> Corsica is only 315 miles and with a plane making 130
> miles an hour we can escape even the pursuit of an
> Italian military plane, provided we had an advantage
> of 15 minutes, which it is logical to admit, considering
> the surprise . . . The time for such an exploit seems
> now most favourable as the situation of the King is
> very tense and ought to be brought to a crisis. A flight
> stirring the citizens to rally around the King would
> face him with a dilemma that he could not avoid any
> longer . . . If the glory or the fun of the enterprise ap-
> peals to you at all and if you might consider it for May
> or June cable me the word.[53]

But within a few days, Lauro told Wood that he had
taken his own decision:

> Just after the last letter I sent you I had a long talk
> with an aviator here and I have decided to become a
> pilot myself . . . After all it is my own business . . .
> Please don't worry about me: I promise you that I will
> not do it until I feel absolutely sure of myself and un-
> til the others too feel that I am an accomplished avia-
> tor. I am going to learn to fly a Farman, because being
> all in wood it floats (sic). Of course I am learning to fly
> in secret.[54]

So the correspondence ends, except for a sad little note of condolence from Wood to Ruth many months later: 'Now that Lauro is definitely no longer with us, I find that he still seems more and more real than anyone I know who has passed on.'[55]

As soon as the decision was taken to be his own pilot, Lauro wasted no time. Early every morning beginning on 16 April he bicycled out to a small airfield near Versailles, at Toussus le Noble, where he took his first flying lessons. After thirty-five days [24 May], the instructor got out of the plane and said to his pupil: 'Allez, Monsieur c'est à vous maintenant.'*

During this period all Lauro's letters to Ruth (quoted in the following chapter) show his desire to convince her of his continuing love for her, and of the happiness they would still have together—and above all, to allay her fears that he was in danger in Paris. But the letters also betray an increasing anxiety that Ruth should not give way to her first instinct to drop her New York season and sail at once to Paris to join him.

The plane in which he proposed to fly was an English Moth bought with money mostly supplied by his friend and admirer Ferrari through M. d'Arsac. Lauro had been to examine the landing ground in Corsica which was in a field called Ghisonaccia near Bastia and had considered it entirely satisfactory. There has been some discussion as to whether Lauro flew the plane there himself or whether an English pilot brought it to him, but there now appears to be no doubt that the pilot was delayed by the English customs because he was carrying so many papers, and it was the pilot who flew the plane over. When he reached Ghisonaccia Lauro was waiting for him, but the ground was not as suit-

---

*'Go ahead, Sir, it's up to you now.'   —Quoted by Franco Fucci, *Ali Contro Mussolini*, p. 170.

able as he had thought and the plane crashed, breaking a wing, scattering the papers over the rocks. Lauro's secret was out.[56]

At this point, perhaps ill-judgedly, he decided that his safest course—to convince the Italian police he had no intention of trying again—was to tell everyone, even his own family, that he would return to America.

On one of his visits to London to stay with Ruth, who had now gone to England, Lauro left with her a long letter to be sent, when possible, to his mother. It is dated 26 June 1931:

> Dearest Caramadre
>
> You must undoubtedly have thought that the letters I have written you this winter were not only scarce but stupid; it is perfectly true, because I was unable to say anything about what was really on my mind, and everything else seemed futile and unimportant . . .
>
> Today, instead, I am writing a long letter in order to tell you everything . . . I wonder how many times you have thought about me with sadness, imagining me nothing but a broken and defeated exile compelled to make a living as a hotel porter, with hardly a hope of betterment or of revenge.
>
> Instead, after the first days of uncertainty, I have for the past six months been entirely absorbed by the great dream, which, unknown to all, was buried deep in my heart. Twenty times it looked as though my dream would be shattered forever; and twenty times I was able to rebuild it anew. What days, what anxiety, what champing at the bit at the delay; and also how much hidden joy!
>
> On behalf of my dream I have crossed the sea seven times; three times I went to London, twice to Corsica.

Does Mussolini really believe that he can prevent me from returning to Italy? Does he believe that he has suppressed the Alleanza and bent me to his will? What do his three hundred thousand bayonets, his fifty thousand spies count against Pegasus? Pegasus is my beautiful winged horse which I finished taming just three days ago and which now carries me far into the skies with a grace all his own. He is all silver with blue harness and has the power of eighty mortal horses. He takes no food, but drinks a sweet and transparent nectar—at the rate of five gallons per hour! His speed is but eighty miles an hour, so that when compared with the Fascist chimeras who can do two hundred and are equipped with machine guns, he looks like a little pigeon or a lamb. This does not matter; thus he can fly over Rome as silently as a shadow. The motor will be stopped over Ostia, when our height will be greater than that of Mont Blanc (5,500 metres), and from there we will volplane until we find ourselves above the terrace of our house where perhaps you will be taking coffee; and you will say: 'I wonder what Lauro is doing now in America?' and all the time I shall be near you and will have a great desire to jump down from my saddle and slip down amongst you in my beautiful white silk parachute. But never mind. I will throw down my two hundred thousand letters (I who never wrote to you!) and I hope that some will fall on our terrace. Will you recognize my style? Not in the letters but in the gesture? Will you understand that it can be no other than I? Will you be worried? Will you be proud? Will you think of Italy? Will you think of the future difficulties you may have? . . . I will spare you the story of all the difficulties I have overcome. The greatest was to tell my angel; but after the first shock she was wonderful, and never said one word to deter me. Just imagine, I passed the medical examination on the day that she arrived in Paris.

In case this letter reaches you after a failure, forgive me for having made such an optimistic digression. I am not counting on failing. Whatever happens I shall have won. It is better to fall in the attempt of flying over Rome than to live for another thirty years as a peaceful bourgeois with utilitarian ideals. Even if the flight ends in a catastrophe, it can only further the Cause, because the dangers are all on the way back, after my two hundred thousand letters have been delivered. And once that has been done, my life will have been justified . . . These letters will make an impression. Will they prick the conscience of my fellow citizens? Will they constitute a lesson in civic spirit? This is hardly my concern. I do my part. The others will do what they can.

As you can imagine, the idea came to me as soon as I read the outcome of the trial . . . It became a definite plan when I heard that the fascists thought I would retract in order to return to Italy. From that moment it became an obsession. I have gone under ten different names; have had to surmount incredible difficulties and find a solution for ten thousand minor problems. It seems only yesterday that you used to tell me about Bellerophon's difficulties in conquering Pegasus. And yet his difficulties were a mere trifle compared to mine.

The customers of the Hotel Victor Emanuel III (what do you think of that name?) who heard the hotel porter call up the stairs: 'Irma, two pats of butter for number 36' or 'Helen, prepare the bath for No. 28' never noticed that on the back of the old bills scattered on my desk I was composing an open letter to the King, and a message for the citizens of Rome.

I do not know today if the thing will be a success or if I will end like Icarus, but you must understand that the enterprise is of a kind which would make any sacrifice worth while. I have thought of everything and would not have the slightest regret. Naturally I am not doing it for my personal satisfaction. I have much more grave, serious and above all sober reasons for making the attempt. It is first of all my duty because I am an Italian; then because I am the head of the Alleanza Nazionale and am free while my two friends are in jail for having believed in me. And aside from the above reasons I must confess to the joy and satisfaction I feel in having a fourth reason in as much as I am the author of Icaro. I hope that no longer will they say that it was full of rhetoric . . . Will you glance once more at the pages of Icarus? In any case when you start looking at the leaflets I shall already be on my way towards the coast without even having troubled to restart my motor. Followed? Shot at? I hardly think so. Perhaps followed by search-lights. But who cares? With the polar star on my right wing and the red light of the compass before my eyes, I will steer towards Corsica. I shall smell her sweet air even before I see her earth. After half an hour the moon will come to my assistance and I will do the rest of the journey singing. Perhaps for the first time I shall be able to compose some decent verses. At midnight a spark! My wings will spurt out a wave of light. For five minutes, enough to enable me to recognize the trees of Fiumorbo, the meadows of Ghisonaccia. And now earth. A little food and maybe a couple of hours of sleep. And before dawn away towards the north! I will

alight at the mouth of the Rhone and renew my gasoline supply, then on towards the north. I will fly over
Vaucluse, Orange, Avignon, Lyons and all those val-
leys for which the Rhone is famous; then to Geneva
where my angel is awaiting me. Oh, why can't I find
you also there to welcome me! But if they haven't
given you your passport until now, they had better do
so now. From now on I shall have the whip hand. With
the prestige of the flight over Rome I shall return
to America in triumph and will go on a lecture tour
which you will hear about![57]

After reading this letter, one would be inclined to believe
that Lauro really thought he would come home again. I do
not think this was so, though in writing to his mother, he
would naturally be inclined to stress the optimism which
they both had in common.

A more significant letter is the one which he wrote to
Ferrari, in London on 22 June, but did not post until he left
Marseilles on 2 October, when he sent it to Brussels together with 'The Story of my Death.'* (Possibly it was a
first draft.)

My expert (in England) has told me that I have not got
one chance in ten of success and, like a proper Englishman, smiles politely behind his spectacles. One
chance in ten! But it's much more than I need. My expert does not imagine that the most convenient road
for me to find my peace of mind again is the road to
Rome. It would take a great deal of courage to give
it up.

And then all the dangers will be on the way back. I
shall undoubtedly reach Rome, and once my business
there is done, I can close the balance of my life . . .

*See Appendix I.

Above all one must show the young that the Liberal cause has still got enough appeal to make a man happy to give up his life for it. For a long time now we have been told that the Liberal idea is bankrupt and has no more attraction for the young. Fascism has made great efforts to attract the young, and with children has been very successful. They are given uniforms, pistols, out-door raids, everything that is barbarous and primitive in every child's mind is brought to the surface and for a few years, they are caught. That is what I most condemn in fascism—that it has brought out all that is cruel and medieval in human nature, to catch men's souls. This romantic corruption of the spirit, this reversal of all essential values—that is the worst crime of fascism and the wound which will be the slowest to heal. Freedom, as exalted for sixty years by old professional politicians, has lost something of its glamour. Fascism was needed so that its bruised splendour might be appreciated again. Mussolini called it 'a decaying corpse' and taught his servants to laugh at it. Boys of eighteen were only ten years old when Matteotti was murdered, they only know the empty but fascinating words of this great corruptor, who attracted them like the pirates they read about in Salgari's adventure books. The myth of Mussolini fascinates them like the myth of Athis, for whose sake we are told that men were ready to endure castration, or like the myth of Adonis . . .

Mussolini has isolated Italy; no news arrives there from abroad; she stews in the barbaric and hypnotic sauce that her chef prepares for her every morning. The earth and the sea are his, but the sky still belongs to free men. Bassanesi has shown us the way—all honour to him! Let his example be followed. If soon there will be five or six 'free lances' prepared to fly across the Italian sky, bringing the glad tidings of freedom, Italy's torpor will vanish and her people will again move forward on the great road to freedom.[58]

This is the letter of a man who does not expect to return—and perhaps does not want to.

After Corsica it was clearly not safe for Lauro to return to England or France, and moreover he had decided to look in Germany for a stronger plane, more suited to the rough ground of Ghisonaccia. Ruth was able to join him in Geneva and from there she was able to follow him in Germany and Switzerland—though always, on Salvemini's advice, in places where they would not be conspicuous. At first they found a delightful little manor-house in the Engadine, near Zuoz, where they walked, talked, played tennis and read aloud. But one obstacle followed another. Lauro had great difficulty in finding a suitable plane at a reasonable cost. Then the German friend, who was to have brought the plane down to him in France, was held up and by then the weather was deteriorating. Both of them found these prolonged delays very trying, and spent part of the time on a bicycle trip in Bavaria and the Black Forest.

At last, in Munich, Lauro was able to find a suitable plane and two German pilots, Max Rainer and Hans Böhning, who also became his instructors. At last, too, a date was settled—8 September—on which the pilots were to bring the plane down to him. But then there were four more weeks delay, which Ruth and Lauro spent between Talloires, Annecy and Geneva, and it was settled for the pilots to meet Lauro in Marseilles, while Ruth waited in Cannes.

The final part of this story should be told in detail, and in the words of the last man who spoke to Lauro—his German pilot, Max Rainer:

> At about two p.m. [wrote Max Rainer to Ruth] we saw a taxi coming. Out of it jumped Mr. Morris [Lauro's

pseudonym] looking very happy and greeting us very heartily. He gave the driver orders to go to the hangar where his machine is and told us he has to start immediately . . . We took out of the bird all our belongings, while Mr. Morris brought several little sacks filled with printing matter to the machine. Of course, we didn't think anything about it, as he had already told us in Munich that he has contracts for advertisements. His nervousness we thought was due to the fact that he didn't fly for about 3–4 weeks, so I begged him to have a couple of trial flights before starting for Barcelona. 'I have not time,' he told me. 'It will be all right!' Now I had to get some oil for the motor, which took about ten minutes. During that time Mr. Morris put all the printing matter on the front seat of the bird, while Mr. B[öhning] was overlooking the machine . . . Filled as the bird was now, it had a cruising radius of at least 8–9 hours, plenty for Barcelona and back to Nice.

Lauro gave the pilots some money for their meal and then another sum, presumably for their journey.

Then he took his place in the machine and strapped himself to his parachute. Along he took an ordinary glass bottle of I think café. We didn't like to let him go, as long as he was so nervous, so I said: 'Mr. Morris, don't forget pumping the gasoline *timely* from the wing tank to the main tank, otherwise the engine will stop.' Then Mr. Morris asked me about the searchlight I brought him along for a present . . .

Now we took the bird with Mr. Morris sitting in it out of the hangar, the taxi-driver helping us. As I feared Mr. Morris will forget the pumping, I told him once more not to forget. By that time he was more calm . . . Soon the engine was running and I said to Mr. Morris, 'Goodbye, good luck and *Aufwieder-sehen* at Nice tonight! . . . ' Then I looked at the bird when it started and waved hands for our dear Mr. Morris. The start was excellent . . . The rest you know.

As, according to the talk we had over the wire from Antibes, you did not know anything about the intention of your friend, I imagine you was stunned like we . . . It is contenting [comforting] to know that at least he achieved what was perhaps his wish for a long time.

I still hope Mr. Morris our dear comrade lives and writes . . . Enclosed you find three pictures which have been in no newspapers, because I declined every offer.[59]

It is very plain from the letter that his German pilots too had succumbed to Lauro's charm; but the only other correspondence between them and Ruth is a sad little answer to a letter of hers of 6 May, asking if Rainer had any souvenir of his: 'Of the personal little things there is in my hands only comb and brush, some toothpicks, a piece of underwear which I always kept nicely waiting for you or your friend to show up some day.'[60]

As soon as Lauro thought he was out of sight, he veered towards Corsica and flew slowly, in greeting, over the villa of a sick friend, Jean Loison, then off to the open sea. The route he had chosen was the following: Capo Carso, the island of Monte Cristo, Rome, Corsica, Ghisonaccia—at a height of 4,000 metres. He prepared to cover the last 20 kms planing slowly down, with the engine kept very low, so as to arrive silently and by surprise on the capital.

According to all witnesses, the plane arrived over Rome soon after 8 p.m. It had been flying for five hours. The sun had set two hours before, but there were still fifty minutes of good visibility. From a height of 300 metres he accelerated again and began to throw his leaflets* over the capital. Their white rain fell, too, on Piazza di Spagna, but all the de Bosis family were away.

The tiny, gossamer-thin leaflets, headed 'National Alliance' and signed 'the Directors of National Alliance' (two of them headed '8th year since the murder of Matteotti') were four: two addressed to the general public, one to the boys enrolled as 'avanguardisti' and 'balilla,'† and one to the King. Lauro scattered 400,000 copies of them, besides some copies of Bolton King's 'Fascism and Italy.'

'Just as one drops food on a starving city, so one must drop history books on the city of Rome.'

The leaflets addressed to the fascist organisations for the young urged all Italian mothers to refuse to let their children be enrolled at the age of eight into the Balilla, 'in order to be made into cannon fodder.'

The two appeals to the Italian people exhorted them to boycott every fascist enterprise and ceremony, and to give up smoking, quoting Bottai's remark that 'The Corporative State is the best police weapon ever invented.' 'For nine years you have been told you have a wise and powerful government. After nine years you realize that you have been under not only the most tyrannical and corrupt, but also the most bankrupt of governments . . . Have faith in Italy, have faith in freedom!'

Finally there was an emotional appeal to the King himself:

> At a sign from you six hundred thousand Italians laid
> down their lives to deliver two cities, Trento and Tri-

---

*See Appendix II.
†Boys from eight years on were enrolled in the Balilla, so-called after a little Genoese boy who threw a stone at an officer of the Austrian occupying army in 1848.

este . . . After Vittorio Veneto are you willing to break the oath with which your great ancestor at Novara kept faith? . . . Your Majesty must make Your choice. There is no middle course. From the depth of their despair, forty million Italians are looking to You.[61]

A great many people picked the leaflets up and put them in their pockets—among them the historian Massimo Salvadori who later on showed them to his sister.[62] On 6 October the London *Daily Herald* published a description of the event, and on the same day *Le Matin* of Paris published an account of 'a mysterious plane,' saying that its pilot, a Mr Morris, had sent a note to his pilots before leaving Marseilles saying: 'I deceived you. I am not going to Barcelona but to scatter anti-fascist leaflets over the capital. I hope then to fly back to Corsica and land there.'[63] Had the pilots known this sooner, they would of course have filled up the extra tank.

In Italy, on 8 October, a cheap afternoon paper, *Il Tevere* (which later on took part in an ignominious campaign against the Jews) gave a brief account of the episode, saying that de Bosis had sunk his plane and had been picked up by accomplices waiting for him in a boat off the coast of Corsica.[64]

Many of the leading European papers published the full text of 'The Story of my Death' at the same time as *Le Soir* of Brussels, including the London *Times*, the *Manchester Guardian* and the German *Vorwärts*, as well as the American *New York Times*. The London *Times* commented: 'So long as there are men like Lauro de Bosis, the safeguarding of freedom is assured.'[65]

On the opposite side, there were plenty of indignant protests. The strongest came from the Italian Ambassador in London, Antonio Bordonaro, in a telegram addressed to the Foreign Office, saying that while he had already protested himself to the editor of *The Times*, he considered that an Italian paper should draw attention 'in appropriate and measured terms' to this publication, contradicting its foolish assertions, and should be given to *The Times* correspondent in Rome. He added: 'If de Bosis is really dead, there is no point in arguing with the dead, but if one simply does not know, it would perhaps be desirable that Italy too should be informed of the absurd and impudent assertions contained in this document.'[66]

In Germany, the two pilots, Böhning and Rainer, were of course interrogated, but, thanks to Lauro's letter from Marseilles, were easily able to prove that they knew nothing of the real purpose of his flight. They were, however, forbidden to enter Italy again.[67] Finally the Italian police were given strict orders not to let Ruth Draper cross the Italian frontier.

Was the effect of these leaflets indeed as great as Lauro had hoped? Were they, as he intended, a turning point, which would lead to the fall of fascism? The question at this distance of time is almost irrelevant, since, as he well knew, the real value of his mission lay in his willingness to die for it.

There are many ways of defending freedom: that of the legislator and the politician, slowly and painfully building up a new manner of life; that of the soldier, fighting under orders to free his country from some form of tyranny, whether foreign or indigenous; and finally that of the individual willing to lay down his life for an idea—not only as a sensational gesture or a personal protest, but in the hope of galvanising others into action.

The effectiveness of such gestures cannot be measured at once, nor the mixture of motives which sometimes lead up to them, but they are still one of the ways by which a man, when all other efforts have failed, may fight for freedom.

The young men who perished as living torches in Poland, Hungary and Czechoslovakia have something in common with Lauro de Bosis, and died for a similar ideal.

The most convincing account of what must have really occurred is given by Lauro's two German pilots, Rainer and Böhning. We must remember that Lauro never told them of his real plans, but merely spoke of a flight to Barcelona and back to Nice, which they calculated as being about 800 kilometres. In addition he was carrying a heavy cargo of papers (about 100 kg, they estimated) and was known by them to be an inexperienced pilot. They therefore did not even fill up the plane to full capacity and Lauro left for Rome with one of his side tanks empty. By the time he had left Rome, after dropping his leaflets (a process which seems to have taken no more than thirty or forty minutes) he had already used up 130 litres of his fuel. In addition, the light fresh wind, the *libeccio*, which so often rises on summer evenings, was against him. His fuel must certainly have given out long before he reached Corsica—probably between 40 and 100 kilometres before his destination. This explains why no fragments of the plane were ever found; for most certainly, if the fascist planes had shot it down, their propaganda would not have hesitated to say so. On the contrary, the Roman papers received orders merely to suggest that an unknown plane had been seen flying towards Yugoslavia.[68]

Before leaving Marseilles, Lauro had many letters to send off, in a great hurry, from the Station Hotel—one to Ruth, one to Paul Winckler in Paris, presumably for forwarding to Ferrari, giving Ruth's Paris address 'in case of death or imprisonment.' The envelope also contained the whole 'Story of my Death,' Lauro's letter to Ferrari already quoted, and a hurried note 'Dear friend, in case of death, will you be so kind as to get these letters posted.' There was also a note for his pilots and the farewell letter to Ruth which she only received after his death.*

To Ruth, waiting with increasing anguish in Paris, a letter came at last from Ferrari, dated 7 October, and gave her the tragic news which she had feared for so long:

> Yesterday, I sent you the letter which my friend de Bosis sent me before leaving. I waited, before sending you his letter, for nearly three days, hoping to receive news of my courageous friend; but, the hope was vain. Even now, I still wish I could hope, but the facts impose themselves and we fear that the expedition, which started so well, went wrong after the flight over the Eternal City.
>
> Yesterday, too, following the wish of our unfortunate friend, I released to the Press the article—a kind of political Testament, which de Bosis sent me from Marseilles on the very day of his departure. It is a magnificent account of courage and abnegation and shows how he coolly and deliberately sacrificed his life for the cause of Italian freedom ... May Providence reward him for his incomparable sacrifice![69]

When the tragic news reached Italy, in the first hours after Lauro's death, his mother was upheld by something resembling her son's own exaltation. But this state of mind could not last and she was left with the stark reality of separation and loss. Several months later, her invincible optimism was still sustaining her, and for over two years these fluctuating states of mind continued.

On 12 November, Lauro's sister, Elena Vivante, received a telephone message from Paris, signed merely 'Hani,' from Hani Rendi Moser, the sister of Lauro's friend Rendi (now

*This letter is printed in the Ruth Draper chapter.

in prison) saying: 'It is known that the pilot is alive; nothing more, they do not know where he is.'[70]

On 28 December, a telegram to the Ministry of the Interior stated: 'We are informed that de Bosis is on an island about 40 miles from the Corsican coast. Immediately initiate intensive search in the Tuscan archipelago to control the above information.'

Later on, Lauro's brother Vittorio heard that the Air Minister had told a friend that the government knew where Lauro was hidden, and were following every step he took. 'I know,' Vittorio commented, 'that this is part of their tactics since the beginning to discredit the whole thing, taking away the tragic and heroic side of it, and [I] don't believe a word they say. But she [his mother] does. She thinks that it may be so and that supports her a little in her sorrow, though she feels that it can't be true.'[71]

    ∽

And now there is an epilogue, rounding up the story as life so seldom does, and as Lauro, in his most optimistic moments, would hardly have dared to hope.

In 1943–4, when the Comitati di Liberazione* (the shadow cabinet consisting of members of each anti-fascist political party who became, after the Allied victory, the founders and constituents of the new Italian Parliament) were being formed in every Italian city, the Roman Committee met, at considerable risk to their hosts, in the de Bosis house, at 66 Via Due Macelli, close to Piazza Venezia. The names of the members testify to their importance—men of such different origins and points of view as De Gasperi, Nenni and Saragat, Bonomi and La Malfa, Casati, Amendola, Fenoaltea and Gronchi; but now all were united by the same purpose as the original Allcanza Nazionale—

*Committees for the Liberation.

to build up a new Italy in a climate of freedom. It is difficult for anyone who has not lived in that period to feel its peculiar tension: the physical danger and the need for secrecy and discretion; the inevitable ups and downs of hope and fear, after so many years of waiting; the contacts with the approaching Allies and the departing (but not yet departed) Germans, and the daily problems of security.

The story has been told me by Lauro's sister Charis—the same sister who, fearing for her mother's health, had persuaded Signora de Bosis, many years before, to write a letter of submission to Mussolini. Charis and her mother were present at almost all the meetings.

The members of the committee—driven by a taxi-driver of the Partito d'Azione—came in discreetly, a few at a time (the de Bosis house had a courtyard giving on to many offices, so that frequent comings in and out were not too obvious). Inside the house there was a passage wide enough to hold a little secret room, for an emergency search, which could contain all the members at a pinch, with supplies of tinned food, biscuits, wine, etc. Usually the Committee met in the family living room where a fine geranium of Charis's concealed a bomb. Another brother of Charis's, Percy, was also staying in the house, with his wife who was daily expecting a baby. Percy was naturally becoming increasingly anxious and finally a family council was held, at which Percy said, 'Now this is enough! You must tell your friends to find another hiding place.' Some of the others protested.

'But do you realize,' said Percy, 'that the baby's birth will give us away, that they'll line us all up and shoot us?'

Signora de Bosis, at whom everyone glanced, was silent for a moment. Then, very calmly and firmly: 'Let them do so,' she said, 'I am ready.'

Surely in that moment Lauro's spirit was very near to his mother's, surely she felt that, at last, her brief hour of weakness long ago had been condoned.

But meanwhile Charis had come to feel that Percy was right, that this was too much to ask of a pregnant woman. Taking aside Fenoaltea (who was staying in the house) the next morning, she told him of the family decision, and he took himself off. But as she heard him reaching the front door, she ran after him.

'Come back this afternoon!' And so they did.

Thus, at the very end of her life, Signora de Bosis was able to recover her image of the son who had given his life for Italy's freedom. When they showed her the letter of thanks of the Comitato di Liberazione:

'Look,' she said, 'Lauro's leaflets are still falling.'

'Chi ebbe mai al mondo sì larga tomba?'*

*'Whoever in the world had so vast a tomb?'

Ruth Draper in 'Vive la France'

III

Ruth Draper

And Her Company of Characters

Our revels now are ended. These our actors,
As I foretold you, were all spirits, and
Are melted into air, into thin air . . .

. . . We are such stuff
As dreams are made on; and our little life
Is rounded with a sleep.
—SHAKESPEARE, The Tempest, IV.1

'My wonderful life goes miraculously on!' So Ruth wrote at over seventy to an old friend. She was right. It had been, and was until the last day, a wonderful life, culminating in a crescendo of zest, activity and success. But there was also, in her forties, a poignant and tragic episode about which only a few close friends knew at the time: just over three years of happiness and fulfillment with the young Italian patriot, Lauro de Bosis, whose story has been told in the preceding chapter, during which she took part in his revolt against fascism, and in the preparations for the daring exploit which brought him to his death. The courage which, after this tragedy, enabled her to pick up the pieces of her life and take up her work again, is a tribute both to her relationship with Lauro and to her own character—and enabled her, at over seventy, to make the remark I have just quoted.

But first I must go back to her own starting point—to the time when she was beginning to call up her 'Company of Characters.' When and how did she begin?

Perhaps she herself could not have said. A cousin, in whose house she often stayed in childhood, recollects that, when she was only nine years old, the other children would gather round her in the nursery at bedtime. 'Do the Channel crossing, Ruth!'—'Do the little tailor!'—'Do Fraŭlein!' And suddenly, sitting on the edge of her bed, the small girl in a nightgown would call up, for the benefit of her beguiled and soon wildly giggling contemporaries, a whole procession of mercilessly absurd grown-ups.[1] A little later on, it was the guests in her mother's drawing room who were portrayed in the sewing room or pantry. It was from one of the servants that, fifty years later, when Ruth was playing at the Gaiety Theatre in Dublin, a letter came: 'I'm not surprised at the Position you took up, as many a time Bridget Broderick was trying to control yourself and Master Paul in the Laundry room with your antics.'

Master Paul was Ruth's brother, the youngest and closest to her in age of the family of eight—Ruth's half-brother and sister, William and Martha Kinnicutt Lincoln Draper, and then Charles, George, Dorothea, Alice, Ruth (born on 2 December 1884) and Paul—who lived in Dr William H. Draper's house in 47th Street, New York. Ruth was born a New Yorker; it was her home, her starting point, the place where she was applauded first and always, and where she died. But New England was in her blood—on her father's side, from Vermont, on her mother's from New Hampshire. This strain was evident throughout her life. Her grandfather was Charles A. Dana, publisher and editor of the *New York Sun*; her father, a gifted musician as well as a brilliant and much-loved doctor, and the guests in their house came from the world of letters and music, as well as from that of 'old New York.'[2]

In the summer and sometimes in the autumn, there were long visits to the family house by the sea at Dark Harbor—swimming, swinging on tall silver birches, drinking in the cool air and light, and wide breakers and salt sea tang of the coast of Maine, putting down roots to which Ruth returned again and again in later years.[3]

One of her nieces, Penelope Draper Buchanan, wrote a vivid account of this place:

> A large grey shingled house with a broad verandah facing the western view, from which one window looks out across the harbor to Seven Hundred Acre Island and beyond that to the Camden Hills . . . Inside, the house was high-ceilinged and comfortable. The living-room and dining-room faced the view and opened into each other to give a lovely sense of light and space. Each had a fireplace. Above were some eight bedrooms for guests. Aunt Ruth's bedroom faced the western view and was simply and plainly furnished with rag rugs on the floor. All the rooms were plain. The great view, the pines and sunlight were decoration enough.

Dark Harbor was Ruth's haven, her fountain of youth.

> She always seemed to be most truly herself there—perhaps because of the associations with her childhood, when she sailed her little boat, the Flickamaroo, round the harbor, exploring every ruck and inlet. Here were so many memories of Paul and the silly games they played together, the role-playing which

eventually grew into her extraordinary art. Certainly one was even more aware there of her humour and tenderness, her deep love of the natural world, and her intense delight in her friends . . .

And it was there that, much later on, her friends from Italy found a safe and warm refuge. Her niece wrote:

> After supper we played games, from anagrams to PIG (a card game using clothes-pins). Salvemini loved playing PIG and scrambled for his clothes-pins as gleefully as the children. He used to throw back his head and laugh—those kind, wise eyes twinkling away behind his glasses. We loved him.

Before World War I, watching Aunt Ruth play tennis was a fascinating sight.

> Mrs. Gibson, Mrs. Howe, another lady and she used to play doubles. Mrs. Gibson wore a large Gibson girl straw hat, Mrs. Howe wore long white kid gloves, and Aunt Ruth sometimes tucked her skirt into her bloomers. Their game was gentle lobs and the conversation was superb. They never stopped gossiping. We used to watch, hypnotized. During the war the tennis court became a hayfield and Aunt Ruth and I would rake it. One perfect Maine day, she and I were raking the hay, each preoccupied with private thoughts and the rhythm of raking. Suddenly Aunt Ruth said: 'When you come right down to it, I don't like talking.' I did not reply and after a long silence she added, 'Or even thinking.' We continued to rake in companionable silence.
>
> Aunt Ruth used to read poetry to us as children, too, sitting on the wide verandah. Usually she read those poems which contained meaning and beauty to her. I remember one afternoon when I was about

eleven, feeling rebellious about the enforced rest. While looking to see if Aunt Ruth were nearly finished with Keats I was curiously embarrassed to notice the tears in her eyes. It was a wonderful thing for us that Aunt Ruth never tried to hide her response to beauty.

> She was always the first up in the morning and would lay the fires to take the chill off. Breakfast was her favourite meal and her special Dark Harbor indulgence was porridge, brown sugar and heavy cream. How she enjoyed it! She usually managed to put on 10–15 lbs. as a result and would fight all winter to get them off again.[4]

Another young relative, Joyce Grenfell, was equally observant:

> Ruth loved her food. Not to put too fine a point on it, she was plain greedy. She ate very fast, with appreciative little noises as she spooned in, and she was always the first to finish and ready for second helpings, before anyone else. I thought I had made a discovery when I told my father that Miss Ruth was a *bit* greedy. 'Well,' he said, 'well, yes.'[5]

As Ruth grew up, there were visits to museums, to concerts, to the theatre, and then her first parties as a debutante. As bright-eyed and industrious as a young squirrel, the girl stored up the inflections and gestures which became her stock in trade: *The German Governess, The Children's Party, The Boston Art Gallery, The Debutante*—all these date from early, ineradicable memories, as well as a few slighter sketches which gradually disappeared from her repertoire. *The Old Jewish Tailor* was one of them—the man who used to come to the house to do the family altering and mending. '"It could be fixed," he would say, "it could be fixed. Little padding on the shoulder. Pearl buttons here. Velvet collar. New lining. Semi-fitting back; box front."' Ruth remembered him later as a 'lovely little man.'[6]

At first it was at home that Ruth's talents were displayed. 'Do something to amuse us, my dear,' her mother would say after dinner.[7] By the time she was twenty, she was already in great demand for charity performances for the 'Junior League,'* and at many friends' parties.

But she was clearly beginning to feel that this sort of desultory work was not enough. She wanted a career and a purpose. She wrote some rather bad verses.[8] But she was still hesitating as to what shape her life should take.

Then three influences, each of great importance, affected her. One was the sight of some monologues performed by an English woman, Beatrice Herford.[9] The second was the sight of a Chinese play, done without scenery, 'small steps that one went up and down, so, when one wanted to enact a mountain—and I understood the extraordinary illusion that can be created with nothing.'[10]

But the third experience was the decisive one. One evening in about 1910 she received the advice which influenced the direction of her life. It was from Paderewski, an old family friend: 'You must do this professionally,' he said. 'Perhaps you should go to Paris to study. Mind you, I am not advising this. You may not need training. You must make the decision . . . from inside.' For the first time she was being spoken to, as an equal, by a professional.[11]

After this, she never looked back. In the spring of 1912 she was in England and during the next two years the circle of her admirers increased. She performed her sketches in many great London houses and in the presence of Royalty;

*The charitable organisation of the New York *jeunesse dorée*.

she was drawn by Sargent (once as a Dalmatian peasant woman and once as a Scottish immigrant).[12]

In 1911 'dear Uncle Henry Adams'* found comfort in her vitality and warmth: 'She is a little genius and quite fascinates me.'[13] Two years later, when she had begun her successful performances, he was able to help her in a charming manner.† H.R.H. Princess Christian of Schleswig Holstein, third daughter of Queen Victoria, asked her to recite privately for a small party of guests, including King George V and Queen Mary. It was then that Uncle Henry came to the rescue:

> We have had various passers by, the last and most vivacious being Ruth Draper . . . to get a dress for to act before the Queen who has sent for her through the Princess Christian. She has rushed my social secretaries about like wild gazelles but goes today, so that I shall probably pass only a part of my time at Worth's henceforward. The two lovely dresses I have made for her are of course too good for Queens, but what could I do?[14]

Early in July 1914, just before World War I began, she sailed for home in the SS *Lusitania*, looking forward to telling her mother about 'kind Uncle Henry.' But her mother suddenly died and she at once devoted her energies to working for war charities across the whole of the United States, for the benefit of the Red Cross and for French hospitals. 'I felt very strongly that I must go on with my work and that I must find new fields among strangers.' She gave thirty-eight performances in large towns in the Middle West, and stayed in a ranch with old friends in New Mexico. 'And

*Writer and biographer.
†'And he wouldn't take a cent, not a cent.'

there I recited to an audience of 200 or so miners, in the grocery store of the rough little town with two counters serving for a platform and the Sheriff with pistols on his hip, keeping order!'[15]

In July and August 1918 she worked, with the same unflagging zest that she brought to any new enterprise, in a munition factory in Bloomfield, New Jersey, standing ten hours at her machine and boasting to Laura White that she had turned out 170,000 percussion caps.

> It is the most satisfying feeling, this expending of physical force and all one's spirit and fervour as well. I really feel, as you say, that I must be winning the war! . . . I am quite used to this strange new life, my old one seems like a dream—Altman's and the Ritz as strange as Ancient Rome! . . . It is undoubtedly exciting to be part of the feverish activity of this great plant. There are 7,000 workers night and day and the morning walk with men and women all streaming one way from different roads is wonderful . . .[16]

But her real desire was to get back to Europe to entertain the Allied troops overseas, and on 12 October she sailed in the SS *Baltic* from England, crossing on the day of the Armistice, to France. There she met Harriet Marple, an attractive woman and excellent singer who soon became a close friend. They performed in Châtillon-sur-Seine, as Ruth wrote to her sister Martha, with four privates who sing together and a cellist, to an audience of three to six hundred every night. She described her surroundings with as much gusto as she accorded, many years later, to her evening at Windsor Castle, 'a little Court with a well dated 1672— moss-grown cobble stones—a walled garden of cabbages and spinach, and red roofs—a bed made for Heaven, and such food! My friends, the old *fabriquant de voitures*, who gives me his best Bordeaux *pour réchauffer l'estomac*, the baker's wife, her four beautiful grand-children and Migrette, the cat.'[17] After World War II she went back, in the hope of seeing them all again, but only found crumbling walls and deserted gardens.

After the Armistice Ruth and Harriet Marple took a bicycle trip in Ireland, met Yeats, A. E. and Gogarty, and took shelter in the house of an old Irish woman, who inspired Ruth's monologue 'In County Kerry.'[18]

Then Miss Marple went home and Ruth settled in a room in Ebury Street, where she took a great decision; she would become a professional. She booked two days in the Aeolian Hall, for 29 January and 27 May 1920, and filled it to capacity. The dates are described in her diary: her first fully professional performances, at the age of thirty-five a woman neither very young nor very beautiful, but whose success was immediate and lasted until the day of her death.[19]

She met 'everyone worth knowing,' and the British public took her to their heart. Perhaps the best way of realising its extent and variety is to look at her fan mail.[20] There are, of course, many famous names—over the years Edith Evans, Sybil Thorndike, Lynn Fontanne, John Gielgud, Laurence Olivier, George Arliss and Leslie Henson express the generous admiration of her fellow actors. Then came the musicians who belonged to the close circle of her old friends: the Kochanskys, the Salmonds, Artur Rubinstein, Olga Lynn, Kathleen Ferrier, Myra Hess. There was also a long list of critics and writers: G. B. S., Bernard Berenson and Isaiah Berlin, Gilbert Murray and Lawrence Houseman, Percy Lubbock and Rose Macaulay, Compton Mackenzie, John Masefield and Hugh Walpole. Some of them told her which their favourite sketches were: Gilbert Murray liked best 'The Lesson in Greek Poise,' Attlee, the study of the village post-mistress ('You contrive to present us with the essence of village life in England'), Rose Macaulay, 'Doctors and Diets.' 'I laughed and laughed . . . You are beyond doubt the most wonderful woman in two worlds, and I wish you were more often in this one.'

But the letters which evoke the essence of Ruth's popularity, and of Ruth herself, are however from the uncelebrated, anonymous admirers who filled her theatres to overflowing, thronged into her green-room, and often became her lifelong friends. There was a little Scottish boy of ten who was waiting for her one day at the stage door and with whom she kept up a close correspondence for ten years; there was a stage-struck Glasgow schoolgirl who was so overwhelmed by Ruth's promise 'to keep in touch with her' that she was ashamed to admit that she lived in the Gorbals, 'a district notorious for its poverty and squalor'—but wrote, the next day, to admit the truth.

And there was Fred Bason, the owner of a secondhand book barrow in Walworth, who wrote to tell Ruth that she was a 'dear sweet lady and the greatest actress in the world,' and who soon became a friend. 'I shall have the pleasure of calling for you around 5.30 on Tuesday, November 25, and if buses too full we'll go by tube to Elephant and Castle and get a bus there. We are working-class and home is humble, but clean and homely, and we are going to get a specially nice tea, with cake and a special treat of Flan.'

Some years later, the friendship was still prospering, and Ruth had sent two seats in the stalls to Fred and his 'lady.' 'It's the first time in her sixty years of life that she has ever sat in the stalls—but I am myself not quite a stranger to the posh seats.'

One of the letters that pleased her most was a little note from Ellen Terry: 'I am more delighted than I can tell you that you should like being at the dear old Coliseum. Of your success I was absolutely certain. *I'm just glad!*[21] This note shows in a very few words why so many people of all ages found Ellen Terry irresistible: it reveals her warmth, her generosity, her unpretentiousness. She once wrote to Bernard Shaw: 'I am happy *not* to be clever. You clever people miss so much, so much.' In writing about Ellen Terry, Virginia Woolf quotes this remark and continues,

> She never had a day's schooling in her life. As far as she can see, but the problem baffles her, the main spring of her art is imagination. Visit mad-houses, if you like; take notes; observe; study endlessly. But first, imagine. And so she takes her part away from the book out into the woods. Rambling down grassy rides, she lives her part until she is it. If a word jars or grates, she must re-think it, re-write it. Then, when every phrase is her own, and every gesture spontaneous, out she comes on to the stage and is Imogen, Ophelia, Desdemona.[22]

Ruth, too, seized the things that the 'clever people' so often miss which chill or warm the heart. Alone in her room, she imagined the people she wished to portray; she thought about them. Then, when she had lived herself into her subject, she worked before the mirror, experimenting with facial expression and gestures. Sometimes the preparation of a sketch, before she was satisfied with it, took eight or ten years. It was all done, she once said to my children, by imagination. 'Think *hard enough* about drinking the juice of seven lemons, and you'll have the right face!'

Where did she find her subject matter? In everyone she knew. Her sketches are a series of delicate, brilliant, utterly convincing conversation pieces—in which the only speaker, with many voices, is Ruth herself. She went round an English garden with her hostess; she sat in an Italian church. Then she went home, and worked. She worked very hard.

Joyce Grenfell, who had known her all her life, has left perhaps the most perceptive account of her technique:

> As well as making one see people and places, Ruth can make us see objects. Marcel Marceau, for instance, was a body mime: Ruth was a hand mime. She dealt with hairnets, hats and combs; knives, forks, and glasses; telephones, buttons and scissors, and so clear was she that there was no possibility of confusing a fork with a spoon or a button with a press-stud. When she cut the big pie to send out to the men on the snow-plough in *Railway Accident on the Western Plains* she used a slicer to put the pieces onto a plate. I swear I saw it. Buz, the boy who helped in the station buffet, had to carry it out. Before he went she scooped up the crumbs and popped them into his mouth, and when she told him to open wide the audience opened wide, too. I also remember the taste of those good brown crumbs.
>
> She came regularly to London and took a furnished house. We didn't always know exactly when she was coming, because she liked to get here and settle in and then announce herself over the telephone in a ringing voice that had no problem getting to the back of the dress circle. 'It's Ruth!' One had to remember to hold the receiver a little further off, but we were glad to know she was here . . . Until I was grown up I called her 'Miss Ruth' because she said 'Aunt Ruth' was false, 'Cousin Ruth' was prissy, and 'Ruth' was too familiar.* We had to be on our best behaviour with her, but it was worth it.

*Ruth Draper and Paul Phipps, Joyce Grenfell's father, shared mutual first cousins. See *Joyce Grenfell Requests the Pleasure*.

I think her most attractive quality was her genuine humility. She really was surprised by her enormous success. She laughed when she told us of records broken at box offices and House Full boards for every performance and she never got accustomed to her repeated triumphs. 'Isn't it *crazy*,' she used to say to my father. 'Paul, they must all be crazy! . . .'

When I was young I found all her love scenes embarrassing, and I couldn't take them because I knew her too well. I squirmed through all the 'Mrs. Mallory' sequence, in 'Three Women and Mr. Clifford' and when she did 'The Return,' about a brave young English woman expecting her wounded prisoner of war husband back to her thatched cottage, I didn't know where to look. [Many young people to whom I have played Ruth's recordings in recent years have felt the same.]

When I went back stage after her last performance at the St. James's Theatre, before it was pulled down, I had been more moved than ever before and I waited in the dressing room, where Gerald du Maurier always dressed, until the crowd had gone. Then I tried to tell her what the performance had meant to me. My diary records that I gave her a hug and said: 'I don't know how anyone dares mention my name with yours,' and she said: 'They don't.' I've been laughing ever since. But ruefully . . .

Nothing appeared to be automatic in Ruth's performances; her technique was formidable, firm as concrete, but it never showed. Her sketches stayed fresh and she played them with a first time quality. I was once in the wings, at the Haymarket, and Ruth was doing a dramatic piece in a three episode sketch. I was so lost in the story and her performances that I forgot it was Ruth acting out there and I was startled, in a brief pause between episodes, when she ran off stage and said to me in a rush: 'I'm starving! Get someone to go and fetch me a ham sandwich. Get two.' *Before* she turned to walk back into the lights she was instantly the next character.[23]

Notes often served merely as an accessory to her memory. The point of her sketches was not in their verbal brilliance—when one came home, there were few sentences that remained in the memory—but rather in the accuracy and delicacy of ear, which enabled her to build up her finished portraits. No two performances were precisely the same. A different inflection, an interpolated sentence, a new gesture—these, after forty years of repetition, still kept each part alive.

One day in the early 1920s Mrs Patrick Campbell persuaded Ruth to perform some of her monologues for Bernard Shaw. 'Have you ever seen such acting?' she demanded at the end. 'That's not acting,' Shaw replied. 'That's life.'[24]

As for Ruth herself, her accounts to her sister and to Harriet Marple of that first season at the Coliseum show how deeply it impressed her.

> It's an immense place and an immense sensation, I can assure you. The Coliseum is a wonderful institution—quite unique in its way, and the audience exceptionally intelligent and well-behaved. One has the sense of feeling, through that mass, all the finest, most endearing qualities of a human being; generous, sensitive, intelligent, kind, and one feels them near and friendly in spite of the vastness. The acoustics are wonderful. I go slowly but without effort, and I'm told every word is heard throughout the house ... You meet no-one, just do your turn, dress and go home.[25]

Two days later, to Harriet Marple:

> I was really very nervous and scared, for me, and you
> can't imagine the sensation of coming out before 2500
> people and facing that vast space and dazzling light . . .
> I did *The French Dressmaker, Three Generations* and
> *Vive la France* (in costume) with the Orchestra play-
> ing the 'Sambre et Meuse' as an Overture and then
> coming in pianissimo with drum beats when I see the
> troops and then crescendo and a final burst as I cry out
> at the end and exit. I never was so excited and moved
> in my life, as I felt them getting it, and heard the great
> wave of applause! . . .
>
> There are many moments of loneliness and weari-
> ness, however, I have to dine at seven which means
> alone in little restaurants, and I get quite blue at times,
> thinking how strangely I have been captured and am
> being led by the demands of this gift—so against my
> desires and longings—and furious with myself for
> my ingratitude for what should fill my life with hap-
> piness. To think I have arrived at a place most women
> would have to pay for, and I've not paid in the smallest
> coin! And without effort or ambition or struggle of
> any kind—but then perhaps it's not always in direct
> ways that life asks a tribute. God knows I've paid and
> am paying, and it looks as if I'd always pay until the
> force of life is spent, and 'I'm nodding by the fire.'[26]

And again:

> As I stood on the great stage of the Coliseum and held
> that audience of 3000 with my *Vive la France*, the rev-
> elation came to me that in thus giving all I had to give
> to those thousands, I must accept it as the alternative
> to giving myself to one. If I possess what you claim
> I do, I should be satisfied—I should be happy—it's a

great and rare power. The point is, I should use it, I should work for it, live for it, rejoice in it—and all the while I'm looking over my shoulder for the other thing. It's this conflict, this choice, this acceptance and renunciation that makes life hard . . . Gosh, I hate you for making me think and feel anew the force of this fear—that what I want can never come because God has given me something else to do.[27]

The most interesting thing about these letters is that already in 1920, eight years before meeting Lauro de Bosis, Ruth was longing for the 'grande passion' which, when at last it did come, she found disturbing. But at this time she seems to have had a romantic attachment, which was a forecast of the future.

Certainly the variety of her performances in England was calculated to make her wonder whether this was indeed what she intended to do all her life. In addition to her 'dramas' at the Coliseum—in one of which she appeared to her great delight with 'an adorable French clown' (the great Grock) with whom she 'carried the show' for two successive weeks, she also, in September, gave performances in the biggest music hall in Brighton, the Hippodrome, following a tame seal. 'Oh Harriet, it's so strange, whatever led me to this Life? I always thought it was difficult to know what "God's will" was—I'd gladly obey if I knew—can it be for me to pursue the career of a music hall artiste? Gosh!'[28]

From then until a few hours before her death at the age of seventy-two, Ruth's story is one of unbroken success. Yet her secret remains elusive. How was it possible for this slight, bright-eyed woman to fill her theatres night after night for nearly forty years, in London as in Paris, in New York as in Polynesia, to be applauded by young and old alike, to be appreciated at Windsor Castle and in a New Mexican mining town? How was so complete an illusion created with such slender means? To a degree, this is always true of the actor's art. 'Every night,' wrote Virginia Woolf, 'when the curtain goes down, the beautiful coloured canvas is rubbed out. What remains is at best only a wavering, insubstantial phantom, a verbal life on the lips of the living.'[29]

If this is true of acting in general, it is peculiarly so of Ruth's vivid impersonations. Since the parts she played were only those she had created for herself, she never identified with any of the symbolic, eternal figures of the stage: she was never Electra, Athalie, or Ophelia. Actresses who play those parts—however variously they may interpret them—take on for a season something of the greatness of the minds which first conceived them: the air they breathe is that of Sophocles, Racine, Shakespeare. And when their voice is stilled, their memory is indissolubly bound to the image they brought to life: we say Sarah's Phèdre, and Ellen Terry's Desdemona.

This world Ruth never entered. Her talent was on a smaller scale, but it was a gift entirely authentic, absolutely her own—requiring few props, no costumes, no fellow-actors, not even a playwright. Scenery? At the end of the script of her monologues there is a list of her stage requirements—as meagre, surely, as can be found in the history of the stage. For 'Doctors and Diets' a small rectangular table and a restaurant chair; for 'At the Court of Philip IV,' two long, low benches; for 'An Italian Church,' a small rush-bottomed chair; for most of the others, nothing at all—a few hats, mostly rather battered—a dressing gown, a waterproof and a collection of shawls. These last were her only indispensable accessories: draped in a hundred different ways, they turned her into an old Irish woman, a young Italian girl in church, a Dalmatian peasant, a great Spanish lady.

As she dispensed with props, so she laboriously worked out for herself her own technique, alone—disregarding the advice of even the greatest professionals. *'Pourquoi ne faites-vous pas la comédie?'* said Sarah Bernhardt sharply, after hearing her. *'Mon enfant, ne faites jamais la comédie,'* said Duse. But she paid no attention to either of them.

Neither did she ever find it possible to act with other people or to take part in someone else's plays. For one reason only, she had accepted a minor part in a play with Marie Tempest, but it was a failure. Ruth became a mere shadow of herself, her whole personality muted.

Even when Henry James, long before her fame was established, wrote a monologue for her, she did not feel able to try it. The letter with which he sent it is highly characteristic and we may perhaps surmise why the monologue was not used, in spite of its author's conviction that it would be just what was required. 'I don't really see,' he wrote, 'why it shouldn't go; and I seem definitely to "visualise" you and hear you, not to say infinitely admire you very much in it.' And he went on to describe his own view of the character he had drawn:

> It's the fatuous, but *innocently* fatuous, female compatriot of ours let loose upon a world and a whole order of things ... which she takes so serenely for granted. The little scene represents her being pulled up in due measure; but there is truth, I think, and which you will bring out, in the small climax of her not being too stupid to recognise things when they are really put to her—as in America they so mostly are *not* ... She rises to that—by a certain shrewdness in her which seems almost to make a sort of new chance for her to glimmer out—so that she doesn't feel snubbed so very much, or pushed off her pedestal; but merely perhaps furnished with a new opportunity or attribute. That's the note on which it closes; and her last words will take all the pretty saying you can give

them. But if [Ruth] takes to the thing at all [she] can be trusted to make more out of it by her own little genius than I can begin to suggest.[30]

But Ruth did not 'take to the thing'—or rather, according to her own account, she tried to force herself into it, but found she could not. Reluctantly—and no doubt, with some discomfort on both sides, she returned it to its author. 'I think he was disappointed,' she said later on, 'but I never learned it or tried it on anyone.'[31]

Henry James, however, was magnanimous—'My dear child,' he wrote, 'you have made for yourself—you have woven for yourself—a Persian carpet. Stand on it!'[32]

It was in the last years of Henry James's life that a close friendship sprang up between him and Ruth. She visited him in his rooms in Carlyle Mansions, she read his novels, she confided in him, and, for his seventieth birthday, wrote some verses for him beginning 'Great-hearted seer, teller of rare tales.' Not good verses, as he was aware, but which gave him great pleasure. 'I feel I am being hugely—and quite exquisitely—celebrated, Dear Ruth, when I receive your slightly overgrown, but all the more luxuriant sonnet . . . Whose excesses I can only blushingly acclaim . . .'[33] He described to her the kind of acting he most admired, which he had found again in her performances:

> They [the great actors of the past] produced their famous effects without aids to illusion. They had no help from scenery and costume; the background was nothing; they alone were the scene. Garrick and Mrs. Siddons, wandering over England and interpreting Shakespeare as they went, represented the visions of Hamlet and the sorrows of Constance with the assistance of a few yards of tinsel and a few dozen tallow candles . . . But the tradition of their influence over their authors has been sacredly preserved.[34]

Ruth Draper in her dressing room with some of her costumes:
"a few hats, a dressing gown, a waterproof
and a collection of shawls"

Ruth's repertory consisted in some thirty sketches in which she played fifty-eight parts—in English, French, German, Italian—with an Irish brogue or a Highland lilt, or in her brilliant imaginary dialects, Scandinavian, Balkan folk songs, or the list of flower names of her English garden. 'Next week my *Funnifelosis* will be in bloom . . . and those darling little pale *Punnyfunkums*. You don't know the *Punnyfunkums*? . . . But my poor *Glubjullas* never came up at all.'[35] She took her audience to an English bazaar, a Southern Dance, a porch in a Maine coast village, a New York hospital, a station on the Western Plains, a windswept beach in Normandy; we shared in a *Class in Greek Poise*, a lunch in a smart New York restaurant, or an English village preparing a country cottage for a soldier's return from the War. Perhaps the most remarkable of her gifts was her power to bring upon the stage, in addition to the part she was playing, a dozen subsidiary characters.

Here is, to take one brilliant example, 'The Italian Lesson.' The curtain goes up: we see a smart middle-aged woman in a dressing gown on a sofa: 'Good morning, Signorina, good morning. I can't tell you how excited I am that we have come to Dante at last!' The lady, at the moment, is alone; but within two minutes the stage is so full that we are craning forward in our seats to prevent the baby from falling into the wastepaper basket, to catch the puppy ('Pat him on his *head*, sweetheart—that's his tail')—to order the dinner ('It isn't fish? I always thought it was fish. It looks like fish, it tastes like fish')—to fill the opera-box ('Oh, anyone, so long as it's a man! No, I picked up a charming young Englishman last week, Sir Basil Something—I put him on a scrap of paper in the blotter')—to design a fancy-dress ('You'll find ten yards of blue chiffon in the sewing room. The figure of Hope—a lady, blindfolded, listening to someone, sitting on a ball')—to replace 'a very dirty lampshade.' And of course to read a little Dante, 'I think, Signorina, don't you, that when one gets to the middle of life one gets a little confused.'[36]

We have seen the picture of a woman's whole life—filled to overflowing, and as empty as a hollow nut.

Her characters, unlike those of most mimics, are never mere silhouettes: we see them in the round, bearing with them their background, their past and future. In 'Three Generations' Ruth comes on to a bare stage, but for a kitchen chair, as the grandmother—an ugly, squat old woman holding a black shawl tightly round her head; beneath it, one has a glimpse of sunken cheeks drawn in over a toothless jaw. She has a low, harsh voice and a strong Jewish accent. She lifts a shaking hand. 'Good morning, Judge. My name is Anna Abrahams—seventy-nine years old. I live at 164 Orchard Street, with my daughter and granddaughter . . . Twenty-five years . . . That's my home.'

She has come before the Judge, in a Court of Domestic Relations, to ask him to prevent her granddaughter, who wants to get married and to go out to the West, from putting her and her daughter in an old people's home. 'I'm an old woman . . . too old to work. And my daughter, she's got heart trouble and can't work . . . We couldn't live without Rosie.' She mumbles her complaints about her granddaughter's flightiness, and the irresponsibility of the girl's young man. 'She go dance every night, she comes home late . . . And the young man—he drinks—he make a very bad husband . . . Rosie she should stay by us. Why she want to go away?'

The daughter rises. As she throws the shawl back upon her shoulders the transformation takes place: in an instant, the stooping, toothless old crone has turned into a tall, middle-aged woman, of dignity and beauty. (One of Ruth's admirers once wrote of her 'genius for assuming physical height—one of the tests of the great ones. The elder Salvini had it, and Irving.') Standing very erect and very still before the Judge, she speaks in a faint flat voice—without acrimony, but without hope. 'I sent Rosie to a business college, so she could have a profession. She has got a wonderful job. But now, she only wants to go . . . No, Sir, I don't like this young man. He don't work regular—and he drinks . . . Please, Judge, tell my girl she should wait . . . She's so young . . . and she don't understand what life is . . . And she owes me something.'

She too sits down, and Rosie springs up, flinging off the shawl altogether. She—how is it done?—is youth itself. Her eyes sparkle, her speech is breathless, even the nervous movements of her hands have the awkward eagerness of youth. What is her name? 'Everyone calls me Rosie!' She is a stenographer, she loves her work, she loves her home— 'We've got a very nice little home'—but yes, she does want to get married. 'I want that my mother and grandmother should go to a home for old people—and they don't want to go!' There is indignation in her voice—and also surprise. But she is a *good* girl, that is plain. She loves her mother and her grandmother and she has taken great pains to find a nice place for them.

'The house has got four sides to it—there's windows all around—and in the room they're going to give my mother and my grandmother, the window looks right straight into a tree . . . They got cretonne drapes and cushions on the chairs. They got a piano, they got a radio and a Victor.'

The old ladies, she says, all seem very contented—'knitting and sitting around.' All this is said with offhand kindliness, in a cool, clear young voice. But when she speaks of her young man, her voice changes, she begins to plead. 'Judge—I can't give him up. I got to go.' They have been offered a job on a Western farm.

'You go for four days and nights—and when you get out there's absolutely nothing to see—only land and sky . . . No, we don't know nothing about it, but we can learn. We're both young.' No, she replies to the Judge's questions, her young man does *not* drink—'Well, he drunk some because he was so discouraged, but he won't drink no more when we get married—he told me.' Yes, she will miss her mother. 'I'll miss her something terrible.' But she must get away. 'I want to get out of this. I want my own life.' And then comes the final, desperate appeal. 'Can't you see? They're different! Judge, don't make me stay!'

That is all. The Judge tells her to come back next Wednesday, and to bring her young man, and it is plain what the answer will be. Rosie will have her husband and her life. 'Come on, Grandma, what's the use of talking now? . . . Come on home.'[37]

The person who could tell this story was not merely a great impersonator, but a woman who loved life and human beings. Bruce Atkinson, the dramatic critic of the *New York Times*, wrote about her: 'She is not astonishing you with the brilliance of her talent. She is modestly asking for your interest in various characters, most of whom represented her respect for the human race.' It was this respect which, for all the sharpness of her observation, took the bitterness out of Ruth's mockery.

It was then that Ruth's public performances in other European countries began. In Paris, in 1921, when she first walked into the Théatre de L'Oeuvre, the famous old actor and producer, Aurelien Francois Lugné-Poe, watched closely 'cette petite, femme brunaude'* as she measured and paced the stage. Presently he asked her what actors and equipment she would bring with her. 'None,' she replied. 'Je suis seule. Je n'ai besoin de personne. Seule—moi—un rideau.' 'Ce "seule" qui revient a chaque minute, en ses propos me fait plaisir,' wrote Lugné-Poe, 'me regaillardit. Il a un je ne sais quoi de fierté, de confortable . . . ce "seule" a

*'a little brownish woman.'

tout l'air d'un défi. J'aime, ca. J'ai toujours estimé les gens qui se croient "seule."'*[38]

For the nineteen years of life that still remained to him he remained her faithful friend. Just before his death in 1940 he wrote in *Dernière Pirouette*:

> Ruth Draper! Without doubt one of the strongest personalities of the contemporary theatre; understanding the ills of the present dramatic art, she walks through it head high, and the contagion has never touched her ... Fierce, admirable North American, Ruth Draper observes herself, knows herself and suffers also like Duse, the Venetian, like Bady, like Réjane. In all her very great afflictions ... I believe it difficult for her not to be objective, to censure and question herself ... In my eyes she is always a great woman.[39]

When in 1923 she was gathering courage for a long journey, a short note came to bless her departure. 'Votre joie de travail m'enchante et je vous fais un bien bon signe à travers les mers et les continents. Amie—au revoir!'†

On that first day they came to terms so rapidly (sixty per cent of the profits to Ruth, forty per cent to the producer) that Ruth was taken aback. 'But you don't know me!' Lugné-Poe answered that she interested him. 'I am not risking much. You will appear here three or four times. If I lose I shall not do it again; if we make a profit so much the

---

*'I am alone. I need no-one. Alone—myself—a curtain.' 'This "alone,"' wrote Lugné-Poe, 'which comes back all the time, pleases me, cheers me up. There is something proud and comfortable about it ... This "alone" looks like a challenge. I like that. I have always esteemed people who believe themselves to be alone.'
†'Your delight in your work enchants me, and I send you a friendly signal across the seas and continents. My friend, *au revoir!*'

better: we'll go on.'[40] The Oeuvre became the place which she called her 'home in Paris.'

This friendship led to an equally exciting encounter. In the late summer of 1927 she met Max Reinhardt in Salzburg and was invited to his Baroque palace, Schloss Leopoldskron, 'A finer guarantee for a start I could not have.' When she returned to Europe in the following autumn it was Reinhardt who sponsored her first appearances before German audiences, in Berlin, in Munich, in Frankfurt and in Vienna.

'I played in [Max Reinhardt's Theater an der Josephstadt] the most beautiful theatre I've ever seen—a perfect gem (about 800 seats) and had *such a thrill* when I learned that it was opened by Beethoven's music, (and he there), the first time it was publicly performed in Vienna! I keep saying to myself, "Be thankful."'[41]

Her oddest private performance was the one she gave for the Duce in Palazzo Chigi—what can he have made of her, with her little bundle of shawls? Professor Neville Rogers has described this scene—perhaps with exaggerated emphasis—as having upset the Duce very much. (Apparently on some other occasion a half-mad Englishwoman had tried to attack him.) When her shawls were brought in, Ruth reported that he was petrified and cried 'Via, via!' (Away with them). But Ruth saved the situation by dropping her handbag, so that all the men bent to pick up its contents.[42] The next morning, however, Ruth's diary says: 'Flowers from Mussolini.'

Of her meeting with Sarah Bernhardt, in 1922, there is only a brief account in her diary:

> I had a very amusing and interesting experience of going to see Sarah Bernhardt and reciting for her . . . Such a scene as her house—her room, dogs, parrots, objects d'art, dust of ages, autographs, photographs,

etc. She, marvellous, vital, keen, enthusiastic, full of force! She was exceedingly kind and said charming things . . . The experience of watching and listening to her, and the whole picture of myself reciting in that room, three feet away from the great old lady, was humorous to a degree. She is superb in her youthful spirit, her vigour and vitality.[43]

About her encounter with Duse later in the same year, she was a little more explicit. During a week's visit to Milan, she saw the great Italian actress four times and recited for her twice. She called their talks 'the climax' of her journey. To her sister Martha she wrote:

> I somehow don't feel the same person, so deeply have I been moved by her tragic personality and her acting—last night in *Ghosts* [Ibsen]. She is beautiful beyond expression, frail, white-haired, but her grace and movement and the line of her throat—her gesture and voice—and a haunting sadness that simply wring your heart, seem to belong to the immortal beauty in the world. I am going to recite for her tomorrow—I suppose my French things as she can't understand much English—and you can fancy how honoured and thrilled I feel.[44]

These were the sad years of Duse's old age, long after d'Annunzio had left her. She was struggling with professional jealousies in Italy and with restricted means, which in the end caused her to embark on the exhausting American tour during which she died.

So far I have chiefly written about Ruth as an actress, and have said nothing about the event, on 14 March 1928, that had changed the course of her life, her first meeting with Lauro de Bosis. This has been fully described in my essay about him, but I did not dwell there on the doubts and uncertainties which were already distressing Ruth during the time in Rome when Lauro and she were first together. Already then she spoke very openly to Marchesa Presbitero, telling her about her great reluctance to part from Lauro, but also about the upheaval that his ardent love making had caused in her. Her friend had replied that she wished that Ruth 'felt more the beauty and wonder of it all, and less the uncertainty and pain,' but she also wisely advised Ruth to try a period of separation in which to weigh her feelings. So Ruth, after a brief visit to Florence where Lauro joined her for three days and some engagements in Paris and London, sailed on 20 June on the *Ile de France* for a family summer. With her sailed Jock, an enchanting Cairn puppy which Lauro had given her, and during the long sea voyage she tried to take stock of what had happened to her in Italy. Then she had been swept off her feet, but now something like panic had overtaken her, and it was to Harriet Marple that she confided her state of mind:

> This radical change of life and surroundings I hope will do me good, yet can I venture to hope for a change in my strange nature? I am baffled by myself, and the way I take life ... Love certainly plays havoc with me—would to God I could take it lightly or that such strong doses hadn't come to me so late ... Don't write to me in sympathy. I deserve none—I deserve lashes for my ingratitude, and mockery of my egotism and selfishness ... Never have I dreamed that such love and such beauty could come to me ... [but] because I'm not convinced of my own feelings and cannot love as he does, I am wretched and almost spoil its beauty with my suffering ... Whatever made me such a fool about life ... I must wait and see what time does to the situation—to me—for of him I am certain ... I was worn out when this last whirlwind hit me in Italy ... I

wonder tho' if I shall ever *know* what I want—ever be sure that I *love enough* to live with a man—either married or not.[45]

She spent most of the summer with her family at Dark Harbor planning to give the children 'a glorious summer to remember.' But still she could not conquer her inner turmoil, and when she heard that Lauro might be arriving to take up a job in New York she even wrote that she dreaded seeing him again. 'I've gotten to the point now of "near" terror at the thought of meeting—and woke at four in the morning, sure that I hated the idea of seeing him and had no love for him at all.'[46]

But when he did come she accepted his love again, and enjoyed his company. Lauro's new job as the Executive Secretary of the Italy-America Society was not an easy one, and his only escape from its anxieties was the time he could spend with Ruth. He became a frequent and lively guest in her charming new apartment at 66 East 79th Street, which had just become her New York home. Here two portraits of her by Sargent faced a portrait of Paderewski by Burne-Jones, and another wall was decorated by a map of the world, which gradually became more and more thickly constellated with stars placed on each of the places where she had performed. Here Lauro was able to forget the numerous problems connected with his new job and his future, but he did not play any important part in her family life. Though he had great charm of manner, it was very much of a Latin kind, very unlike the Drapers and most of their friends. Ruth's nephew, Bill Carter, remembers Lauro coming to Sunday lunch in the country in his mother's house—'rather pale with his black moustache' and 'not dressed for a country walk, with his Sunday suit and black shoes.' But he does not remember any conversation with him and 'the idea of a romance hardly entered my head.'[47] Once, but only once, Lauro stayed for a few days in the place nearest to Ruth's heart, Dark Harbor, and later on its doors were always open to any of his friends—and every day the bond between them grew stronger.

After a sensationally successful season in the spring of 1929 in the Comedy theatre of New York, Ruth sailed back to France on 18 May—and this time Lauro, too, was on board. On arrival they had a wonderful day together at Mont St Michel, but still Ruth's doubts were haunting her. 'I despair of understanding myself and Lauro grows to me in beauty all the time and I remain hateful to myself.'[48]

Then Ruth set off for engagements in Poland and a trip to Russia, but already after a week in Warsaw was writing 'I am awfully lonely for Lauro and the week has seemed like a month.'

As for Russia, she spent four days in Moscow and one in Leningrad, but only wrote that the three weeks away from Lauro already seemed like three months. Russia was '*awful*, so depressing, so uncomfortable.' And when the time came at last for her to fly back to Lauro, she wrote to Harriet, 'If this is my last night on earth, tell everyone I was terribly happy, flying to join my lover, and what a lover! I can find no flaw in him—this separation has taught me so much.'[49]

She spent a night in Vienna, getting thoroughly washed and tidy, and the next morning flew to Venice, landing at the Lido. 'As I descended from the machine I heard a whirr above me and said, where does that machine come from?— "from Rome, Signorina"—and in three minutes Lauro and I were rushing toward each other ... It seemed miraculous!'[50]

They had six enchanting days in Venice, and then flew down to Portonovo. And when it was time for her to sail to New York from Genoa, in the SS *Augustus*, Lauro sailed with her.

During this whole year—according to their letters—the thought of marriage had often filled the background of their thoughts. The previous year Ruth had received a letter from Marchesa Presbitero from Rome saying how much she hoped that the wonderful gift Ruth had to give 'might not be fruitless and only a memory of incompleteness.'

But there were anxious doubts in Lauro's mind, too. We have no letter from him asking Ruth to marry him, only a quotation of what had been said to him by Ned Sheldon, the blind and paralysed friend in New York whose wisdom and friendship they both deeply valued: 'Ned says,' Lauro wrote, 'that whatever we will chose will be perfect, so we must feel confident and happy . . . that our present freedom is of great value for love . . . Marriage would hardly add anything *except* we felt we wanted [it] for the sake of a child . . . The ultimate decision must lie only in your having or not having a craving for a child . . .'[51]

It is easy to imagine the discussions between them on this subject—dictated, on both sides, by unworldly generosity; on her part, that she was seventeen years older than he, that she wished always to leave him his freedom; on his, that he might be drawn into a political struggle of which he could not forsee the outcome. But this is only guessing. For nearly three years the bond between them grew stronger. Only a few months before his death Lauro wrote of her miraculous gift for constantly renewing herself and their relationship, 'this elusive and thrilling sense of being always in a perpetual flash . . . You give trust without habit.'[52]

But now many doubts were certainly troubling Lauro's mind, as he wondered whether it was right to involve Ruth in complications of which she had as yet no notion, and which would also bring him many new responsibilities and duties. Even after their weeks at Portonovo, in 1930 when he was already planning and writing the pamphlets of the Alleanza, he kept all the political side of his life as far away from her as possible and she seems to have remained untroubled by his increasing disquiet. Perhaps, being herself entirely unpolitically minded, she saw in his increasing rebellion against fascism and his determination to fight it, only an extension of his general idealism. Certainly his letters all reflected his determination to keep their relationship, for as long as possible, on another plane. 'You are all yourself, I am so mixed up in so many things alien to you . . . that it must be quite distressing and disheartening to love me. You are in the frame of your art, I am in the frame of Balkan politics.' (1931)[53]

Even when he had become so deeply involved that she could not fail to feel his anxieties, and he told her that he might soon be obliged to resign from his post in the Italy-America Society, he minimised the situation for as long as possible, and only told her that he might have to return to Italy almost immediately. He sailed on 26 November 1930, saying goodbye to very few friends and telling even Ruth very little of his plans. But as he approached Southampton, bad news reached him: the arrest of his mother and of his two friends Vinciguerra and Rendi.[54]

The story is told with honesty and generosity in a little volume called *Italy Today*, published by 'Friends of Italian Freedom,' which contained accounts of Rendi and Vinciguerra and also of Lauro himself.

Lauro's first reaction to the news of the arrest of his friends was naturally to hurry to Italy, to join his friends and share their fate, but he was persuaded that this would be folly, his whole movement would then come to an end. His first letters after the trial, his disappointment at having had no part in it even *in absentia*, are quoted in the previous chapter. But now Lauro had a new problem: how to prevent Ruth from joining him.

She, meanwhile, had read in the American and English press the story of the arrests and of the subsequent trial, and had also had to face the violent attacks on Lauro as a traitor by those who mistrusted him, and the inquiries of his faithful, but puzzled friends. She knew that he had got a job as a concierge in a little hotel off the Champs Elysées, that he was working at an anthology and continuing to post his anti-fascist pamphlets from different countries, and that he saw hardly anyone except Salvemini. But she knew very little else. All his letters were concentrated on keeping up her spirits and convincing her of his love—and on preventing her from joining him:

> I think that when you read this, your season will already have begun. You will feel me, won't you, all around you? God bless you, adored Angel. If even at 3000 miles your angelic influence overflows my life with sweetness, can't you imagine what it is when I can hear you? *Que ton sein m'était doux, que ton coeur m'était bon.* Sweet Angel, *je sais l'art d'évoquer les minutes heureuses.* And equally well, I knew the art of anticipating them.

In yet another letter he begs her not to send any money, except to Rendi and Vinciguerra; it might be useful one day for the Movement. In another he denies a rumour that he is proposing to throw bombs: in yet another he thanked her for 'a Rolls Royce of typewriters,' which must have looked very incongruous in his little porter's lodge:

> Please don't think, not even for an instant, that our sweet peace is gone. It is hardly begun. Many things we will not be able to do for some time (like going to spend the summer at Portonovo or going to Venice) but there are many others that we could not do before that we will be able to do now: for example be in London together for all the time of your season . . . Darling mine, believe that the nicest part is still ahead . . .

> Please, darling, keep gay; everything is for the best. Of course ousting tyrants is not as simple as cracking a nut and it is long, but still it must be done.

And again:

> I am sorry to disappoint you in another point, but your fears about my dangers are *phantastical*. Good gracious! even kidnapped! There are here thousands of exiles . . . I have a lovely room in a respectable street and go nowhere else except the Curtis house and the Library . . . The Movement has found another director and it goes on . . . Darling, it would have been terrible if you had left everything to join me. Especially with the bad feeling against me in America. It would have been terribly compromising. Do everything as if I did not exist, then dash to London. I will take a room near you and we will be happy as GODS. I swear it to you.

Sometimes he even tried to cheer her up by gently mocking her, 'Darling Angel, you do make me laugh when you regret not to be like Cavour's Egeria. First, I should have to be like Cavour! Your regret is nothing compared to mine.'

But of his own deep discouragement and loneliness, after one or two letters in the early days, he said hardly anything, nor did he hint at what was going on in his mind, except that each letter betrayed an increasing anxiety that Ruth should not give way to her first instinct to join him. 'Your sweet cable is just arrived telling me of your successes and of your sailing on the *Berengaria*. I am excited, but I really wish you had postponed a little more. Darling, let's be on the safe side, postpone until you absolutely long entirely to sail . . .' And again: 'If there was a chance of your ever doubting my love,' he wrote, 'even for an instant, I would not dare say this, but I feel I can tell it safely . . . You must come *only* if you want it very badly for yourself. Otherwise don't come.'

Ruth realised that Lauro could hardly bear to drag her into a world which he felt to be so essentially alien to her. 'How you must hate Politics and Problems,' he wrote, 'which interfere with our quiet life!' 'Arrests, prisons, tyrannies, exiles; it must all seem so alien to your life! What right had I to dump it on you?'[55]

But day by day, Ruth's anxiety increased. She could not help feeling that there was something in Lauro's mind that his letters did not say, something that terrified her. At last she wrote to beg him not to lull her into a fallacious security—and this letter at last provoked a full and sincere reply:

> You say that things are terrifying, that there can be no peace. You are perfectly right. But I must make a bit clearer what my optimism is [based on] ... In this world there is always a fight going on. With or without violence, it hardly matters, but it has no pauses and will never end. It is right that it should be so, because in history there are no definitive positions and no millenniums (which would mean stagnation) ...
>
> It is possible (and sometimes necessary) to obtain peace by isolating oneself or one's circle of friends and ignoring the fight that rages all around. But one must choose and look at life from either one or the other of two angles, either putting one's own peace and comfort first by shutting one's eyes to what is happening in the world, or feeling it a duty to join the fight ...
>
> If one takes the first angle, it is obvious I can only be considered an irresponsible man who has brought serious trouble on his friends and family for the sake of something that is very dubious and intangible. If one takes the other angle, then one must view the

whole field, and look ahead at the generations still to come, with even the remotest results in view . . . It does not depend on whether we are successful or not. We must regard this terrible tragedy as an episode in the long war which the Risorgimento has waged for a century. In the last war we spent six hundred thousand lives to free three provinces and now it is a question of freeing ninety-three. The unhappiness of the dozen people who are nearest to us is a tragic thing, but the Cause that we have espoused . . . involves the happiness or unhappiness of forty-two million people. The price seems not out of proportion.

Of course there are things strange to be said by a man who remains free alone while his companions are in gaol and if there was a drop of egoism in what I have said it would be monstrous. But God knows how torn I am by the grief of being free and by the regret at not having been at the trial instead of the others . . .

Of course it is easy to say now what a terrible mistake it was for me to leave Rome. But [I went] also to get a position without which it would have been absolutely impossible to carry on the work in Italy, and the person I had arranged to take the place of my mother withdrew after I sailed . . .

On the whole, things are less terrifying now than a year ago, because something has been done. Italy is not entirely dishonoured as it was a year ago . . . Believe me, one must *either not look at all or look at the whole*. Both positions are permissible but nothing in between. Please read Thayer.* I'll write you tomorrow. Pardon this explanatory note. It is not a letter. Love, Lauro.[56]

*Thayer's book about Cavour.

After reading this, Ruth can hardly have failed to realise that something crucial was about to take place—and perhaps this fortified her to meet the news of Lauro's plans, which she received as soon as she arrived in France in April, to play for a short season in Paris in Lugné-Poe's theatre. To his mother Lauro wrote later on from England, that his greatest dread throughout the winter had been the breaking of the news to Ruth. 'But after the first shock she was wonderful, and said not a word to deter me.'[57]

But a letter written by Ruth to Harriet Marple on 18 April 1931, a few days after her return to Europe, shows how clearly Ruth had now become aware of the dangers ahead. 'I count each hour of happiness—that's all I can say. It's all as if these five months had gone up in smoke—and we are so close; I feel less than ever worthy . . .'[58]

And in May of the same year:

> Lauro is more wonderful than ever, but his situation is terribly difficult and I find I'm deeply troubled by all it involves, and it's hard to cast off the shadows . . . and the actual question of daily bread! One can hardly advise . . . where such a nature is involved—and such ideals at stake . . . There are moments when I feel that I must marry him—to have him more and closer—and throw in my lot with his; but always comes again the reasoning that warns me, that shows the many dangers and *impasses* . . . One thing I know, that if I lose him—not having married him—the anguish will be far greater![59]

Though this, of course, she could tell none of her friends, she now knew that he had been in correspondence with his old Harvard friend, the professional pilot Eric Wilmer Wood, which has been quoted in the last chapter, asking him to find a pilot who would fly with him to Rome. But

Wood could not come himself, and in the end Lauro's decision, against Wood's advice, was to learn to fly himself and be his own pilot. The decision was taken only a few weeks before Ruth's arrival and it may well be imagined how inconvenient her presence was, since he bicycled every morning to a small airfield at Toussusle-Noble to take flying lessons.

At one moment, when Ruth was in Paris and she thought Lauro had already started, she wrote:

> I'm writing in a kind of mechanical way—I'm sort of dazed, recovering from hours of agony when I thought Lauro was going, with very insufficient training but such will and confidence I could do nothing. I feel I have been very weak and stupid in not being firm with him—but he is like one possessed, so impatient to be off, and not realizing the gravity of it all and the necessity for perfecting the mechanical end ... It's all a nightmare to me, what is a dream of glory to him. I try to see his vision and God, I love him so![60]

They did, however, still manage to have a few happy hours together. Ruth's Paris season was a great success, to the delight of her old friend Lugné-Poe—and Lauro had left his job as concierge, so that they were able to spend one long happy day at Chartres together and one at Fontainebleau.

Then Ruth had to leave for London and took a little house in which Lauro occasionally stayed with her, though they did not think it wise to be seen too often together. Lauro was also making a series of practice flights in different airfields, each time under a different name, but occasionally they managed to get away—to row on the Thames, and (incurable sightseers still) to visit Runnymede and Stratford-on-Avon and Oxford.

During this time Lauro also made a brief trip to Corsica,

to explore the terrain where the Moth, the English plane he had chosen, was to be brought to meet him. It was at Ghisonaccia—little more than a farm field—near Bastia, but the landing-place was much rougher than Lauro had realised—and the plane crashed on arrival, with his secret disclosed.[61]

It was at this point that Ruth showed the stuff she was made of. When Lauro was obliged to leave his grounded plane, it was not only Ruth's courage but her determination that sustained him in his decision to try again. How many women in love would have the courage to do the same?

After the failure, Lauro decided that the Moth he had used for his first experiment was not sufficiently strong and that he must look for a German plane. His friends in Belgium and a Dr Sica in London supplied the necessary funds and he went from town to town until he found a satisfactory secondhand plane whose trade mark—by a strange coincidence—was Klemm Pegasus, which a friend was to bring to him at Marseilles. Then there was yet another delay. The friend fell ill. Finally it was settled that Lauro's German instructors, Max Rainer and Hans Böhning, would bring the plane to him at Marseilles, but there were numerous other obstacles and delays which became increasingly a great strain to them both.

But in September Ruth was again writing: 'The delays and things that happen are fantastic and fate seems to mock us . . . He is upheld by his burning desire and his confidence. We read Cavour aloud—it's a great book—a great story—and P. G. Wodehouse for lighter moments.'[62]

During the time of waiting Ruth joined Lauro again, but always, on Salvemini's advice, very prudently; first finding, by great good luck, a quiet little manor house in the Engadine near Zouz, where they walked in the forest and played tennis and slept and Ruth even temporarily caught some of

Lauro's optimism, and then taking a bicycle trip in the Black Forest and Bavaria. 'If all goes well we may come home, too good to think about. I long to take things easily, cheerfully, bravely and optimistically, and be full of confidence and faith and fervour . . . Well—one is thankful for such interludes as this past week has been.'[63]

At last the date was settled, 2 October, and, having received confirmation that the plane was ready, Lauro returned to Marseilles to meet his German pilots, while Ruth waited in Cannes. The story of his departure is told in the preceding chapter, in the words of Max Rainer, the last man who spoke to him.

Before the plane arrived Ruth and Lauro had ten last days together in Talloires, Chambéry, Annecy and Geneva. From the station hotel at Marseilles, Lauro wrote her a short note of farewell to Cannes, where she thought it wiser to wait. 'If I close my eyes I feel you so close as if I held you in my arms—I think I could live 100 years on the sweetness accumulated these days.' But he admitted, too, his interest and eagerness to get off, 'I burn to go and be through with this thing. I feel absolutely sure of this success and am I not even excited about it. It has become almost a matter of routine.'

'He was wonderfully patient and calm,' wrote Ruth in a comment on this letter, 'but inwardly restless, eager to get it done with.'

Then Ruth travelled back to Paris, where she stayed for a month with a close and faithful friend, Léa Dessay, who once ran a lingérie of her own, in her house in Avenue Wagram, and there spent five agonising days of waiting. Ruth had chosen to stay with Léa, of whom she was very fond, partly for reasons of security, but chiefly because she needed to be with people who loved her and *cared*. Aileen Tone, most faithful and understanding of friends, joined them, and she saw Salvemini daily, while she also received a visit from her devoted young nephew Bill Carter, on his way to Geneva. He was soon to render her a great service.

Ruth was desperate, fluctuating between hope and terror: 'I'm nearly wild with apprehension,' she had already written to Harriet Marple from Geneva before Lauro set off. 'A thousand terrors assail me, but I can do nothing—he is confident, courageous and calm . . . If only he succeeds—that's all that matters. Love me—and pray for us—if you can. I hope I don't fail—or even regret what I've done.'[64]

At last, in a letter dated 7 October, from Ferrari in Brussels, the news came—and it was the worst. His letter has already been quoted in full in the preceding chapter.

He enclosed a copy of 'The Story of my Death,' and Lauro's final letter of farewell. It was a plea for courage.

> *Be happy for my sake*! not only proud, but happy: you wanted me to play a role in the life of my country. I can assure you that not even in 50 years of successful work I could have attained such a role. Wait and see! Not right away, but I will become a symbol and achieve one hundred times more this way than if I were alive . . . I could not have wished for a happier solution of my wish to serve my country and my ideals. If I had come back alive, it would have been only a *beau geste*. In this way it is much more. If I had lived you would have done thousands of things for me. Won't you do only one more? My last and deepest desire? Be happy and continue your glorious life not as if something had been taken away from it, but as if something had been added.
>
> You have made my life a real paradise for over three years. Don't make me now the injustice of rendering me a cause of sadness. I am happy. Be happy.

'*Sta allegra*' and work. You will have given me then your crowning boon. If you do that, I will feel that my love continued after death to protect you, otherwise my soul never would have peace. Never until you are again happy. And *please* love somebody else. I will consider [it] indirectly as love to me.

I embrace you with all my adoration. Lauro[65]

For the first few days Ruth was overcome and seldom left her bed, but she was still not entirely deprived of hope. If the fascists had shot him down, it would surely have been announced as good propaganda, but it seemed possible that he had made his way to Sardinia, or had been picked up by fishermen on the Corsican coast.

She reported to the Préfet de Police to explain why she was being followed by the Fascist Intelligence in Paris, and frankly spoke of her love for Lauro, but said she had not taken part in his political activities. The Préfet came from behind his desk saying 'C'est un amour extraordinaire!' and kissed her on both cheeks.[66] But she was longing for more details of what had happened in Rome and her young nephew, Bill Carter, courageously came to her aid—going to Rome for thirty-six hours to talk to friends of Salvemini's and learn all he could.

His account of the visit is inevitably incomplete, since he naturally saw only a small number of the opponents of fascism of whom the most important, Umberto Zanotti-Bianco, the founder of the Associazione per gli Interessi del Mezzogiorno d'Italia (ANIMI), was an ardent anti-fascist, who after the fall of fascism became the President of the Italian Red Cross. From him and from one or two other friends whose names Salvemini had given him, Bill learned of the effects of Lauro's achievement, as told in the previous chapter, of the fact that no plane rose in time for his pursuit, that Mussolini was very angry, that an artificial pro-fascist demonstration was organised, and that an official of the Air Force lost his post. But whether the psychological effect of the exploit was, at the time, as great as his friends hoped, must remain a moot question, since we know the story from one side only, and from people who were at that moment very much on the *qui vive*. Certainly Bill himself drew a great breath of relief when he crossed the French frontier and, on reaching Paris, entered Salvemini's little house, just as he was climbing into bed.[67]

In Paris, on 13 October, Ruth wrote to Harriet that she had no desire to come home:

> My only comfort is to be near friends who knew and cared for him—to go over his papers—to work for as wide a publicity as possible. At home I'd feel so cut off from sympathy with his ideals. Dear old Salvemini is like a loving old uncle to us both—so proud and full of tenderness it comforts me. Léa is an angel . . . I feel I never want to leave. You speak of hoping still—others do too—I try to, but dare not really. There are still mysterious rumours and speculations.[68]

And indeed on 16 October the French police provided Ruth with a series of false hopes.

> My whole state of mind has changed now [Ruth wrote in an hour of optimism] about the possibilities that Lauro is safe. These are the hypotheses: 1) that he flew east, was picked up by fishermen in the Adriatic and is being hidden, or got to Yugoslavia—2) that he was picked up in the Mediterranean and is on a vessel bound for a far off port, and can't communicate with anyone, 3) that he got to Algiers and that the French police are hiding him until Italy is less angry . . . The

police have strongly hinted that he is alive—but have told me *not to tell* save to my close and *trusted friends* ... I feel ashamed now that I didn't trust him more and trust his skills and his lucky star and everything.[69]

These methods were very similar to those used—as we have seen—to wake false hopes in the de Bosis family, and especially in Lauro's mother, for from the first his brothers and sisters felt very sceptical. Ruth, more credulous, at once felt 'almost happy again' and able to enjoy life 'as if nature commanded me to make use of this "pause" to recuperate my forces,'[70] staying in the country with an old Boston friend, Miss Cushing, who had lived near Fontainebleau for over forty years.

A close childhood friend of Ruth's, Malvina Hoffman, was travelling around the world with her husband, Samuel Grimson, and had therefore not heard Ruth's news until she was reached by a telegram in the Pacific. To her Ruth wrote more fully, enclosing a copy of 'The Story of my Death' in the London *Times*:

> The destiny that I foresaw has fallen on me—to overwhelm me with intolerable grief—and lifted him to glory. I try and catch the light in my darkness—I struggle to believe the sacrifice has not been made in vain—to feel the pride and happiness I should in his achievement—but it's as yet a losing battle ... O Mallie—how I need his courage and his will and his faith and his love of life to lift me from the horror of this suffering ...
>
> I've lived in alternate despair and hope—for five days was sure he was alive—told by the Ministry of the Interior ... that he'd been picked up by Algerian fishermen! It was Machiavellian in its cruelty ... I

only hope he was drowned quickly—without knowledge perhaps and without pain. I love to think of the ecstasy he must have felt when he saw the lights of Rome and flew over the city . . . So he tasted, thank God, the glory of achievement and the fulfillment of his desire.

But—oh—he loved life so—he was sure of coming back—quite fearless—and quite confident—and he had *so* much to give, and to achieve; such beauty and such enthusiasm—he'd been so hurt—so terribly hurt—and lived to cast off the burden he carried in this one gesture—and then face life again, a free man, . . . Added to my grief and loneliness is the burden of regrets and questionings . . . I was terribly aware always of the beauty of what we had—aware of our happiness—of its poignant and constant reality—but I did not suspect that the regret that I had not married him—and *had* him more . . . could take such possession of my mind. I know our love would have been strong enough to overcome the obstacles my 'reason' used to find . . . but I failed—thro' fears of various kinds—and a constitutional baulking at committing myself to any bond. O well, I must grit my teeth and know one can't recall the past, and have a second chance—with all my weaknesses and failures he loved me—and regretted nothing—that I know . . .

Dear friend of my childhood I cry out to you in my pain— send me a word.[71]

As soon as she could draw breath from her first shattering pain, Ruth began to fulfil Lauro's requests. But first, she found it possible to help someone else in his sorrow. It was then that her nephew, Bill Carter, received a piece of tragic family news and that Ruth, in the midst of her own suffering, wrote to him asking him for his help, finding the right words to bring him to her. 'Now it is your turn,' she wrote, 'you stood by me in my darkest hour, now I long to be near you.' 'Happiness,' she said Lauro had taught her, 'is also an act of the will.'

She persuaded Bill to join her in London and then in Liverpool, and though she was already translating *Icarus*, as well as giving nightly performances, she found that her need for support had been the right appeal. Bill joined her, and she worked on her translation. She referred constantly to the Morocco note-book in which she had written passages that reminded her of Lauro and helped her to build up her courage.

To his mother Bill wrote that he was helping Aunt Ruth with her translation of *Icarus*, 'with the wording and the cadence of the sentences . . . Few of us, I think, realize what Aunt Ruth has been going through this winter; but now I can see the power she has found in having conquered sorrow in a fine poetic memory.'[72] Ruth reminded Bill, too, of the bicycling trip she had once taken in Ireland with Harriet Marple, meeting an old Irish woman whose dead son had appeared to her in a dream, saying 'Give over weeping, Mother, or me wounds will never heal.'[73]

So, in Ruth's little room in Liverpool, the middle-aged woman and her young nephew supported each other. Ruth was fulfilling Lauro's other requests to return to her art and her work, to promote the diffusion of his writings and finally, to found in Harvard, in Lauro's memory, a 'Chair of Italian Civilisation,' of which the first holder was a close friend of Lauro's, Gaetano Salvemini. His letter to Ruth in 1934, written just before beginning his first Seminar at Harvard, must be quoted:

I was deeply touched by your letter of December 27. Lauro's memory and your friendship have become two sources of inspiration and courage in my life, and I will do my best in order to remain always at the same level in your friendship and in the esteem he had for me.

My Seminar will start on February 6, and my first public lecture on the Italian Commons will begin on March 5 ... [Here followed his list of dates, in the hope that Ruth might be back in time to attend one of his lectures.] The President wrote me a letter in which he said that he was happy to have me teaching here and he was very sure I would not make political propaganda. I answered by the letter a copy of which I enclose.

The Department of History is in my favour. The fascists have not been able to prevent my appointment this year. They will start a new fight next time. Of course I am sure that I never will utilise my position as a teacher for political propaganda. I never did so in my life. But the fascists want to reduce me to starvation so that I could not carry on my political work *outside the school*. Perhaps they would agree that a Lauro de Bosis lectureship existed in Harvard, since there is somebody who supports the lectureship by his money; but on condition nobody knows who de Bosis was, and that a fascist teacher is appointed.

You understand that I must avoid both the charge of utilising my Chair for propaganda purposes and the cowardice of concealing who de Bosis was in order to avoid the charge of making propaganda. You will see from the enclosed clipping the attitude I am taking. And I hope you will approve of it.

As regards my first lecture, I discussed the letter with La Piana, after receiving your letter. We reached the conclusion that it would not be advisable to challenge the fascists from the first moment by devoting the preamble of my first lecture to de Bosis. The best method is to give my lectures; to show that I have done a scholarly work; to conquer the confidence and the approval of my audience; and at the end of my final lecture, when they have realised that I am a scholar and not a politician, then I will thank the unknown donor who has made my lectures possible, and European friends.[74]

But what, during all this time, was happening to the de Bosis family? In the days after Lauro's flight they had been waiting for news with an anxiety equal to Ruth's. On 13 October—ten days after the flight—Ruth wrote to Harriet Marple, 'His family know—except his mother—they have not told her yet.' But they must have done so soon after, and by the beginning of 1932 Ruth had managed to get a letter by hand to Lillian de Bosis, receiving from her a letter in which grief mingled with pride and tenderness.

> My darling blessed Ruth,
>
> I cannot tell you how deeply I feel the dear letter you sent me. It is balm to know that you had those beautiful weeks in the summer, to strengthen and bless him, to sweeten your bitter cup. His was a perfect life, but without you and all that you gave him it would never have reached this height, nor have been complete . . . I am unspeakably grateful to you and I love you in a way I cannot describe. I hope you will understand. I know you will . . .
>
> Later I shall feel the pride more fully. Now I must slowly become accustomed to the severing. But perhaps I shall never realize it. I have not given up hope. A spark remains and will burn until positive proof comes—or at least for a long time yet.

Dear, I am glad he told you to go on with your life happily. So my Dear [her husband] begged of me as a proof, as a continuation of our love. I have tried to do it: but at the age when he left me, happiness can only be sad. You will do better: you are an artist, and so vital, and have so many years before you to make rich and beautiful. The pain will subside and the happy memories will glow brighter as time passes . . .

M. will tell you all about us. But indeed what is there to tell? Nothing matters but that we are proud and grateful, and that we love you . . . Mostly I think of what those last hours of flight must have held for him of triumph, beauty, exaltation. Valente, Shelley, the beauty of the earth, the sea, the sky, the night—solitude harmony. Perhaps—he was content to end life so . . .

Dear Ruth, I love you, Your Lillian de B.[75]

A few days later, another letter from the de Bosis family reached Ruth, this time from Elena Vivante.

My dear dear Ruth,

You know that all the time our thoughts are with you . . . never should we have lived to see his death—beautiful as he has known how to make it—we are left without our pride and our love and our youth and everything that made our family bright—what can ever console us? There is no consolation. We shall cry bitterly when we feel weak but also often, as he taught us, strengthen ourselves in the pride of what he did, rejoice at the beauty of his death and at the supreme joy he felt—be happy as he so often was and as he would have liked everybody to be is no more possible—he was a beloved child to each of us.

All our thoughts of love, your Elena[76]

In the same year Vittorio de Bosis wrote:

> Dearest Ruth,
>
> It has been impossible for me to write—mentally impossible—to you or anybody I love. But you have been and you are always near my heart. My love and devotion is beyond words, and even the sad side of your remembrance is dear to my soul. Everybody at home feels the same way, and the only reason we don't rush to see you is that there is no chance of getting a passport.
>
> Mother went through many terrible moments and many times her hopes have been raised by vague news or rumors that made her hope again. She is beautifully strong and brave—ready to hear any tragic definite news, and thinking that *logically* there is *no* hope whatsoever. But in the deepest of her heart she has a faint but continuous hope. We don't encourage any illusion, but as there is nothing really *sure*, we don't think that we should insist on her dropping that tiny light which supports her in her last struggle. She knows that there is nothing to hope but she can't help hoping. What should we do?
>
> But on *May 24th* we had a telephone message from Paris which upset us terribly. Please let me know by any means how things are.
>
> Dear, dear Ruth! You can't imagine what you mean to us and how I love you. V.[77]

Early in 1933, Lillian de Bosis had another opportunity to send a letter to Ruth:

> Here at last is an opportunity to send you a letter freely written, at least without the chilling sense of its being read by alien eyes. A sense quite futile now, for we have ceased to be interesting—alas! . . .

Oh my dear—can you realise the yearning re-morse at what I did, what I had to do, that hurt him so much? For myself I do not care—nor, except just a little, for what people think of me . . . but for the pain it must have given to him, the disappointment, the shock. I can find no relief for that, save at long inter-vals, for a short time—when I can keep present all the loving words he wrote me still, *after* that—and the tones of his voice in those precious telephone talks . . . There, it will help a little to have written this to you— I think.

But—dear—I am unable to believe for long that all is over. Partly because of the vivid reality, spiritual and sensible, of those thirty bright years—still occu-pying all my being—partly because I follow the radi-ant spirit as constantly as I do Adolfo's,* partly be-cause of instinct and cowardice I suppose, and because of the fact that no one ever *saw*, and of the many re-ports. My reason would force me to accept—but it too falters at times and unwittingly I look forward. Lately I have been cataloguing his books—and that has brought such a feeling of security, of nearness. You must be patient with me, all of you. But who ever could have imagined that at seventy one's interior life could be such an infinite turmoil![78]

In 1934, Charis de Bosis succeeded in getting a passport with a visa for England and stayed in London with Ruth, to attend her recitals at the Haymarket. It was a great occasion for them both. 'And did we see London!' wrote Ruth. 'She is a wonderful person—more and more I realize what Lauro's youth and inheritance was . . . I am happy that we are such good friends—like sisters too—and no cloud between us.'[79]

*Lillian's husband.

At moments, however, the memories that Charis's presence evoked, became almost too poignant. 'She has many little resemblances to Lauro, and it's a kind of agony, yet joy, to be with her—certain tones in her voice—certain pronunciation of words—and her hands.'[80]

For Charis the visit was an unalloyed delight, and on her way home, from Paris, she sent Ruth a loving letter of thanks:

> I think we could not be fonder of each other than we are. I am so proud of my sister Ruth! I feel you as a continuation of him [Lauro] in the deepest sense of the word so much of him is still left in you, now and always. You carry on, Ruth, the flame of his life! . . .
>
> Thank you for so many lovely things. Thank you for that paradise of flowers, for the magnificent Mantegnas, for your art, for the hearty laughs that your characters aroused in me, and the tears that they made me shed. Thank you for the tenderness with which you surrounded me in your lovely little house. Thank you for everything, my dearest . . . Your sister Charis[81]

In January 1936, there was another letter from Lillian, in reply to Ruth's cable on the anniversary of Lauro's flight: 'Your dear faithful telegram found me still here with Vittorio—in the quiet rooms where the memories seem more peaceful, so little of the outside world reaches me here . . . I am surrounded by tokens of you, of our days together, Dear. The purple shawl, the mauve bed-jacket, the green basket, the photos accompany me everywhere. And you are in my heart . . . Your own Caramadre.[82]

At last, in the following January, the Aldriches arrived, to reopen the American Academy on the Janiculum. It was a great day for Signora de Bosis, for Amey brought with her some letters about Lauro's flight and *Icaro* which Ruth had copied out for her. She was driven up to the Academy to see them, and saw a framed portrait of Lauro 'with a tricolour riband around it'—and then carried the letters back with her. 'Then at night . . . a few of them only, for they are too vibrant to read all at once.'

A few days later she was writing to Ruth about them:

> Darling, I have just finished reading all the letters, after midnight, with silence—and no danger of interruption—all around me. I must try to tell you a little about the rapture they have given me . . . They are the confirmation of all that my heart desires . . . 'Sorrow' is not the word—now and for some time past I have left sorrow behind me and live in the presence of such unspeakable beauty and greatness . . . I know, I feel that you too have come to the same triumph of life over death, not in every hour, but in many hours. So all is bright and clear between us and I need not try any longer to tell you nor to thank you for what you have done for him and so for me . . . God bless you my dearest Dear—and keep all your days bright with the consciousness of this great beauty and truth which it is our privilege to serve, to live in. Please, dear, when you receive this, read *all* these letters over again, feeling me read with you, word for word. Then I will know all is actually said between us by them.
>
> With tenderest love, yours, as his Caramadre, L de B.[83]

Everything had been said, but there is a postscript to Lillian de Bosis's letter—the story of an occasion, many years later, when the torment of her sense of guilt about the pain caused to Lauro about her letter to Mussolini, was at last set at rest. The occasion is described by Lauro's nephew, Arturo

Vivante, who was staying in his mother's country house near Siena. He was only a child at the time but must have heard the account from his mother, Lauro's sister Elena. They were awaiting the return of Gaetano Salvemini—who had been the first occupant of the chair of the Lauro de Bosis fellowship at Harvard, and who was now, in 1949, returning home after twenty-four years in exile:

> In a letter to my mother [wrote Vivante], [Salvemini] wrote he would be passing through Siena, and hoped to see her. She wrote back, inviting him to stay . . . My grandmother feared that the professor might resent her conduct of long ago, and be hostile to her, and she was visibly nervous about his visit. She expressed her apprehension to my mother. Should she stay in her room when he arrived, should she go down to meet him, should she not go down at all? Half amused, my mother tried to reassure her, but she would not be re-assured. Repeatedly she asked when he was coming, 'You must excuse your grandma, she has such a poor memory,' she would say to us, speaking of herself in the third person, and again she would ask the time of his arrival. The old Professor postponed the trip two or three times, adding to her discomfort.
>
> When at last he came, she was at the front door with the rest of us. Though they hadn't met for more than twenty years, he immediately recognised her and went over to her first. He embraced her and shook her hand with both of his. It seemed it was just what she wanted—a comfort, an unhoped for absolution, something she had long despaired of, but that had finally come. Side by side, they passed into the house.
>
> Later, when he went up to his room, she drew a sigh—a great long sigh—and, beaming as though the

sun had come out after a month of rain, said: 'Listen to me, but he really is a magnificent person isn't he, that professor.'[84]

During all those years Ruth—though she always kept in touch, as we have seen, with the de Bosis family—was constantly on the move. In 1933, she started for the first of her long tours, and we owe to Neilla Warren a full description of her 'strictly functional' luggage. Two large suitcases and a square Vuitton hatbox for the extraordinary hat she wore in 'Opening a Bazaar,' while three other suitcases held her coats, shawls, jackets and semi-costumes. Always she took a cooking kit and a small electric hot plate, and on long tours a briefcase, a typewriter and often a bookbox. On her trip to South Africa she had eleven pieces of luggage.[85]

Her first long journey started, on 11 December 1933 from Southampton by sea. We are also indebted to Miss Warren for the full itinerary of her long African and European journey: to Cape Town and then by train to Johannesburg (two weeks' performances) followed by other recitals in South African cities and then South Rhodesia, Salisbury, Kenya, Khartoum and Wadi Halfa.[86] She was especially fascinated by the 'High Veldt' near Kimberley, and by slowly moving down the Nile.[87] Then Paris and London and a season at the Haymarket in May and June, with a return to America on 23 June. In 1935 she took a nine days' trip to Mexico, staying in Cuernavaca with Mrs Dwight Morrow, 'interesting and picturesque and very strange . . . one feels one's ignorance'—a brief trip to Scandinavia in 1936, and again a four weeks' season at the Haymarket in June and July. Then in the spring of 1937 she was off again, giving sixty-seven performances all through the Northern States to San Francisco.[88] Her letters during this time are scanty and hurried; one has an impression of breathlessness, and this increases when she takes off, with Mary

Erdman as a companion, on 31 December 1937 round the world. One feels that she is always running—not perhaps away—more like Alice, to keep in the same place.

The itinerary for her next journey is again recorded by Miss Warren. Sailing from Marseilles on the last night of 1937, her first stop was Ceylon at Colombo, then Kandy and the jungle ('Last night I heard a leopard snarling, but in the morning found that it was a buffalo.'). On by sea to Madras —Mysore—Bangalore—Bombay, where she performed in the ballroom of the Taj Mahal hotel; Udapur—Delhi—Benares—Calcutta—Darjeeling, where she saw 'the whole Mount Everest range'; then by air to Burma—Rangoon—Mandalay—Massua—and on again by Bangkok to Malaya and by train to Kuala Lumpur. By boat to Java—Bali—('idyllic') and from Java to Australia. There she saw Sydney — Newcastle — Melbourne — Adelaide — Canberra — Sydney—and went on to New Zealand, performing in Wellington — Christchurch — Dunedin — Auckland — and finally in the Fiji Islands, and so home by Honolulu to Los Angeles—nine months in all. In practically every town she gave a performance, and wherever there was a Government House, she stayed in it. Everywhere 'wonderful audiences,' but the incident that moved her most was at Suva in the Fiji Islands, where she was asked to permit a broadcast of the recital. 'She was heard in isolated coconut and sugar plantations, in the gold mines of Tavua, in remote islands, in ships at sea, and in Tonga, 1600 miles away.'[89]

Only a few months rest at home, however, and then she was back in Europe again (June 1939)—first in Paris ('shampoo, slippers, hats') and again a brilliant season in London. She decided to stay on there because Lauro's sister, Elena Vivante, had come there with her husband and four children. Since he was a Jew they had been obliged to leave their beautiful place in Siena. Most unfortunately in June

A montage of Ruth Draper in a selection of her roles.
This gives some impression of the variety of
characters and moods she portrayed

1940 one of the boys, Arturo aged seventeen, as dear to Ruth as a 'member of my own family', had been interned in a camp for aliens and then sent to Canada.[90] In her desperate anxiety about him, Ruth wrote to Mrs Roosevelt, to plead for him to be admitted to the United States. His actual liberation took place after a lunch in Ottawa during which she spoke to Prime Minister McKenzie King about the case. A place was found for him at McGill University where Ruth assumed full responsibility for his support and education.[91]

In May 1940, Ruth discovered yet another new world, that of South America. She gave recitals in Brazil, the Argentine and Uruguay, then crossed the Andes to Chile and Peru and Ecuador—and so at last back to the haven of Dark Harbor.[92]

During World War II she accepted many engagements across the States and Canada for the benefit of war charities, and recited in military camps and hospitals. In Ontario the news reached her that her beloved nephew, Sanders Draper ('Smudge,' Paul's son) who was on active service in the R.A.F. had been killed in an accident caused by engine trouble at Hornchurch, in England. He manoeuvred so skilfully that he avoided a school containing a thousand children, but his Spitfire crashed, and he himself was killed.[93]

After the war, on every visit to Italy she managed to see again some members of the de Bosis family—which she still felt to be her own—staying with the Vivantes on their farm near Siena, and sometimes coming to stay with us on our Tuscan farm.

From there she wrote a long letter to her sister Dorothea, ecstatic about the beauty of the country and the work of reconstruction done after the war:

> Yesterday after tea Iris drove [us] through the country at sunset—I think the most beautiful drive I've

ever made, high up, thro' winding precipitous roads, past tiny villages, farms bathed in golden light—everything is in summer glory . . . laughing children, splendid youths and curly headed girls—one is *drunk* with the beauty of it all. And *how* they work, what vitality and sinuous rhythm as they swing the scythes! And the amazing building they've done—roads and bridges and new houses—after the destruction of the war.[94]

In March 1946, she started a new season in London at the Apollo Theatre. The last decade of her life had begun—and perhaps it was the one that brought her the greatest success. The audiences that gave her so great an ovation were now not only admirers, but old friends—and sometimes their children and grandchildren.

But the London she returned to this time was not the city she had known. 'I've driven to the City and seen St. Paul's and all the devastation,' she wrote to her sister Dorothea. 'The churches are tragic evidence of the horror, yet strangely enough the lovely steeples stand, and much of the walls, the roofs all gone . . . I was near to tears those first days, and still am.'[95]

From America the news had come of the death of her wise, unfailing friend and counsellor, Ned Sheldon. To his sister she wrote, 'I have been so shocked and saddened by the news of Ned's death. Somehow I never thought he might die,' and to her own sister, Dorothea, she wrote 'I used to tell him that going to see him was like going to Heaven and talking to God in a cosy way.'[96]

It was just after arriving in England, where she had received so much affection and applause and which she now deeply loved, that she felt she must try to express a little of what she felt in a broadcast [BBC 16 March 1946].

I am glad to have this opportunity to come before a larger audience than I face four times a week in the theatre, because I feel that I should like to convey to as many people as possible who know me in Britain, my deep emotion at being here again. The welcome I have received this week has been overwhelming, and it is difficult to express just what it has meant to me . . .

Apart from this personal gratitude, I can't refrain from thanking you as an American for your great kindness to my compatriots during these past years. I am sure they will take back most happy and lasting memories, even as I hope your men will hold the same, of their brief sojourns in my country. England is a second home to me, and I am thankful that so many Americans have now experienced something of its character, its beauty, and its heart-warming, kindly and inspiring qualities. For the tangible and intangible things that you have given to them, and to me, I thank you with reverence and humility, with pride, and with most true affection . . .

Please think of me more than ever before, as an American—understanding and fraternal. One of the old links—a small one—among the many new ones in the chain that binds our two countries, but none-the-less a symbol of endurance, of confidence in the future, and abiding good will.[97]

The storm of applause that greeted her return had been overwhelming. To her sister, Alice Carter, she wrote: 'My welcome is perfectly terrific! The theatre was sold out at once for all twelve performances. It holds about 800, a perfect place for me, and hundreds are turned away . . . I am so filled with emotion and gratitude and wonder and humility

. . . I only wish you were here—you would understand and weep and rejoice with me.'[98]

At this point she made a tour in the United Kingdom, from Brighton to Edinburgh, and everywhere she received the same welcome. On her return she characteristically sent a generous cheque to the Mayors of each of the sixteen cities she visited for 'civilians who had suffered from enemy action' and for children, the blind, the aged and the crippled.[99]

Honours, in these visits to England, descended upon her. In 1951 she was awarded the CBE (Commander of the British Empire) by King George and Queen Elizabeth in a private audience at Buckingham Palace. 'It was moving and lovely . . . and I just can't get over [the Queen's] beauty . . . we talked alone for a few minutes. Then the door opened and the King walked in, with the little box in his hand. He stood by the fire, talking pleasantly . . . and gave me the medal . . . [He said] something about how few had been given and how well I deserved it . . . He has a winning charm and no pomposity or aloofness.'[100]

On 11 June 1954, another honour: Cambridge University awarded her a degree of Doctorate of Law, *honoris causa*. 'Unforgetful and heartwarming,' she wrote to Dorothea, 'all very solemn and slow—no music—and the Orator . . . speaks in *Latin*. He quoted Shakespeare "One man in his time plays many parts," but added, "It is unusual to find one who plays . . . (several parts) at once, as does our talented guest."'[101]

One of her last public performances in England was for the women in Holloway Prison who were struck by the shabbiness of her shawls. 'I like to have them near me,' she said, 'they have been my faithful friends.'

But this was not her final memory of English life. In 1951 she was invited to dinner at Windsor Castle for a Command Performance and, in a letter to her sister, Dorothea, described the scene with the same gusto as she would have felt thirty years before, her bright observant eyes taking in every detail of the scene:

> It was a glorious sight! Thirty-six at a beautiful mahogany table, the famous gold plate—*everything gold*—pink and mauve sweet peas in showers, nectarines and strawberries . . . real candles . . . I never saw such splendour! The Queen a dream in pale grey and silver and diamonds, Princess Elizabeth in blue taffeta, Princess Margaret [in] white satin, Princess Mary in pale blue crepe—Duchess of Gloucester in dark blue taffeta—me in yellow chiffon . . . all I had that was long . . . I did six monologues: they howled with laughter—it was a young party, not a bit stiff as in 1926, just a lovely gay and happy group. A superb piper . . . the food was wonderful—the servants in knee-breeches and scarlet coats, all covered with medals (all had been soldiers) . . . I had a lovely chat with the Queen and Princess Elizabeth—they're 'just *lovely* people' . . . [102]

She went on to describe how, at the end of the last scene, as she was running out, her foot slipped on the floor and she fell on her back 'and thought I had broken it.' But the Queen and Princess ran to pick her up, 'they were so human and dear and solicitous' and gave her some whisky—and so all ended well.

This was not snobbishness. It was just one side of Ruth's unfailing capacity to assimilate *every* aspect of life, as it presented itself to her, and also to take 'the great and the good' at their own valuation. When, for instance, she stayed with Berenson, after World War II, in his villa near Vallombrosa, 'Casa al Dono,' her letter describing the visit was precisely the one that B. B. himself, had he been reading over her shoulder would have most enjoyed. 'At eighty-two, his mind clear, incisive, his vast knowledge, his un-diminished passion for beauty, his beautiful speech and voice.' Nicky Mariano, 'B. B.'s devoted Egeria,' was 'an angel of selfless devotion'; the food was delicious and the talk brilliant, and though she did admit B. B. to be vain, she added, 'one sits gladly at his feet.'[103]

Sometimes her more critical friends wondered if in so much enthusiasm there was not a certain lack of discrimination. But now I think they were mistaken: it was Ruth who ended by seeing most.

Twice, in 1951 and 1954, she was billed as giving her 'farewell season.' Critics, reviewers, interviewers, all protested. At the performance on her seventieth birthday, the audience shouted 'No! No!' She changed her mind. 'I dread the thought of what I'll be should my wings be clipped.'[104]

～

On several occasions, interviewers asked her what she considered the secret of her art to be. She replied that it consisted in three things. The first two, she said, were her own vitality and curiosity; the third was her audience's imagination. 'One *must* have vitality to project oneself into an imagined life and then to project this across the footlights into the minds of the audience . . . It must somehow always be there to draw on at a moment's notice, so that any fatigue, distraction or other preoccupation can be disregarded.'

By curiosity she meant, she explained, an unquenchable interest in human beings and the ability to awaken it in others. 'What I had as a child,' she said, 'I've never lost—the child's ability to *pretend*, to *be* what he imagines he is. Your curiosity must take you out of yourself.'

But the essential element, she maintained, did not lie in

herself alone: it lay in an audience's capacity 'to supply the imagination':

> All I can do myself is to make the audience give it to me . . . The great trouble today is that so much entertainment—cinema, radio, television, makes people passive, deadens their imagination . . . In the older drama—Oriental, Greek, Medieval, Shakespearean—the audience had to supply what wasn't there. The poet or dramatist gave the cues . . . but it was from the audience that the experience of truth had to come. What has encouraged me most in my work in these later years is that young people who have never seen anything but films or television find, when they see me, that they are expected to share in what I create, and to their amazement they discover that they can do so . . .'[105]

A stage doorman at the Vaudeville Theatre said once to Joyce Grenfell's father: 'She mass-hypnotises them.'

One day she showed a friend one of her commonplace books, which contained a passage from Conrad's Preface to *The Nigger of the Narcissus*. 'My task, which I am trying to achieve, is . . . to make you hear, to make you feel; it is, before all, to make you *see*. That—and no more, and it is everything.'

'That,' said Ruth, 'is one of the greatest things that has ever been written about art.'[106]

The origins of the drama, in Western lands, are rooted in one great theme: the journey of Everyman between Good and Evil. Ruth Draper's sketches, too—slight as some of them were—followed that great tradition. They too were Morality Plays, stories of Everyman meeting with Vanity and Passion, with Folly and Despair—but always moving in an ordered, stable world, in which, at last, it is goodness that prevails.

Perhaps it was this belief—as well as her own courage—that enabled Ruth, in spite of her own encounters with anxiety and tragedy, to preserve all her life, together with 'a child's gift to pretend,' a child's power of enjoyment.

If her audience rejoiced in her, she was no less delighted by them. 'Weren't they wonderful tonight?' she would say as she left the theatre—and the same zest endured, on this side of the footlights, in the company of her friends. The moment would come after dinner when, 'Do you really want me to?' Ruth would ask as she rose, and the chairs would be pushed back into a semicircle. 'Well—just one before bedtime—which shall it be?' And again, as in her own schoolroom days, children's voices would clamour: 'Please, please, *The German Governess*!'

Now and again, though not often, a life closes in a manner entirely fitting: the pattern is rounded, complete. To Ruth, whose life had been as active as a bird's, the lean still years of old age would have been unbearable; the generous hands, always extended to give and to gather in, could never have lain folded.

In the summer of 1956, just before her seventy-second year, she gathered round her at Dark Harbor those of her friends with whom she had so often shared the beauty and happiness there; many of them were Italian.

The description of her last summer comes to us from her niece Penelope:

> The last summer before she died was full of signs and portents of the end . . . Aunt Ruth complained of feel-

ing odd in the early morning and avoided the scramble to the beach. She drove around the island a lot seeing the few island people whom she had known since childhood. One day she went sailing—a 'blue' day with a light breeze. The little boat barely made head-way across the harbour. Aunt Ruth told me that she planned to sell the boat as she no longer had the strength to sail it alone. Then she said in a most curious tone of voice, 'Isn't it a shame that one has to die and leave all this?'[107]

Her last season at the Playhouse began on Christmas night in spite of bitter weather. She had a great ovation, but she told her dentist that she was tired, at the Saturday matinée she was feeling very queer and found that she was going on talking without quite knowing what she was saying, and indeed her performance went on for longer than usual. That evening, 29 December, after the performance, she drove back by Rockefeller Plaza to gaze at the bright lights under the stars, with laughter and applause still ringing in her ears. When the maid came to wake her the next morning, it was to discover that she had died peacefully in her sleep.

In London, a Memorial Service (organised by John Phipps, Anne Holmes and Joyce Grenfell) was held in St Martin's in the Fields, with Bill Carter representing the Draper family. In New York, at the funeral service in Grace Church, the Bach Passacaglia in C minor was played, and Ruth Draper was carried head-high above the congregation, her 'worn shawls' draping the coffin. Her sisters walked close behind, followed by the rest of her family and her closest friends.[108] The great light over the theatre marquee, spelling out simply RUTH DRAPER, remained up until after her funeral.

Her family were directed that she wished to be cremated,

and to have her ashes strewn over the sea at Dark Harbor—
the scene of her pranks with Paul in childhood, the place to
which she had welcomed Lauro's friends, the haven to
which she had returned, between all the triumphs of her
later years. Her sister, Alice Carter, and one of her nieces
rowed out in a little boat and carried out her desire. For her,
too, 'la mer fut sa sépulture.'

Gaetano Salvemini in middle age

Gaetano Salvemini

The Man Who Would Not Conform

*The truth is that Salvemini did not sow for
the satisfaction of picking the fruit. He planted
the tree, in the hope that it would not be
uprooted by the storm, and that one day men
who came after him, would rest in its shade,
even if none of them had ever heard his name.*

—NELLO ROSSELLI

I

In the first lecture that Salvemini gave in his old chair in the
University of Florence, after over twenty years of exile,
*Una pagina di storia antica**, he said:

> On the first day I went to school, at the age of five, the
> teacher asked me: 'What are you coming to school
> for?' And he taught us to answer in chorus: 'To read,
> to write, to do sums and to behave like a gentleman.'
> Reading, writing and arithmetic I learned, more
> or less, down there. To 'behave like a gentleman' I

*'A page of Ancient History.'

learned here. This knowledge is not always convenient in life, but it gives one a sense of self-confidence that makes up for many disadvantages. The method of our teachers was to behave as *'galantuomini'* not only in their teaching, but in their daily lives.*[1]

What Salvemini meant by 'here' was Florence, where he had entered, at the age of seventeen, the 'Institute for Higher Studies' which formed both his character and his mind. What he meant by 'down there' was Molfetta in Apulia where he was born on 8 September 1873, and where he was instructed, but not taught to be a 'galantuomo.'

He was the oldest of nine brothers and sisters, in a family—according to himself—'rich in children but poor in purse.' His birthplace was a small town between Barletta and Bari, of which the population consisted mostly of small landowners, peasants and fishermen. Salvemini's grandfather was a fisherman owning a small sailing boat, and two of his aunts married fishermen. His father, Ilarione, was given some schooling, like himself. His mother, Emanuela, belonged to a family who transported goods by sea as far as Trieste; Salvemini suspected that sometimes they did some smuggling. Emanuela was intelligent and astute, and took an interest in politics. His uncle was a priest who taught him Latin and transmitted to him his obstinacy, but not his reactionary views. Loyal to the Bourbons, he hoped that the boy would have a successful career in the Church, but was first disillusioned when Gaetano, at the age of nine, came back from school full of the liberation of Italy by King Victor

---

*Salvemini's expression *'procedere da galantuomo'* is particularly difficult to translate. 'To behave like a gentleman' has, unfortunately in English, class connotations which are inappropriate. 'To behave like an honest man' is accurate but weak. Salvemini was more than an honest man. There was in him also a touch of Don Quixote, which made him a *galantuomo*.

Emmanuel and Garibaldi. His uncle lost his temper. 'Shut up, Heretic and Manichee! Victor Emmanuel is a usurper!' When, after eight years in a seminary, already dressed as a priest, the boy passed his final exams brilliantly and heard from a schoolmate that it was possible to get a scholarship in Florence to attend a college, he was determined to try his luck. His family, with great difficulty, collected the money for his ticket, and he set forth for Tuscany.[2]

What sort of men were formed by the education he received in his new school Salvemini has himself described. He became a celebrated historian, a Socratic teacher, and a man whose whole life, from boyhood to the grave, was singularly consistent, showing an unswerving loyalty to the same ideas.

He became a historian whose view of history was influenced by his roots as a countryman from Apulia, and by the Marxist doctrines acquired in his youth, even if he sometimes looked back upon them 'with a touch of indulgent irony.' A historian who said, 'Impartiality is a dream, honesty a duty.' A historian who considered that the supreme purpose of life, 'the only purpose that really distinguishes a man's life from a beast's,' is the search for truth.

He became a teacher who said that teaching was 'his delight and his pride,' who obtained from his pupils not only respect but love, and inspired them—in spite of his severe demands upon them—with his own passion for hard work. A teacher 'who could not tear out of his heart the peasants of his land and the pupils of his school—of the colleagues who had placed their hopes in him, and of the young men who believed in him and in life.' A teacher who worked incessantly, persistently, for school reform—for a school which, in his own words, 'would give his pupils a key to open locks, a compass to direct them across a sea of facts, to guard them against improbable or false assertions and to teach them to think for themselves.' A teacher who observed that in most Italian schools only facts were taught, 'an inorganic chaos of disconnected information,' with the result that too many pupils 'took their final exams in order to be done with studying—as often they received their First Communion to be done with faith, and some took a wife to be done with love.' A teacher who wrote in his essay on culture, 'God said to man "You shall earn your bread by the sweat of your brow." Culture is the bread of the soul . . . One must work, suffer, and give things up to be worthy of conquering it, and capable of retaining it.'[3]

It was this conviction—'an almost religious sense of a teacher's mission,' that enabled him, as Eugenio Garin has said, 'to face threats, danger, unpopularity.'

> No-one has dared as he did to run the risk of making mistakes, of becoming absurd—and often he did make mistakes and say absurd things . . . He dared to remain alone, cut off from any group or party, without heroic poses, fighting heroically even for small, apparently insignificant things . . . When, in his essay about the meaning of culture, he ended it with the word 'justice,' he was expressing what he considered the social duty of an intellectual—to show, at the risk of being always against everyone, what is fair . . . to exercise the right of criticism without which a man ceases to be human . . . This is the justice without which it is unbearable for men to live together.[4]

Ernesto Rossi wrote,

> Like Socrates: [Salvemini] only wanted to be the obstetrician who helps to bring the truth into light: the truth that every man bears within him. In speaking to a young man, he never made use of his own superiority: he tried, instead, to find in his pupil what was worth taking seriously.

'That is what you want to say, isn't it?'—he would ask, and even in the mire of the most confused ideas he always succeeded in finding a little golden straw. And the young man he was speaking to, recognized that this golden straw was his own, and gained confidence in himself. And so gradually he learned not to accept any statement without first weighing it in the light of his own reason. He learned to ask himself what the use was of established habits and conventions, even the most venerable; he learned to knock his knuckles against the plaster of words, to find out what was inside them; plaster, real stone, or emptiness . . . He learned not to be ashamed of saying a thousand times that he didn't understand, even when others said that they did. He learned not to conform.[5]

Ernesto Rossi has left us a description of his appearance which I will not try to better:

Like Socrates, [he] was like an old Silenus: a large skull, rendered wide by his baldness; small eyes, filled with kindness and intelligence; a snub nose; high cheekbones; a wide mouth, which when he smiled showed a great fence of teeth; a pointed beard; wide shoulders; a thick-set figure; a heavy step. A man from the fields, not from literary drawing rooms.[6]

This was a man enriched by the warmth and variety of his friendships, never allowing his political opinions to obscure them. A man passionately attached to his children, but whose love for them was cut short by two tragedies. 'A sentimental man with the mask of a rationalist'. A man who tempered vehemence with laughter. A man who did not consider success important, who knew his own limitations and recognised his mistakes, but never desisted from his quest for truth. A free man, who said what he had to say both to enemies and friends. A man for whom, in the words of one of his students, 'freedom counted more than life.' A socialist who in his last years broke away from the framework of his party, but never betrayed the ideals of his youth, and who in the end—in spite of the devoted friends around him—trod a lonely path. 'The truth is that Salvemini did not sow in order to pick a fruit: he planted a tree, in the hope that it would not be uprooted by a storm, and that the men who came after him would be able to rest in its shade, even if they never remembered his name.'[7]

When he entered the Florentine School for Higher Studies, at the age of seventeen, which formed both his character and his mind, Salvemini was embarking on a new phase of his life. He has described it himself in his famous first lecture after his return to Florence, after twenty years of exile, 'A Page of Ancient History.' Alessandro Galante Garrone, who was present, has described his appearance on that day—'very serious, with a pale waxen face, contracted by the effort to conceal his inner emotion.'[8] 'A man cannot return,' Salvemini began, 'without a throb of emotion to the school which received him as a schoolboy, and made a man of him, and then took him back as a teacher, and to which he now returns after a long landslide of events . . . Memories flock to the door of his heart.'

He then proceeded to describe these memories so vividly that one feels bound to make use of his own words.

> Imagine what a seventeen-year-old schoolboy was like in the autumn of 1890, who had wasted the eight best years of his life in a horrible *ginnasio-liceo* in Southern Italy! Among my masters in these eight years I only remember three with gratitude. One taught me privately the elements of Greek, one . . .

explained to me the first book of Euclid's geometry. That miracle of clarity, order and good sense had a decisive and permanent influence on my subsequent development: if I have ever succeeded in expressing myself in a clear and orderly fashion, I owe it to Euclid. Finally, during the three years of the *liceo*, an open-minded priest presented historical events to us in the form of cause and effect. Some of these connections, now, seem to me rather questionable. For instance, he said: 'Christ was born—and the Roman Empire fell.' Four centuries of cause and effect, concentrated in so few words, obviously represented an excessive synthesis.

Except for these three teachers—really not many for eight years—the others were miserable hacks, who taught us nothing, because they could not teach what they did not know.

Salvemini went on to say that, as there was no library in the school or in the town, he spent his first five years in the *ginnasio* suffering from intellectual starvation.

But in a large basket of religious works belonging to my uncle, I discovered six volumes of the Bible in Latin. I did not learn anything in them about Hebraic history, but the psalms, the prophecies, the Gospels, with their moral force and poetic beauty, left on my mind a great impression, which endured and later on helped me very much with my studies in medieval history. I also found, in a great chest, 32 dissertations (I don't remember whose) which informed me, among other things, that Adam and Eve in the Garden of Eden spoke to God the Father and to each other in Latin, and that Joshua, in order to defeat the Philistines, had indeed held up the course of the sun.

During the last three years of the *liceo*, however,

French novels translated into Italian began to be handed around in secret. The history professor explained cause and effect, but *The Three Musketeers* made us share the intense life of Richelieu and Mazarin at the Court of Louis XIV. Then came *The Count of Monte Cristo*, *The Mysteries of Paris* and *The Wandering Jew* by Eugène Sue. I read *The Wandering Jew* in circumstances that no-one could imagine.

Every year at the end of Lent, the boys were required to perform spiritual exercises, ending with Confession and Communion. Salvemini said that he would never have thought of avoiding these duties, but that when one of his schoolmates offered him *The Wandering Jew*, honestly warning him that it spoke against the Jesuits, he decided to read it, even if he was committing a sin. 'But I had to finish the sin before the spiritual exercises were over, to be able to confess it when I had committed it completely.' In every spare moment, day and night, he perused the ten volumes in very small print. His eyes survived the merciless test and he was able to make his confession and be absolved by 'a very sensible priest.'

The next books that came his way—since he had no money to buy them for himself—were those of Jules Verne, and he remained grateful for them all his life. This was his reason:

> The protagonists of these stories always found themselves facing a mysterious and menacing world with the sole help of their intelligence and character; but they were never discouraged and always won in the end. The generation after mine read instead Salgari's tales of pirates looking for gold without any moral purpose with a dagger in their teeth. Jules Verne, 1880–1900; Salgari, 1902–1920. These names and dates explain many Italian events.

Finally, in the third year of the *liceo*, he discovered another 'mentor.' He said that, beside the Bible, Euclid and Jules Verne, he owed all that was good in the early development of his mind to Francesco de Sanctis.*

> This was the intellectual luggage that I brought to Florence with me in the autumn of 1890. The moral content was not too bad: the prophecies of Israel, the Gospels, the stories of Jules Verne and the books of de Sanctis had done a good job. The intellectual content was rambling, untidy, full of gaps or rather enormous caves. For instance, nobody had ever mentioned to me either D'Annunzio or Carducci. In the case of D'Annunzio I am convinced that I did not miss much. But to come to Florence to study literature and never to have heard of Carducci! . . .

He had been told that the Institute he hoped to enter was offering twenty scholarships—the most successful competitors received ninety lire a month, those in the second category, seventy, and the least brilliant, sixty.

> I believe [he said], that I owe my good fortune to Euclid, to my history teacher and to de Sanctis. They helped me to put together an Italian essay in which a certain good sense was not lacking. But I think I was saved by an answer I gave in the oral examination. One of the examiners asked me 'what the kernel was of the legend of Aeneas.' I was startled.
>
> With a sob in my throat—for I already felt that I was done for—I replied that I did not understand the question. 'If you want me to make a summary of the Aeneid or if you want me to translate any unseen passage at sight, I think I could manage it. But no-one has

*Great historian of Italian literature.

ever taught me that legends have kernels.' One of the three examiners smiled, and they awarded me the lowest scholarship.

Without those sixty lire, I should have had to return home, the eldest son of nine brothers and sisters, and to become a priest—for that was the fate in Southern Italy then of boys in poor families who were not entirely unlettered or stupid. This school saved me from that fate, and I think probably spared the Bishop of my town some trouble.

Salvemini then went on to describe what it was like to attempt to live on sixty lire a month—even if it was worth more at that time:

The man who has always been certain of his bread, says scornfully, 'Man does not live by bread alone.' That is true, but without any bread one does not live at all . . . Sixty lire a month, turned into fifty-six by taxation, were not enough even then to make both ends meet. The evening meal alone ate up one lira.

His books were provided by the library of his school and the National and Marucellian Libraries, which in winter even provided heat until ten p.m. After that the boys ran to take shelter in bed 'with steam pouring out of their mouth and nostrils.' He found help in private lessons: six hours a week, at twenty-five lire a month, to tutor a boy in Latin. 'My budget was balanced.'

At the end of the first year, his fifty-six lire were increased to ninety, or, after taxation, eighty-four. 'With what was left over from my private lessons, I occasionally visited my family, bought a book, and, once in a blue moon, went to a theatre.'

Salvemini then described his teachers and their influence. It is impossible not to be impressed by the high standards of the teachers, the industry of the pupils, and the passionate enthusiasm of this particular boy—as described by him with gratitude and nostalgia. 'His teachers' first lessons were moral ones,' commented Galante Garrone in his introduction to his collection of Salvemini's scattered writings. 'They had an unwavering scruple about the truth, and the courage always to tell it . . . They were, in other words, *galantuomini* in life as in letters.'[9]

Salvemini declared that his first year in this institute was the *'annus mirabilis'* of his life. Geography was taught to him by Bartolomeo Malfatti, who began by explaining the theory of evolution from the simplest forms of organic life to the appearance of *homo sapiens*. While taking notes the boy was uneasy, still weighed down by the precepts in his uncle's chest, and at one point he muttered, but loud enough for the professor to hear, 'So we descend from worms?' 'The dear old man stopped, and said quietly, "What harm would there be in that?" I was deeply shaken. Farewell, Adam and Eve speaking Latin in the Garden of Eden!'

Another teacher who stimulated his mind in a new way was the professor of Latin Literature, Gaetano Trezza, who made his pupils translate Catullus. And Catullus gave him the opportunity to bring to life the world in which Catullus lived:

> Lesbia, whom Catullus hated and loved, and Caesar, against whom Catullus launched violent attacks, and Cicero, who was always disagreeing, and Horace, who ran away at Pharsalia, and Lucretius, the philosopher-poet, who passed on to us the wisdom of Epicurus . . . He taught us the story of men who have loved, hated, believed, suffered. It was a new window opening on the world . . . and I would discover it. At seventeen the whole world lay before you. You have only to hold out your hands . . .

Yet another teacher who kindled dry wood—and into what a blazing fire!—was Pasquale Villari, the teacher of Medieval and Modern History. He was a tiny man, as lively as a cricket, who showed nothing but a bald forehead above the green table behind which he spoke. He explained to us the theories about the history of humanity which we owed to the great thinkers of all periods: Saint Augustine and Bossuet, Dante and Machiavelli, Vico and Montesquieu, Buckle and de Tocqueville. He didn't offer us ready-made ideas, to repeat like parrots, or to cushion our intellectual laziness. He launched us into the open, dangerous but fascinating sea of a great historical synthesis. If we could swim, so much the better, if not, we could always go back to coasting along the shore . . .

One could hardly describe Villari's lessons of history as methodical. This was seen to by other teachers of the Institute. By common agreement, punctual, inflexible, each one of them took a room in the unfurnished or ill-furnished houses of our culture and taught us to keep it tidy, to restore the crumbling furniture, to transform or eliminate what was in bad taste. Villari entered all the rooms, opened wide all doors and windows, let in air and light everywhere and sometimes even upset the order produced by one of his colleagues. In short, he taught us an infinite number of things, including modern history. He taught us above all not to be mummies, to become men.

It was Villari who advised Salvemini to read *L'Ancien Régime et la Révolution* by de Tocqueville, 'one of the most genial books ever written about a great historical event,' and who pointed out to him Taine's *History of English Literature* and *Critical Essays*.

And not only was he our teacher: he was our great friend. He went for long walks with us, a persistent asker of questions, criticising our work, advising us what books to read, asking about our families, scolding us for our youthful follies. I, for instance, worried him on account of my political ideas, like a chick running away from the hen ... but when, in the third year of my studies, I fell ill, owing to too much work and the habit of living on nothing which one acquires when supplies have run low ... he recommended me to a family of one of his friends, who asked me to stay with them in the country, and so helped me to recover and come back to work.

Salvemini remembered, however, that his 'annus mirabilis' contained one black spot: the lessons about the theory of philosophy of Augusto Conte. He had, and always retained, an unconquerable distaste for abstract philosophical theories. Professor Conte said that the teaching of philosophy had, among other purposes, also that of teaching young people humility, putting before them problems whose solutions they could not understand: 'During the three weekly hours of the theory of philosophy, I was taught humility for a whole year by Augusto Conte. And I did not take to it . . .'

Finally he came to 'the kindest teacher of all, the one of whom I cannot think with dry eyes,' his teacher of paleography, Cesare Paoli.

I used to go to his house in the evenings to read him my homework by the light of an oil-lamp, while his children romped in the next room ... At the end of the first year he put a big book in my hand, Imbart de la Tour's *Les Eléctions épiscopales dans les églises de France du IXème au XIIème siècle*, telling me to prepare a review of it. I knew nothing either about the episcopal elections nor about the eleventh and twelfth centuries. I worked on it all the summer—and Paoli printed my six pages and paid me 18 lire. In those days of formidable appetites, our currency was not the lira but the steak. One lira, two steaks; 18 lira, 36 steaks. Not to speak of the honour! I have written many reviews and books since then, but none of them has given me so much satisfaction. To complete my happiness, the book's author wrote me a letter congratulating me on the diligence of my review.

Finally Salvemini attempted to define the general attitude of his old teachers, who almost all belonged to the current of thought which was despised later on as 'positivist,' 'illuministic,' 'intellectualist.'

Intellectual fashions pass. The positivist fashion passed and the idealistic one will, too ... Even after the upheavals of the French Revolution and the Napoleonic Empire, in the first half of the nineteenth century, the Illuminism of the eighteenth century was overwhelmed, but it came back again with fresh vigour in the second half of the century, and got rid of Romanticism. Perhaps we, the archaeological remnants of today, will, in half a century, become the latest fashion—cured, I hope, of our exaggerated faith in science and willing to admit that men allow themselves to be led more often by intuition—that is blind passion—than they are led by reason. *Multa renascentur quae iam cecidere.**

Salvemini's last tribute in his 'Page of Ancient History' was to his fellow-students—most of them from Central Italy or from the North. 'My habits were far from refined—

---

*'Many things are born again, that once fell to pieces.'

they were frankly common. The behaviour of these friends made me follow their example. When, having trained me, they accepted me, one of them paid me the backhanded compliment of saying: "It seems impossible that you are a Southerner."'

Among these friends the one who influenced him most was a girl from Cremona who became his friend in his second year, Ernestina.

> I called her Ernestina then, and still call her so. She had great dark eyes, a very fine complexion and a gentle voice. Please free your Latin minds of all superfluous ideas: there was fortunately nothing between this girl and me but friendship. I say fortunately because the friendship of a boy and a girl, when both of them behave themselves, always gains strength from a vein of tenderness, which might suddenly become love, but if it doesn't, it remains a source of poetry in one's spirit for all one's life. That is better. A proof of it is that when Cesare Battisti, with his virile good looks, turned up from the Trentino and Ernestina and he fell in love, it was a great joy for me.

At once Salvemini sent her a letter of congratulations that had no touch of envy:

> Dear, good Ernestina,
>
> I can't tell you how happy I am. I would like to say a thousand things to you and Battisti, but I am too delighted to be able to write anything. I don't know if in life you'll be as happy as I wish you to be, but you certainly deserve it. I don't know which of you is most fortunate, certainly you are worthy of each other. The handwriting of your letter is too excited; one must be calm, one must not be too happy. Hurrah! How much I wish I were in Florence now—to Hell with poverty

> . . . I was as happy as this only on the evening on which I realised that Maria loved me. Devil take it— but what a wonderful thing![10]

Twenty years later Ernestina, whom Salvemini had warned not to let herself be 'too happy,' saw her happiness brought to an end with the death of her husband, by the hands of an Austrian hangman. Battisti, who had fought for the autonomy of the Trentino from Austrian domination, had enrolled in the Italian army at the outbreak of war. He was captured and executed as a traitor.

Salvemini wrote in Battisti's honour perhaps the most emotional article he ever published, but, while he could not fail to admire his courage, he reproached him for going on fighting a losing battle. His duty, according to Salvemini, would have been to leave even his wife and children as soon as the war broke out, in order to put himself at the head of the other emigrants from the Trentino, and to convince the rest of the world to oppose the Austrian tyrant. 'His glory does not console us for his death.'[11]

In the days of Salvemini's and Ernestina's youth, the young people who met in Via Lungo il Mugnone had all turned socialist.

> In the evenings we settled all social problems with such vehemence that the owner of the house threatened to expel Marx and his female and male congregations if they did not become less noisy. The teachers of the Institute knew what we were up to . . . But neither to Villari nor to any of his colleagues did it occur to interfere with our liberty or to make any political distinctions between us.
>
> Ours was a real religion, with its dogmas and priests. Not all religions remain unchanged, the dogmas crumble, the priests often show themselves to be mere sacristans. The Marxist doctrine is a wonderful

filter to wake up sleeping souls, but if you overdo it, your mind becomes blurred. Yet the man who has once discovered in his spirit the source from which religions spring up, will never see that source dry up. He will never betray the ideals of his youth, even when he may remember them with a little indulgent irony.

The believers of the little congregation that met in the evenings of 1894 in Via Lungo il Mugnone have never betrayed their youthful ideals. In the winter of 1944, talking to an American friend, I said that the group of friends in Florence from 1892 to 1895 could not complain of having had bad luck. One, Cesare Battisti, had been hung by the Austrians; his wife Ernestina had had to take refuge in Switzerland; one had been pushed off to South America, I myself to North America. Two of the Rosselli brothers had been murdered on Fascist orders by French assassins; Berneri had been murdered in Spain. Two others stayed in Italy; I know nothing about them, but I feel sure they have kept their self-respect. To close one's eyes saying: 'Cursum consummavi, fidem servavi'*—what greater success can there be in life? ... My friend looked at me, disconcerted and speechless. Two years later he said to me: 'I have often thought about what you said that day. You were right.'

'People of Anglo-Saxon origin,' Salvemini commented, 'sometimes take a little time to accept a new idea, but they always end by getting it right.'

He brought his first lecture to an end with the words: 'Instead of giving you a history lesson, I have wasted an hour praising the good old times, a sign of premature senility. You must forgive me. I won't do it again.'

*'I have run the race, I have kept the faith.'

II

When the years of Salvemini's scholarship were over—
('the marvellous years')—he went back to his birthplace,
Molfetta, and was extremely unhappy there. He admitted
in a long letter to Carlo Placci in Florence that this sudden
change of atmosphere had aroused in him a deep depres-
sion, such as he had never known before.

He only remained at home for four days, and then went
on to Palermo, where he had been given a post as teacher to
boys of eleven, and from there wrote a long letter to Carlo
Placci in Florence, saying what had upset him so much. His
father had fallen so deeply into debt that it had become impossible to save any of his property, but—according to his
mother—a part of Gaetano's own income (of about 700 lire
a year) could be saved by a trick which indeed showed some
financial ingenuity, but which would deprive his creditors
of about forty per cent of their due. This caused a violent
argument with his mother, and left him in such a state of
moral confusion that he turned to Placci to know whether, if
he agreed, he could still call himself an honest man.

> Forgive me, dear Placci, if I say certain things to you;
> but you cannot imagine what I have suffered while I
> was in Molfetta. From the first moment I found my-
> self fighting with my mother—my father, poor man,
> has made so many mistakes that he does not dare
> speak ... Who is right, dear Placci? ... Am I to
> become a *thief*? ... Would Signora Elena* continue
> to think well of me, and what would my Maria† say?
> Take care, Placci; look at the matter from a moral point

*Elena French, an old friend of the Placci family.
†Maria Minervini, the young girl from Molfetta who was then living
in Florence, and who later on became his wife.

of view, consider the difference between the world I have made for myself with my studies and my friendships, and that in which my mother lives . . .[12]

In the following Spring, he sent Placci a horrifying account of a sulphur mine near Palermo which he had visited, and of a boy who showed him round it: the heat, the stench, the dark descent underground, in such a position that the children inevitably became stunted. Salvemini asked the boy:

'Do you earn enough to live?'
'No.'
'Did you have an insurrection here?'
'No, but at Favara they burned some houses and killed some people.'
'And why did you do nothing?'
'Because it's no use. The owner is like the king, he makes the laws and, as he gives us food, we have to obey. And if we make an insurrection they put us in prison and we will be hungry all the same.'
'Does the *padrone* seem rich?'
'Yes, very rich. We can't know how rich he is.'
'And how did he get rich?'
'Oppressing the poor—lending money.'
'And yet you respect him very much?'
'He gives us bread.'[13]

This letter upset Placci's equanimity. He answered: 'I should have liked to organize at once one of those protests that English people sometimes draw up in cases of obviously gross brutality and in which every class, whatever their party may be, unite. And this I did not do. I really believe that a sense of compassion is very superficial in Latin peoples, still too pagan, sensual and egotistic.'[14]

Salvemini's greatest hope was to get back to Florence as soon as possible—this time as a teacher: 'Villari has written me that there will be a free post next year in the Galileo [Institute in Florence] and that he is trying to do something for me in Rome. You cannot imagine my agitation . . . These seventy-five days that separate me from Florence are counted on my fingers and I can hardly believe that they will end.'[15]

It is plain from all these letters how much the young Salvemini trusted Placci's opinion and advice. His own scrupulousness in money matters is shown in another letter written three years later about some money which Placci had given to him, but which he insisted on considering a loan:

> I want to speak opening my heart to you, in the certainty that you will not misinterpret my words. My circumstances are such that even ten lire are a help on some days, and I must not let a crumb fall from my table. But I wish to pay my debt to you in full. This is the first *real* obstacle that I have met in my life, and I want to show myself that I am capable of overcoming it . . . The gift you offer me would make my victory easier, but would diminish my own satisfaction at having won it . . . If tomorrow I needed something, I would at once think of my friend Placci, and would turn to him, feeling that to ask him a favour would not be undignified; I would turn to you as one turns to a brother . . . But now, I feel a painful pleasure in meeting my whole difficulty and fighting against it.[16]

Who was the man to whom Salvemini owed so much? In Florence and Geneva, in Paris and London—in every place where political life was interesting and social life entertaining—he was a well-known figure. His manservant, who followed him everywhere, said 'My master is not rich or noble—but he has such good connections.' He would look in on Berenson saying that he had just come from Duino, where he had been staying with Princess von Thurn und Taxis, and where Rilke, poor fellow, was very ill again, or from Paris, where Clemenceau had told him . . . or perhaps (for his range was wide) from Hatfield, where Lord Salisbury . . .

After he left I Tatti Mr Berenson would laugh and say, 'Poor old Placci, no pudding is cooking in Europe without his stirring it!'

It was to Placci that Salvemini owed an entry into many social circles that he might otherwise never have known. He introduced him to the distinguished historian, Francesco Papafava, and to his daughter, Margherita Bracci Testasecca, whose whole family became his lifelong friends, and also to Bernard Berenson, the celebrated art critic and connoisseur, with his wife, Mary. The latter did not at first take to him. In 1895 she described him as 'a rabid Socialist' and 'a fanatical enthusiast,' adding that several friends had implored her to 'pull Placci out of his claws.' She thought that the best way of achieving this would be to give him 'a sensible Fabian book.' But by 1912 Salvemini was firmly established at I Tatti as a family friend, was asking B. B. for 'the autobiography of an American writer who wrote with great warmth about Mazzini' and receiving in return the Autobiography of Jane Addams. He also confided to Berenson his unhappiness at returning to Molfetta, saying that he was losing his faith in everything, even in himself—'that is, losing every reason for living.'[17]

During the terrible months of the Italian retreat on the Piave, and the subsequent humiliation of the peace treaty, it was to B. B. that Salvemini poured out his grief, disillusionment and resentment, and we even find Berenson subscribing to the *Unità,* a socialist weekly started by Salvemini and offering one of his farms to house a refugee family from the Veneto.

But before this time many changes had taken place in Salvemini's life, of which no trace appears in his correspondence with the Berensons. Soon after his return to Sicily to teach there, in 1897, he had married, after many scruples, a simple, loving girl from Molfetta, Maria Minervini, and wrote to Placci that he was completely happy with her.

> If you know what a great change has taken place in my character! I spent the last days of my bachelorhood in a deplorable state. I wept, I could not eat, I repeated to myself a hundred times the long word 'responsibility.' Now everything is changed: I don't think any more about the future, or rather I think about it with confidence. I feel strong and sure that I shall be victorious in the battle of life. Maria is so good and she loves me so much that it is impossible that things should not go well with me. As for Socialism, I have become more Socialist than ever since my marriage. I said to myself: 'Look, you have had to wait for this happiness for so long. Why? Is it fair? No. So down with Society and long live love!'[18]

In an article entitled 'Amico e Maestro'* Maria's much younger sister, Lidia Minervini, described Maria's first meeting with Salvemini who, when he first came to Florence, was only seventeen, while Maria was thirteen.

> From that time Salvemini was a frequent visitor to our house, many years before. So he saw the child turn into a girl, and was captivated by her great sweetness. Everybody said that she was so good and he

*'Friend and Teacher.'

adored her. 'Mariolì mia' he would say. She wasn't a cultivated person. In the South, then, a woman didn't study, she only prepared herself to look after the house. But she played the piano very nicely and he listened, enchanted . . .

A letter of Salvemini's has been found, written a few months before the disaster of Messina: it said: 'In my family life I am so happy that I am frightened.' It was a presentiment: disaster was awaiting him in the tragic night of December 28, 1908, the night of the Messina earthquake . . .

Lidia also remembered the earthquake:

I was only eight years old, but I remember my childish anguish. I guessed that something very important had happened. I remember spelling out the headlines of a paper which said: 'The family of Professor Salvemini completely wiped out' . . . I remember something else: a telegram from Mussolini: 'Gaetano Salvemini, one of the finest figures of Italian socialism, has disappeared.' But Gaetano Salvemini was not dead. He had been miraculously saved.

Having come home late, when the family was already fast asleep, he was alarmed by the warming signs of the earthquake—the ringing of electric bells and the desperate howling of dogs. A moment of terror, and then he leaped towards the window while the outer wall came down like a pack of cards. It was a house of five storeys on the promenade which was hit simultaneously by the earthquake and tidal wave. Gaetano was thrown down from the fifth floor, but the architrave of the window miraculously broke his fall . . . his family was swallowed up—five children, his wife and his sister, all taken unawares in their sleep.

Strangely enough my father, W. Bayard Cutting, who was then the American Vice-Consul in Milan, was in charge of the American rescue ship which arrived in Messina. Many thousand dead lay beneath Messina's ruins— perhaps as many more were buried there alive. One of the things that first struck my father—apart from the sheer horror of the human suffering before his eyes—was a strong impression of the Oriental affinity of the Sicilians: 'Their mood was one of submission, unsurprised and unassertive, to the hard hand of fate. They did not rebel or complain, and on the other hand they would not strive. It was folly to think of building a comfortable house, when there was no-one left to occupy it, or to earn money which could bring no sweetness. So most of them sat idly in the streets, or under the roof of the market, and took what food was put before them. The few who worked, like our boatmen, did not care what pay they received. A piece of bread they were glad to get; but when it was a question of money, one lira or five were all much the same.'*

Salvemini, however, was not one of the men who sat idle and passive in their misery. Lidia Minervini says 'Gaetano, together with my brother Ugo, groped for days among the ruins to try and find some of his family, and only found corpse after corpse. Not all the bodies were found, neither Maria nor Ughetto—the youngest of his five missing children . . .' She vividly remembered the days after Salvemini's return:

> Our dinner table, the table laid and all of us silent . . . I can still see his face turned to stone, without that dear smile, sealed up in hopeless sorrow. He would remain

*This report brings out how very swiftly relief ships—British, Russian and American—reached their destination. In particular my father was impressed by the Russian sailors, who were a revelation, he

with his fork in the air. Somebody said 'Gaetano, have you eaten anything?' Perhaps he didn't realise how it was possible that he should still be alive, he the only one still left of his whole family . . .'[19]

Whenever he heard about the survival of a little boy of the same age—Ughetto was only three—he hurried to the spot or sent a telegram, only to meet with disappointment. He continued to be haunted by the fear that Ughetto, too small to explain who he was, had been taken away in one of the rescue ships. To the philosopher Giovanni Gentile he wrote:

> If I had ever tried to imagine a terrible misfortune hitting me, I could never have imagined what has really happened. If only one of those beautiful children had been left! . . . I go ahead, work, make speeches . . . in short, I go on living. And people think I am strong . . . I have on my table some letters that my wife, my sister, or the children wrote. They are like their voices. And when I have read one of them, I have to stop, because a great fit of weeping overcomes me, and I should like to die . . . [20]

Many years later, when he was staying at the villa of Donna Titina Rufini at Sorrento, her daughter Giuliana, who slept in the room beside his, would hear the sound of his voice at night, crying out in his sleep 'Maria, Maria.'[21]

This tragedy became a turning point in Salvemini's life. To Giustino Fortunato* he wrote: 'Life for me can now have

---

wrote, 'to those who did not know the quiet common sense, the tactful sympathy and the unassuming heroism of the *moujik*. The Russians were the only people who had always everything on the spot.'

*Giustino Fortunato, one of Salvemini's closest friends, was one of the greatest *meridionalisti* of his time.

no other purpose than to forget myself in work that binds me to other men, while waiting for the final hour which will free me from the constant burden of my grief.'[22] He returned to Florence and at once resumed both his lectures in the University and his political work.

In the summer of 1911, he started a campaign against the Italian invasion of Libya in *La Voce*, a periodical directed by Papini and Prezzolini. Writers of very different views were contributing to this review and although Salvemini's favourite themes—the policy of Giolitti, the Southern question and the problems of education—were discussed; there were also many articles on philosophic, literary and artistic matters.

After the war against Libya had actually been declared, the other contributors to *La Voce* forgot Salvemini's anti-Libyan campaign, and he ceased to write for this review, starting a weekly paper of his own, *L'Unità*, which became the mouthpiece of young liberals and socialists—such men as Antonio Gramsci, Piero Gobetti, Ernesto Rossi, and Carlo and Nello Rosselli,* and was the first paper to tackle objectively and concretely the problems of the South. Its first number appeared on 11 December 1911, three months after the declaration of war against Turkey. Rather than declare the programme of his new paper, Salvemini preferred to enter *in medias res* and discuss the attitude of the socialists and the nationalists towards the war on Libya. He hoped to enlarge the horizons of the Italian ruling class by

---

*Carlo and Nello Rosselli were close friends and disciples of Salvemini. Carlo collaborated in Piero Gobetti's paper *La Rivoluzione Liberale*, joined the socialist party after Matteotti's murder and became one of the founders of the clandestine paper *Non Mollare*. One of the founders of *Giustizia e Libertà*, he was the first Italian anti-fascist to fight in the Spanish Civil War. He was murdered in France, with his brother Nello, by the *cagoulards* (a right wing terrorist movement) by the order of the Italian fascist government.

educating a group of young men from different origins who would be less superficial, less ignorant and more honest and active than their contemporaries. All this was in line with his teaching at the University, with the advantage that it gave him several thousand readers instead of a limited number of students. Benedetto Croce himself sent a letter of support and some financial help. The greater part of the work was done by Salvemini, often under different pseudonyms, and as the subscriptions were not sufficient to meet the expenses, he sold a tiny piece of land which he still possessed in Molfetta. At times he let himself be carried away by the strength of his feelings and became too personal: but even when he was most violent, his defence of truth and justice was always the real cause. Moreover no man was more conscious than he of his own limitations, or admitted to them more frankly. He wrote to Giustino Fortunato:

> I am frightened by my responsibility towards the men who love me and think highly of me. I feel that I shall never be able to give them more than a minute part of what I should; I almost feel that I am deceiving them . . . by not saying that they are mistaken, that it is not fair—if I dare say so—that they should expect so much from me!
>
> I would like you to judge me at my true value. I am not stupid, no . . . but my culture is full of terrifying gaps. And my temperament is not properly balanced. If I were a steady man, in control of my nerves, capable of always behaving firmly and steadily, I would certainly be more valuable. Instead . . . I am worth a great deal less.[23]

The expedition in Libya had been preceded, he wrote, by propaganda saying that it was a promised land, overflowing with water, sulphur and minerals, 'and ready to absorb in a few years millions of immigrants with open arms and little flags to welcome the kind Italians.' Salvemini's campaign against this war was caused by a realistic assessment of the needs of Italian foreign policy as opposed to insane nationalist and colonial dreams, which would waste the nation's meagre resources and would only serve to divert the country's attention away from its real problems. This led him to give a vigorous support to Italy's entry into World War I, which he saw as a necessary step towards the realisation of democracy and socialism.

During Italy's nine months of neutrality the Austro-German alliance had been trying to persuade her to enter the war on their side with the offer not only of Nice, Corsica and Tunis, but also of the Croatian and Dalmatian coasts, where there had been small Italian communities since the time of the Venetian Republic. Some interventionists (the men who wished to enter the war on the side of the Allies) were even in favour of occupying Dalmatia, but Salvemini remained firmly against it.

His political career was necessarily affected by his personal unpopularity and his constant defence of the underdog. Already in 1913—after a dearly won struggle for universal suffrage—he had stood for Parliament in Apulia and was even shot at by one of his opponents. There was a scandal in the press about the incorrect behaviour of local officials in favour of the government's candidates, but Salvemini was nevertheless defeated, and when, in 1915, Italy did enter the war, he felt compelled to join the army himself. Fernande Luchaire, whom he afterwards married, wrote sending his military address to a friend:

> He says that he already hears the guns, and will soon be in the trenches; from what he writes I imagine that he is already near the Isonzo, as he spoke of walking in the mud . . . I am torn between a feeling of profound happiness and bitter, constant anxiety. I fear that his

nervous system, which is just beginning to recover from the shocks of the past, will not be able to stand his new life, and I can't help feeling that a man who has suffered what he has suffered should have been spared certain trials, *in spite of himself*. He says he is feeling well and is passionately interested in all he is seeing.[24]

Fernande was right in her forebodings. Salvemini's health could not stand life at the front and he was told by the doctor that his heart had been injured. But he could not remain inactive and in 1919 he was standing again as a candidate for Parliament in Apulia—this time as an ex-service man—and was elected with a large majority. From the first he opposed the fascist movement. In Parliament he accused Mussolini of having stolen 480,000 lire collected in America to help D'Annunzio in Fiume. Mussolini challenged him to a duel, but Salvemini's seconds maintained that it was first necessary to ascertain whether Salvemini's accusation was true or not. Mussolini's seconds refused the investigation and so the duel did not take place.

Salvemini considered the Fiume incident* to be 'a source of dishonour and ridicule for Italy,' and he refused to collaborate with those who supported it. In 1921, ill and discouraged (after only two years of parliamentary life) he decided not to stand for Parliament again, thus avoiding, perhaps, the same end as Matteotti, since undoubtedly, if he had remained in Parliament, he would have attacked the crimes committed by Mussolini and his 'squadristi.'

Ernesto Rossi has vividly described Salvemini's unpopularity at this time:

The first time that I observed his strange figure, he was wearing a black cloak such as even cabbies had

*See Foreword.

ceased to wear, and the sugar-loaf hat of the peasants of Apulia. It was in 1919 in a tram. A violent opponent leaned out of another tram to insult him by calling him 'turncoat—renegade!' For in the Italy of the 'elmi di Scipio,'* someone like Salvemini was a pain in the arse. He wanted the few available resources to be used to build roads, aqueducts, drains, council houses, to fight illiteracy and to help the lowest levels of the population to free themselves from the bestial conditions of their lives. He was a pain in the arse who showed that Libya was not a promised land, and who explained in his paper that the annexation of Dalmatia demanded by the Higher Command in order to increase their staff, would make the defence of Italian territory even more expensive and difficult. Such a man was inevitably considered a turncoat and renegade, indeed, as *the* renegade.[25]

III

While all this political activity was going on, Salvemini's private life had also taken a new turn. The moment had come when he found life without any children unbearably sad. Madame Fernande Luchaire, the former wife of a French colleague, had become a family friend and gradually he became increasingly attached to her two children: a pretty little girl, and Jean, a highly intelligent schoolboy of fourteen. When they all came to call on my mother at Villa Medici in 1914 Jean was already running a school newspaper in which he expressed his belief in the need for a united Europe, to include both the Germanic and the Mediterra-

*The reference is to 'Fratelli d'Italia' the *Inno di Mameli*, now the Italian national anthem.

nean peoples. Salvemini spent many hours arguing with Jean about his views, and was troubled by realising; even then, that they were not only wrongheaded but dangerous. He could not yet foresee to how great a tragedy they would eventually lead.

His affection for the Luchaire children did not mean that he ever forgot those whom he had lost. I remember that when he and the Luchaires came to see my mother during the summer in the little villa she had taken in Marina di Massa—Salvemini dressed up for the occasion in his best black suit—it was always late in the afternoon. 'You see,' Salvemini explained, 'I always hope that the second post will bring me news, direct or indirect, of Ughetto.' And a look of great sadness would cross his face.

Soon after, he and Madame Luchaire threw in their lot together. But Fernande's anxiety about Salvemini's health and spirits did not decrease:

> He needs rest, but he won't accept it. He says it will do him more harm than good. You know him, know well the intensity of interest that he brings to all he does. All that we call entertainment bores him stiff—even going out to see friends, chatting with them—all that fatigues him; and when he sees me looking sad, he says 'How unwell I feel.' 'I don't feel well'—sometimes it is the only phrase he utters for hours at a time . . . Perhaps when we are married and I can have him close to me, I shall be able to look after him better. But we still haven't settled the date . . . Just as I did not wish to accept the responsibility of a marriage of which evidently many people disapprove, so I don't want to show undue haste. Salvemini loves me and I love him, so it's up to him to decide, both the date and the marriage itself which he does so obstinately want. For him, the sooner the better.[26]

In the autumn of 1923 Salvemini was invited to London to give a series of lectures on Italian foreign policy at King's College and, in spite of Mussolini's refusal to grant him a passport, determined to go there all the same. He met a friend in Modane who helped him to cross the frontier by the simple device of getting out of the train on the wrong side, and then bought (for 150 francs) a clandestine passport from the Italian Consul in Paris which enabled him to get to England. His lectures in London caused great indignation in Florence. A highly rhetorical article in *La Nazione* proclaimed that 'in the sacred name of our betrayed Dalmatia and of the martyrs and soldiers of Italy, the Florentine fascists take up the challenge of Gaetano Salvemini.'[27]

When Salvemini announced to Lidia Minervini, his sister-in-law, in a laconic postcard that he was about to return to Florence, and told her to go to the University and tell them that he would resume his lectures on a certain day, he caused her considerable dismay. The walls of Florence, she said, were then plastered with manifestos saying 'The ape of Molfetta shall not re-enter Italy.' She gave a vivid picture of his return.

> I shall never forget that day. The stairs and the courtyard were full of menacing fascists with truncheons, while Salvemini's lecture hall was incredibly crowded. In the front bench sat, together with the students, his colleagues and old students and faithful friends . . . I met Padre Pistelli, a nationalist and a fascist, but a man who esteemed Salvemini and who was against any form of violence. When Salvemini arrived in his coachman's cloak, with his round hat jammed on his bald head . . . Pistelli, without a word, came up to him and shook his hand. This was enough for the fascists not to use their truncheons and to limit their opposition to booing in the passages . . .

The door into the lecture room opened, and in came Salvemini. A hurricane of applause broke out, and out in the passage protesting yells. He went up to his chair, pulled out his old silver turnip watch . . . and said, as calmly and clearly as ever, 'Neither applause nor booing will change my opinions. The Florentine Commune . . .'[28]

For some months Salvemini continued his lectures, but in 1924 the murder of Matteotti* gave him a severe shock. A month later he held a meeting of about two hundred anti-fascists in a Florentine cinema at which a pamphlet in honour of Matteotti signed by Salvemini was distributed, and then the whole company, led by a beautiful English girl carrying a wreath,† walked in procession through the streets of Florence crying 'Evviva Matteotti!' and placed their wreath on Cesare Battisti's bust in Piazza San Marco.

From then on Salvemini became the leader of the anti-fascist opposition in Florence. He advised his friends to display the highest contempt towards the fascists in public and to break off all personal relations with them, and on several occasions he embarrassed some of his colleagues by refusing to shake hands with those who had gone over to fascism, looking them straight in the eye with the words 'We do not know each other.'

That autumn Salvemini's lectures were frequently interrupted by blackshirts, who tried to force their way in. 'I was never certain,' he wrote afterwards, 'that I would get out without a broken head!'

Early in the following June 1925, realising that Florence was now too hot for him, Salvemini made his way to Rome, but was arrested there on the grounds of having collab-

*See Foreword.
†Miss Marion Cave, who afterwards married Carlo Rosselli.

orated in the anti-fascist paper *Non Mollare** which had been founded in Florence by the Rosselli brothers and Ernesto Rossi, and spent a few weeks first in the Roman prison of Regina Coeli, and then in Le Murate† of Florence. He wrote later on that this was among the happiest times of his life. 'What a welcome rest,' he exclaimed, 'after so many months of constant anxiety!' A fellow prisoner, a young man from the *Ciociaria‡* who cleaned his room, gave him news of the other political prisoners, brought him their greetings and supplied him with books. When the time came for him to leave for Florence the young man said in a low voice, 'Let's hope that in Purgatory the holy soul of Lenin is praying for us.' Salvemini commented: 'Thus Catholicism lived on in the Communist religion, as many centuries earlier Paganism had been absorbed into Christianity.'

When he got to Florence, an absurd incident occurred. His 'guardian angels' (two warders who subsequently accompanied him everywhere) got out with him at the first Florentine station, that of the Campo di Marte, while they were expected at the central one. 'Never mind,' said Salvemini, 'I'll take you to Le Murate myself'—and, still handcuffed, led them across the whole of Florence to his prison. Here he was given a little cell which he liked because from his window 'one could see the sky, the Fiesole hill and the swifts whirling in the air.'[29]

He made friends with an international thief, who told him about the different ways adopted in other countries to prevent prisoners from escaping, when they were being transferred. Sometimes their braces were taken away, so that they had to walk holding up their trousers; sometimes

---

*'Stand Fast.'
†So called because it had previously belonged to an 'enclosed order' of nuns.
‡A region in the hills south of Rome.

two warders held them on each side by a little chain fastened to the prisoner's wrist. In Italy they used very painful handcuffs, and these Salvemini wore.

Salvemini's sister-in-law, Lidia Minervini, has described her persistent efforts to visit him in prison. 'I was such a nuisance, so insistent, that I obtained permission.' He told her that everyone was nice to him in prison. They taught him to play cards, to steal, and to break safes open. And she brought him welcome insect powder to destroy his bedbugs.[30]

From the prison he wrote to his wife:

> You must not worry about my long silences. My daily life is not at all painful . . . after all, we scholars are voluntary prisoners: our enclosure, which might be terrible for a peasant who is accustomed to living in the open air, is not at all heavy going for one of us. It is true that I can say this because I have a private cell: two lire a day. Don't worry about the cost . . . In short, dear old girl, imagine that I am not in the Murate in Florence but in London, in a pension room no bigger than this one, and hardly more comfortable, but very much dearer. My only regret is that I cannot work. I should like to correct and send off the new edition of *The French Revolution* . . . What worries me is that my friends may try to stir things up about me and exaggerate the drama of the situation. I am certain of you, dear old girl. I know that your intelligence and your character will lead you to face with dignity this absurd adventure of mine, even if your affection and your pride are wounded by it.[31]

Then came the day of his trial, 13 July 1925. Lidia wanted to be present but Salvemini dissuaded her, telling her to lunch instead in the house of his defending counsel, Advocate Marchetti. While Lidia and Signora Marchetti were eating, the maid came in, crying 'In town they're saying that Advocate Marchetti and Professor Salvemini have both been killed!' They hurried to the Court. When they got there they found a state of chaos. The fascists had set up barricades and were hitting everybody with their truncheons. Then they saw the imposing figure of Padre Pistelli once again trying to reestablish order. When at last the two women reached the door of the Court they were told that Salvemini and Marchetti were safe, in the basement. But the fascists had beaten and wounded several other men. Two days later, Advocate Marchetti was so brutally assaulted in Siena that he died soon after. 'It was not prudent in those days,' Lidia remarked, 'to be a friend of Salvemini's . . .'

In the trial he was not acquitted, but granted provisional liberty, which meant that, wherever he went, he again had two guards at his side, in theory 'for protection.'

At this point Fernande, who rightly feared that Salvemini would never get permission to go abroad, took a step which would certainly have horrified Gaetano. Relying perhaps on the slight physical resemblance between Berenson's and Salvemini's heads (but only their heads), she asked young Count Umberto Morra di Lavriano, a great friend of Salvemini's and a fervent anti-fascist, to go up to I Tatti and give a message to Berenson: would he be willing, since he too had a beard, to let Salvemini use his passport. Morra, very glad of this opportunity to meet Berenson, complied; but Berenson's only reply was a hearty laugh and an invitation to Morra to dine at I Tatti, where he became a lifelong friend.[32]

After several weeks spent travelling for the express purpose of giving his guards as much trouble as possible, Salvemini realised that in the atmosphere following the murder of Matteotti more serious measures were likely to be taken against him soon. So he succeeded in giving his guards the slip and, zigzagging across the North of Italy in a series of trains, managed to arrive in France on 16 August 1925.

In Paris Salvemini found a small group of close friends, among them Ernesto Rossi and Giuseppe Donati. He longed to get back again to Italy and to his lectures, but was afraid to do so, and went on hesitating until an offer from the Italian Minister of Education, Fedele, precipitated his decision. Fedele told him that the Ministry was prepared to grant him two years' leave to study abroad, if he asked for it. 'That offer,' Salvemini wrote, 'struck me like a slap in the face. If I had accepted it, I would have had to abstain from criticism of the régime that was granting me this favour and, while my friends in Italy were risking their freedom and life in resisting fascism, I would have spent a pleasant time abroad at the expense of the fascist government.' He hesitated no longer, but immediately sent in his resignation to the Rector of the University of Florence:

> The fascist dictatorship has now completely suppressed in our country the existence of freedom, without which there is no dignity left in the teaching of history as I understood it . . . I am therefore obliged to part with deep sorrow from my pupils and colleagues . . . I will return to serve my country in a school when we have got a civilised government again.

In a letter to Piero Calamandrei he was more explicit: 'A complete break, and then let's not speak about it any more. I don't think that the fascists have made a good deal in forcing me to take this decision. They would have done better to kill me.'[33]

Both letters were sent from London, where Salvemini went as soon as he had made up his mind. The 'Academic Senate' of the University (composed of the heads of the various faculties) 'deplored the calumnies' in Salvemini's letter, and protested against 'the insult to the National Government.'

Finally, on 4 December 1925, Salvemini was relieved from his post in the University and on 30 September 1926, after a lecture given by him in the National Liberal Club of London on 'Italy and the fascist régime,' he was deprived of his citizenship. The threats against him in the fascist press were numerous and violent. One paper wrote: 'It would not be surprising if some fascist, with guts and a heart, lost his temper, and sent him to reflect about his affairs in a quieter and more peaceful world than this.' Another, 'Go ahead, you fascists who love the Duce with passion and dedication! Cross the frontiers. In the sacred name of Italy and of the Duce, smite, without respite, without remorse . . . Go ahead, fascists, and kill.'[34]

IV

As early as 1922 Salvemini and Fernande had been quietly preparing for a possible move to England, and it was at this point that his correspondence with the Berensons revived. In the autumn of 1922 he told B. B. that he had sold a small piece of land at Molfetta to enable him and Fernande to live abroad for six months, and that in the Spring he proposed to go to England, having learned English in the interval, to look for a respectable job there. 'Certainly it is not amusing to have to begin one's career again at the age of fifty. But having chosen to fight, it is fair that I should suffer the consequences.' In the same letter he warned the Berensons to observe the greatest prudence in their conversations, 'in front of the servants and of all the people who are not intimate friends, whether Italians or foreigners. No-one will trouble you, so long as they do not have a pretext to do so.'[35]

He then hurried to England to start learning English and wrote to Mary Berenson from Brighton to describe his first experiences, saying that he had at last found a lodging in which no-one could speak a word of Italian or French. In London, he said, his landlady, the cook and the waiter all spoke Italian; in pubs, on buses, even at the meetings in Hyde Park, everyone recognised him as an Italian. (If we bear in mind his appearance, this was hardly surprising.) 'In short, to learn Italian one must go to London, and to learn English it's better to stay in Florence.' But now in Brighton he was having a real chance to master the English language; he spoke to his landlady; he went to the play or to hear sermons, he read the papers in the library. 'In short *"All right."* I like this sentence and these people more and more. They are people of great kindness and hospitality. I feel surrounded everywhere by an atmosphere of courtesy and warmth, which goes straight to my heart.'[36]

As to his progress in English, his first spirited letter to B. B. can testify:

My progress in English is dreadful. I speak now and—as you see—I write English with a brave and barefaced unconsciousness. And when I am speaking all the bones of Westminster Abbey tremble in their burials. And the unknown warrior asks from day to day to himself what new greater war lately lost England, if such barbarous people has gone in it, speaking such an unheard idiom. And they shall not enjoy peace before I leave this country.

But the living . . . calm down after the first astonishment and they are very kind to me, and even can understand my story, and heroically forgive my faults. They overcome my impudence with their gallantry . . . May our Lord and Saviour likewise forgive my sins in the Judgement day.

My woes begin for me . . . when I must understand people speaking. No longer then the bones of Westminster Abbey but my own bones, tremble like Falstaff's bones on the camp of Shrewsbury. For almost always I catch nothing at all . . .

I have discovered that the preachers of the English themselves speak a delightful English: that is a English in which I can grasp, like a quick fowl, a little word here and there: for example, 'Christ, hevens, soul, let us pray' . . . And when I am understanding in these conditions, that is without being controlled, I am happy and triumphing like Baron Sonnino after having pocket[ed] the London's treaty of Versailles, like Mr Lloyd George building and admiring the treaty of Sèvres. Moreover people in English churches sing many hymns and psalms and recit their prayers 'ad alta voce' (let good God blind me if I know how I may translate this). And I find that is a very useful practice, singing and praying together . . .

I should have many other things to tell you about my English life and experiences, and the horrible cooking and the lovely country, and the curious faces of this wonderful people. But to write this letter I have been working like a dog, in fighting with a whole library of dictionaries and grammars, and am tired like the Creator of nature after six day of his work. And I also rest like him. Blessed be his name. Amen![37]

In the summer of 1923 he was again briefly in England and writing to Mary Berenson about the meetings in Hyde Park 'at which I understood almost everything'—but after his return to Florence in 1924 he was writing to Mary about a severe illness of Fernande's and, for the first time, applying to the Berensons for financial help: 'As to expenses, dear friend, we have made arrangements so that we hope to manage with our own resources for usual matters. But we are in deficit; we shall run short for doctors and medicines. We shall be short of 1500 lire at the end of the month when these payments are due. Then we shall turn to you fraternally. B. B. and you are the only people in the world before whose generosity we do not feel humiliated in our need.'[38]

Then came Salvemini's arrest and his trial for *Non Mollare*. Undoubtedly the Berensons sympathised, though we have none of their letters at that period. But in 1925, after sending in his resignation to the rector of the Florence University, Salvemini sent a copy of it to Mary—and with it a passionate expression of his feelings:

> Even if my life and freedom were not threatened, I could not teach history in the present climate in Italy. I have never worked only to earn my bread. I have simply earned my bread, *working in my own way*. Teaching was my delight and my pride, because I taught *what I wanted*, because I felt I was my real self in my school. What could I do there now? I would have to measure my words, one by one. I should have to amputate myself of everything that made my name with my pupils . . .
>
> This is my fortune. If I gave it up, (could I?) what would be left to me? . . . What example would I set to my pupils? they would say, 'He is afraid of losing his bread.' I would rather shoot myself.
>
> Dear B. B. and Mary, don't grieve over my exile. I would feel far more exiled in Italy. In London I am not an exile: I am at home, I am in the country of my spirit, free among free men . . .[39]

On his arrival in England, in 1925, he received a warm welcome from the small, tightly woven society of English intellectuals and anti-fascists. He was beginning a new life again, for the third time. The first had been when he came to Florence, at seventeen; the second, after the tragedy of

Messina; the third, at the age of fifty-two with a new language to master, was his move to England. Within eight years, there was to be a fourth change, when he began his career at Harvard.

At the time of his first visit to England, he had received letters of introduction from the Berensons to some of their friends, and now it was to Alys Russell (Bertrand Russell's wife and Mary Berenson's sister) that he turned. She took a vast amount of trouble to find him a decent cheap lodging, and to arrange lectures for him. 'The fee for each lecture,' he wrote 'was usually five guineas, and one guinea covered my expenses for a week.' Then there was Miss Isabel Massey, who translated his lectures and articles and letters to the papers into English and made him say his lectures to her beforehand to make sure that his audience could understand him. (This admirable aim was not entirely achieved. When I heard him speak in America, many years later, his wording was still highly idiosyncratic, and his accent that of Molfetta.) There was also Mrs Crawford, who later on edited the green pamphlets of *Italy Today*, which gave much information (mostly provided by Salvemini), which would otherwise never have reached England, and which devoted special numbers to the heroic enterprise of Lauro de Bosis, to the arrest and trial of his mother and friends and to the Rosselli brothers. Her niece, Miss Marion Enthoven (later on, Rawson)—a highly intelligent and cultivated young woman—became perhaps his closest friend in England. She sat beside his bed when he had bronchitis, typed out his manuscripts, and later on translated *The French Revolution* and his short study of Mazzini.

'It is the custom,' Salvemini commented, 'in English cultivated classes, to help causes which they consider right. Those two young friends of mine [Miss Enthoven and Miss Massey] thought it their duty to help me, and did so without sparing their brains or their time. Without those generous friendships, which I shall remember as long as I live, I do not know if I could have managed to survive.'[40]

Speaking later on about *The French Revolution* and *Mazzini*, Marion mourned deeply 'the historian we have lost.' But Salvemini had a different yardstick. He wrote that he would be ashamed to steal a single hour from his political activities, while in Italy his friends were fighting for the same cause at the risk of their lives. All his life this painful dichotomy tormented him: on the one hand his inner conviction that his true métier was to be a historian, and on the other, the feeling, in all the long years of his exile, that he must continue the political activity from which he was cut off at home.

Another person whom he saw often in England and whom he greatly admired, in spite of their unbridgeable differences of both opinion and temperament, was Don Sturzo, the founder of the Partito Popolare,* and a sad and lonely man. 'Poor Don Sturzo,' wrote Marion Rawson, 'was neither well nor happy here. He never succeeded in speaking adequate English, and his lectures were not a success, being given in incomprehensible French ... I have often found Italians sceptical about any real friendship between these two [Don Sturzo and Salvemini] but I saw too much of them ever to doubt the genuine trust and friendship that existed between them.'[41]

Salvemini's own reminiscences confirm her opinion, though he deplored Don Sturzo's total absence of any sense of humour. 'With that truly good man one could not joke, and I never did ... and I believe that it was due to the respect that we both had for really serious matters, that I owe a

---

*The strongest left-wing Catholic party in Italy, of which the leader was Don Luigi Sturzo, who returned to Italy after the fall of fascism. He could not accept the fascist dogmas—especially with regard to Catholic education—and had been exiled for his outspokenness against the régime.

friendship which I consider one of life's best gifts to me. We never argued. Before that Himalayan peak of faith and will, any argument would have been senseless. When we reached a debatable point . . . we stopped in a friendly way, each one taking his own path.'

The greatest bond between them was that Don Sturzo was not, in Salvemini's sense, a 'clerical' but a 'liberal.' 'He trusts in the methods of liberty for everyone and everywhere . . . This common respect for freedom made our friendship possible.'[42]

So, though once Salvemini stormed out in a rage, because Don Sturzo had brought a friend whom he thought untrustworthy, they spent many evenings in talking amicably by Marion's fireside. This was the more remarkable in that, when irritated, Salvemini did not mince his words, even with old friends. To Umberto Zanotti-Bianco, the founder of the National Association for the Welfare of Southern Italy,* who insisted on staying on to fight against fascism in his own country instead of emigrating, he wrote:

> If, instead of obstinately staying on in Italy to blow the noses of snotty children† while a horrible storm is raging around you, you would come to work abroad among the millions of Italians who need a guiding hand . . . you would be doing something very useful. But you won't do it . . . You will only come abroad, if they let you go, when it will be too late to prepare anything, for events will not wait upon our convenience . . .
>
> There are abroad thousands of Italians ready to hurry to Italy when a crisis comes. Some of them have

*Associazione Nazionale per gli Interessi del Mezzogiorno—ANIMI.
†The reference is to the numerous nursery schools founded by Zanotti-Bianco in the south to give a civilised preschool education to small children and freedom to their mothers for a few hours a day.

communist ideas and, if they are left alone, will organise a communism worse than Mussolini's . . . You
cannot believe what bitterness there is in my heart
against you all, who have lost a year in waiting for
someone to hit you over the head and turn you into
unknown martyrs. Yours is the courage of the Italian
people—a fatalist and ineffective courage. But you
have not got the active courage to take the initiative. Mussolini had this initiative, not you. You will
not play cards unless you have three trumps in your
hand . . . [43]

Zanotti, however, stayed on in Italy, fighting his fight
there in his own manner, and bearing Salvemini no grudge.

Marion Rawson, whom I had had the pleasure of meeting some years before, was so kind as to send me an account
of Salvemini's daily life in England:

At that time he was in splendid health and full of
physical and intellectual vigour. He was able to work
far into the night, but very much enjoyed whatever
relaxation he allowed himself, particularly meeting
English friends with whom he could talk freely. He
was deeply interested in English traditions and institutions . . . and his admiration of English political
freedom, and of the power wielded by public opinion,
was unstinted.

According to Marion Rawson, Salvemini was impressed
by two crises during his brief visits to England—the attempted revision of the Prayer Book, and the abdication of
Edward VIII. What he liked about these episodes was 'the
freedom of expression and the moral strength' shown by
the English people. 'Altogether there was a great deal that
he enjoyed in England. He liked the English countryside:
Miss Massey used to drive him about in her little car, to ex-

clamations of "Che bella campagna!"* He also liked living in a Protestant country where "there were no priests looking over your shoulder." '44

What he really valued most in England was this sense of freedom, of spiritual independence:

> I did not play the part of an 'exile' [Salvemini wrote in his memoirs], nor did I care for the title of 'refugee.' When Turati had to leave Italy, he refused to call himself by either name, but preferred that of 'fugitive,' a man who had escaped from the great prison that Italy had become ... I preferred the term 'fuoruscito',† a man who has left his country to continue a resistance which had become impossible at home ... I did not suffer from nostalgia. My spirit went on living in Italy. I received half a dozen daily papers of different trends. I eagerly read all the reviews I could find. This was living in Italy, not being an exile in America, England or France.45

Such an attitude was calculated to please English people and won him their respect, instead of their compassion. The element of an *enfant terrible* in him—always more popular abroad than at home—amused them, his frankness was reassuring and very unlike the mental picture of a 'wily Italian' that some of them had formed, and his sense of humour was disarming. The chief fascist propagandist in London at that time was Luigi (Gino) Villari, the son of his old teacher and friend, Pasquale Villari. Salvemini wrote later on that at first he 'felt a certain repugnance' about attacking this man's son, but he got over his scruples by the

---

*'What a beautiful countryside!'
†*Fuoruscito* implies a deliberate choice on the part of the exile. It was first used by Machiavelli and, subsequently, by fascists as a term of abuse.

simple means of referring to him in print as Luigi XXX. At the political meetings where they crossed swords Salvemini would pretend that he did not know who Villari was: 'Will ze gentleman in ze back row kindly explain why he thinks . . .', thus telling the audience that Villari was not the Englishman he appeared to be. He was so adept at turning the tables on Villari that, far from being made impatient by his constant heckling, the audience was glad to have an excuse to laugh.

Salvemini also had some lighter diversions. Political strife, exile and poverty had not destroyed his eye for a handsome woman or a pretty girl, and he found English women attractive. Among the few letters of his which Ernesto Rossi kept there was one describing a holiday at Hindhead with Carlo Rosselli:

> Rosselli was a great success in the feminine world, and I, poor old man as I am, have no complaints. A junoesque widow, between 35 and 45 years old, waited on us at table and was also a delightful pianist and singer. Well, Rosselli admired that lady very much; and so did I. Rosselli, with youthful energy, launched his attack; I stumbled in the background. On the last evening she asked us both for a moonlight walk. Rosselli was aggressive, I silent. In the end the fair lady said she liked me best. Irreparable disaster! Rosselli went off on his own. I remained the sole master of the situation. What happened then, in the presence of only the moon, I cannot say . . . because nothing happened.

In a subsequent letter to Rossi, Salvemini said that, if he found it quite impossible to take up his old life in Florence, he would like to live in London, even if he were obliged to shine shoes or play the clarinet in the street. 'You will say, "How would you manage to play the clarinet?" "Don't worry," I reply, "Here you can do whatever you like. The worse you play the clarinet, the more people will be sorry for you, and will leave a penny in your plate."[46]

When the summer of 1926 came and no more lectures could be held, Salvemini went back to Paris where life was cheaper. But he returned to England again in 1927 and for almost the whole of 1928. In Paris he again found Italian friends who had been obliged to leave fascist Italy—Alberto Tarchiani,* Luigi Albertini, the director of the *Corriere della Sera*, and the whole Nitti† family. But except for Tarchiani, Salvemini saw little of them, being absorbed in his book, *The Fascist Dictatorship in Italy*. In the same autumn he accepted an invitation to give a series of lectures in America, obtained a visa for his passport with the help of Walter Lippmann, and sailed for New York. Fernande, with her children, remained in Paris.

V

Salvemini has left us a vivid picture of his first impression of America: a country where political discussions were conducted while digesting a good meal. On the first evening after his arrival, he was invited to the Knickerbocker Club in New York for a debate, presided over by Walter Lippmann, in which Thomas Lamont, the director of the Morgan Bank, started by asking him whether the loans which Mussolini

---

*A journalist, he returned to Italy to take part in World War I. From 1919 to 1925 he was the chief editor of the *Corriere della Sera* which he only left when the paper had changed its character. As an exile in France, he helped to organise the flight of Rosselli and his friends and was one of the founders of Giustizia e Libertà. After 1943, he became a Minister in the government of Salerno and Italian Ambassador to Washington from 1945 to 1955.
†Nitti had been a politician and a Minister.

had been able to negotiate in America were not a proof of the prosperity which Italy enjoyed under Mussolini. He was then taken by his manager for one night each to Columbus, Ohio, Boston and Montreal, spoke in all these places and returned to New York. 'How I survived, I do not know.'

In New York he at once found himself at one of the Sunday lunches of the Foreign Policy Association for a debate with the leader of the Anglo-American fascists in New York, Thaon de Revel. Since I am not concerned with Salvemini's political campaign in America, I will not attempt to summarise the debate, but only observe, as Salvemini himself did, that after it the Board of the Foreign Policy Association decided to increase his fee from 100 to 150 dollars—'a kind of applause that I had never experienced before, and that meant for me a fortnight of life in America.'[47]

This tour, after which he called himself 'the wandering Jew of anti-fascism,' was repeated in 1928, taking him as far as California, and in January 1930, he was invited, on the proposal of his friend Professor La Piana, to lecture at Harvard on Italian foreign policy between 1871 and 1915. To Roberto and Maritza Bolaffio, he wrote from Paris: 'A great piece of news: I am invited to teach in the University of Harvard for four months! They will give me $4000; that is a year of life . . . I want to see you and no-one else . . . *Tell no-one.*'[48]

He returned to America for five months between 1932 and 1933 to lecture at Yale, this time receiving a fee of 5,000 dollars—while living 'in complete happiness with a wonderful library and with courteous, generous colleagues and willing, grateful students.' But the rest of his time between 1929 and 1932 was spent in Paris, taking an active part in the anti-fascist Resistance.

The number of his old friends there had now increased, but there were also many fascist spies. Shortly after his return from America in the summer of 1929, Salvemini had one of the 'greatest joys' of his life—the arrival of Carlo Rosselli and Emilio Lussu,* who had succeeded in escaping from the island of Lipari, where they had been banished by the fascists for their participation in *Non Mollare*. They had got away in a motorboat and found Salvemini and a group of other friends anxiously awaiting them in a Parisian café. 'It was worth having been through so many trials to enjoy happy moments like these.'[49]

Two days after arriving in Paris, Carlo Rosselli telephoned to Salvemini to tell him that Marion Cave, now his wife, had been arrested in Aosta. 'She will soon be freed,' said Salvemini, and set to work. At his request all his friends in England sent telegrams to Marion in her prison, protesting against the arrest of a British subject because her husband had escaped from Lipari. The telegrams were signed by such names as the Archbishop of Canterbury, the Duchess of Atholl and others, and, as Salvemini had hoped, did not reach Marion but Mussolini, still extremely sensitive to criticism abroad. Three days later Marion was in Paris.

It was then that Salvemini, together with Emilio Lussu, Alberto Cianca,† and Carlo Rosselli, founded an anti-fascist

*Emilio Lussu had been banished to Lipari with Carlo Rosselli and escaped with him to France. He was one of the founders of Giustizia e Libertà and of the Partito d'Azione. An active member of the Resistance, he became one of the men who drew up the new Italian Constitution.

†Alberto Cianca was the director of *Il Mondo*, a paper founded by Giovanni Amendola. After the suppression of this paper he escaped to Paris in 1927 and became one of the founders of 'Giustizia e Libertà.' After his return to Italy he became a member of the 'Partito d'Azione' and a Minister under Bonomi and De Gasperi.

organisation that they called 'Giustizia e Libertà,'* which soon became the focal point for all anti-fascist thinkers of the left, in France, England and America.

> We agreed that we exiles could not take upon ourselves the right to organize revolutionary expeditions to Italy from abroad; it would have involved technical and political absurdities. No bombs in France: Mussolini's consuls were seeing to that. No bomb-throwing in Italy: that might endanger innocent spectators . . . The émigrés could and should do abroad what could not be done by anti-fascists who were still in Italy: that is, help them to keep the democratic tradition alive, thus preventing the victory of dictatorship from becoming total and final. The anti-fascists who lived abroad in freedom had to work on this basis and import . . . into Italy as much clandestine press material as possible . . . The distributors of this material formed a network of men who, in a moment of crisis, would emerge from obscurity and come to the fore with clear ideas about what should be done.
>
> 'Giustizia e Libertà' summoned men in Italy from all anti-fascist parties to active resistance against the dictatorship . . . It did not require the acceptance of any economic dogma, whether of free trade or of government control. It only required a commitment to re-establish in Italy the personal and political freedom of its citizens . . .[50]

Later on, in America, Salvemini elaborated the aims of this organisation:

> Giustizia e Libertà is not a party . . . It is an anti-fascist organization in Italy which brings together for this

*'Justice and Freedom.'

purpose men from all left-wing parties, and those who do not belong to any party, on the sole condition that their ideas are democratic and republican. There are many anarchists, socialists and republicans, but those who are disposed to plunge into the struggle *in Italy* are few. At best, it will be possible to gather together a hundred men in a large city, a few dozen in a smaller city, and two or three in a village.

We who are abroad can enjoy the luxury of holding meetings to discuss the future. No meetings are held in Italy: three friends may meet for a few minutes, give a password, exchange news, and immediately separate. How can one expect, under these conditions, that anybody should discuss whether anarchism is preferable to socialism, or socialism better than the republic? . . . While the parties are permanent organizations, Giustizia e Libertà is provisional and will last only as long as the struggle against fascism lasts . . .[51]

Salvemini added in his memoir: 'I do not wish to dress myself up in peacock's feathers. Having lived most of the time in America I took little part in the concrete activities of 'Giustizia e Libertà.' I acted as the "noble father," i.e., I gave my opinion when I was asked for it, and collected money in America and England . . .'

In 1930, Salvemini suffered a severe blow. He heard that all the members of Giustizia e Libertà in Italy, including Ernesto Rossi and Riccardo Bauer,* had been arrested. They were tried, in the following Spring, by a 'Special Court for

---

*Riccardo Bauer was the founder, in Paris, of the anti-fascist weekly, *Il Café*. He was banished for two years to Ustica and Lipari; he was arrested in 1930 with other members of Giustizia e Libertà and was sentenced by a special tribunal to 20 years of imprisonment. Freed in 1943, he took an active part in the Resistance movement in the Partito d'Azione.

the Defence of the State.' This year—1931—was called by Salvemini in his Memoirs 'un 'annata maledetta,' a cursed year. At the time of the arrest of his friends he had been in Paris recovering from a severe heart attack and bronchitis, and according to himself, 'breathing like a pair of bellows.' But as soon as he could get up again, he set to work. He feared that Rossi and Bauer would receive a death sentence, because the special court would be trying them with closed doors, with no defending counsel who was not an officer of the army or of the fascist militia. The only hope of saving them would be to collect protests from abroad. Salvemini succeeded in getting the *Manchester Guardian* to publish an appeal signed by thirty prominent English intellectuals, asking that the prisoners should be given a public trial, be allowed to choose their own counsel to defend them and in-form them in time about the evidence against them. This successful appeal was also signed by foreign journalists, whose presence at the trial ensured that the accused were not sentenced for having thrown a bomb in 1928, an offence which they had not committed. They got off with a sen-tence of twenty years' imprisonment, to be followed by an indefinite period of *confino*.*

On the 4 October of the same year, Lauro de Bosis—as we have already told—was drowned in the Mediterranean, after dropping his anti-fascist pamphlets over Rome. His political opinions were the exact opposite of Salvemini's, and they argued about them continually, but this did not prevent the older man from forming a close friendship with Lauro in the months before his heroic gesture; he also watched over Ruth Draper during her terrible weeks while waiting for news. One more tragedy in this 'accursed year.'

Finally, before the end of 1931, Salvemini had a great disappointment. All University professors were called upon

*Banishment to remote islands or villages.

Gaetano Salvemini listens to Ruth Draper
reading to her niece at Dark Harbor

by their Rettori (Principals) to take an oath of fidelity to the King and the fascist régime, or resign their posts. This oath included a clause stating that they would undertake 'to fulfill all Academic duties with the purpose of forming active and valiant citizens devoted to the country and to the fascist régime.'* Most antifascists abroad were convinced that at least fifty teachers would refuse to take the oath—thus causing Mussolini to draw back—but those who refused were only thirteen! Salvemini, while showing himself indulgent to the needs of some of those who gave way, nevertheless considered this to be, for all anti-fascists, 'a great desertion.' 'So the "annata maledetta" came to an end.'

Two years later, in the autumn of 1933, Salvemini returned to America, and this time was met by a welcome surprise: the news that the first Chair of History of Italian Civilisation, which Ruth Draper had founded at Harvard in memory of Lauro de Bosis, would be awarded to him.† His letter of thanks to Ruth also enclosed a copy of one to Dr Conant, then President of Harvard, in which he undertook only to 'carry on his political work *outside* the school,' and this he faithfully did—though the *slant* of his history lessons can have left his students in little doubt as to his opinions.

As soon as his nomination was known, trouble arose. The Italian Consul in Boston opposed it and sent 'a prominent Bostonian' to Dr Conant. The President's reply was to ask Salvemini to dinner. Then 'a stroke of lightning fell.' The *New York Times* published the news that Salvemini had been an accomplice in the explosion of a bomb in Saint

---

*The Pope tacitly approved this measure by publishing in the *Osservatore Romano* a communiqué permitting Catholic professors to sign.
†The endowment was for a Lectureship in the History of Italian Civilisation. Ruth Draper did not actually endow it until 1938, but gave a yearly sum of 2,000 dollars to cover Salvemini's salary.

Peter's. Salvemini at once went to see President Conant, who said quietly that the American government had no obligation to extradite him, until an American judge had accepted the evidence against him. 'Wait for the trial, and defend yourself. We shall wait, too.' Salvemini hurried to tell La Piana, who advised him to send a telegram to Mussolini, challenging him to ask for his extradition, and also to send a copy of his telegram to the Press. 'Mussolini did not ask for my extradition, because there was not even a shadow of evidence about me that could be shown to an impartial judge in a civilized country. And so this storm, too, blew over.'[52]

For the next thirteen years, from 1934 to 1947, Salvemini lived and taught at Harvard. It was a turning point in his life. When he reached the age limit for teaching (sixty-five years) he received a letter from the Chairman of the History Department saying that it was not possible to continue his appointment. He was also told that the Corporation was so grateful to him for his 'splendid services' that they had voted to award him, as a pension, the income of the Lauro de Bosis lectureship—2,000 dollars a year.

Salvemini felt very uncomfortable about this pension, telling the Bolaffios how much he regretted that he was thus depriving Harvard students of a course of lessons. 'But I needed that money to keep alive.' He added, 'Harvard is rich. But if I take from a rich man something that does not belong to me, that is wrong,' and as soon as he was awarded the International Prize for History of the Accademia dei Lincei (8,000 dollars) he refused to accept anything more from Harvard. 'You must believe that this money was a burden to me. Now that I am rid of it, my heart feels much lighter.'[53]

There were many things at Harvard to make Salvemini happy. The first was the Widener Library. According to Roberto Bolaffio, Salvemini would say, 'I am the richest man in the world, the Widener Library is mine, really mine!' It was indeed largely on account of this library that he had decided to move from Paris to America. In Paris, an hour was needed to go from his own house in the XVIIème *arrondissement* to the Bibliothèque Nationale, an hour to get out a book and another hour to get home again. Three hours of work wasted every day!

> At Harvard, instead, he could walk from his rooms in Leverett House across the splendid Yard* to a place where there were no cars, no crowds, no noise, in short a place where nobody disturbed him, where he wasted no time in getting books. In Widener he had his own private study, next to the section of Italian history. He could keep all the books he required in his study as long as he pleased.
>
> Some students who worked in the library were always ready to help him both to look for the books he needed, and to replace them. If he wanted a book that was not in the library, he only had to ask for it, and it was ordered by telegram and arrived free by airmail, even from California or England.[54]

'A library,' Salvemini wrote in amazement, 'actually made for scholars and not for its staff!' He asked his friend La Piana what happened to all the books 'that were thus entrusted to the mercy of heaven.' La Piana answered that sometimes a book did disappear, but it was not worth while, on account of this infrequent inconvenience, 'to give up the advantages of that noble hospitality.'[55]

The second of Salvemini's pleasures at Harvard was his

---

*To be precise, from Leverett House to Widener Library Salvemini did not need to cross the yard, though he must have done so whenever he went to the Faculty Club.

relation with his students. Though he admitted that they arrived from their High Schools knowing almost nothing, and that many of them underwent what was called 'the freshman's crisis' during their first year before they had learned to work seriously, he felt that this was fully compensated by the 'civic sense' that their High School had given them—'Freedom of speech, freedom of the Press, freedom to form associations, were taught in the High School not as an abstract precept, but in practice.'[56] Moreover, he deeply approved of what he called their 'right to ignorance' which was officially recognised in their written exams. In these they were given a number of questions or subjects, among which they might choose the one about which they had something to say. The student was not required to know everything about the subject he chose, but merely to state what was essential and to express his own thoughts sensibly and tidily. Moreover he added that—*mirabile dictu*—the students were left to themselves during the exams, yet no cheating took place.

How much his students both liked and admired him, is shown in their letters after Salvemini's death. One former student, Louis Lyons, has described how, when he first arrived at Harvard, he had asked the brilliant lawyer Felix Frankfurter what courses he should follow. 'He only had two names to give me as *musts*. One was Salvemini's.' Lyons said that he had been disappointed to discover that Salvemini was giving a course that year on Medieval Italy. 'Never mind that,' said Judge Frankfurter, 'whatever Salvemini teaches will be *current*.'[57]

The testimony of many other students bears this out. They were impressed by the way in which Salvemini presented medieval history so that it reflected their own problems; they were grateful to him for being always at their disposal; they admired his fire and zeal, 'a combative commitment, a sort of consecration of history.' 'Now,' one of them wrote, 'Professor Salvemini is certainly giving lessons in the other world. I wish him every success in his enterprise.'[58] 'To his students,' wrote Professor Murdoch, 'he was always kind if they seemed to him intelligent and willing to learn, but he was sharply outspoken in his criticism of those who did listen to both sides of a question, but remained too indifferent or too lazy to take sides themselves.'[59]

When in October 1948, the sad day came on which Salvemini left Cambridge for good, it was his students who helped him to clear his study of the accumulation of fifteen years of work, 'the books that I should have liked to finish and now will never write.' 'It has been a piece of donkey work, which tore at my heart.'[60] When Niccoló Tucci handed the key of Salvemini's study to one of the librarians, the young man said, 'We have many great scholars in our library, but the greatest *man* is Salvemini.'

Finally, Salvemini derived great pleasure from the social aspects of Faculty life. He lived in Leverett House and took most of his meals in its dining hall, or sometimes in the Faculty dining room. According to Professor Murdoch, he was happiest in the evenings in the Leverett Common Room, silent with closed eyes, apparently asleep, while the talk went on around him. But when an ill-considered or foolish remark was made, his eyes would open and the room would ring with his 'Nonsense!' And if something that really interested him was said, he would sit bolt upright, or jumping to his feet and pacing to and fro, would burst into excited and exciting eloquence.[61]

Another admirer of Salvemini's was Professor Morison, who at first sight seemed to Bolaffio 'tall, strong, as stiff as a statue of granite from the rocky coast of his own New England, gruff, cold and laconic.' But as soon as he heard

Salvemini's name, he melted. 'I was not only his friend; I loved him. He often came to my house.'[62] Another historian of great standing, Professor Langer, wrote with equal warmth: 'Salvemini had no enemies at Harvard, only friends. He was one of the few men who not only believed in freedom, but was willing to fight for it . . . There was in his class no trace of political, anti-fascist propaganda. He made a very clear distinction between his work as a serious historian and his political activity.'[63]

After Salvemini's death, the *Harvard University Gazette* printed a tribute signed by his closest friends,* which would assuredly have pleased him, because it was both unrhetorical and true.

> Through a long life, checkered with personal tragedies and disappointments, he never ceased to be a fighter against all forms of tyranny and oppression whether of the right or of the left; his voice became an expression of the conscience of the people of his native land—not the Italy of pagan or Christian Rome, nor even the Italy of the Renaissance nor of the Risorgimento, but simply that 'humilem Italiam,' of which Dante and Virgil spoke . . . His mocking and moving eloquence, inspired by indignation and common sense, triumphed in the most famous polemical encounters . . . He always fought with Dantesque disdain against the lukewarm and the neutral . . . He said of his own philosophy of history, 'We can only be intellectually honest—that is, aware of our own passions, on our guard against them, and prepared to warn our readers of the dangers into which our biased views may lead them.'[64]

*H. Stuart Hughes, Giorgio La Piana, Renato Poggioli and Myron Gilmore. *Carte Bolaffio*.

Professor Schlesinger's wife was fond of telling a story about Salvemini. One evening, when they were talking about Mussolini, suddenly Salvemini stopped talking, pointed his finger at his own forehead and said, 'Oh, when you speak about Mussolini, you, Salvemini, should realize that you are prejudiced!'[65]

After Salvemini got back to Florence, he presented to the Widener 2,000 dollars which had remained in a bank in Cambridge—they were used to buy some books of Italian history which are still there, marked 'Bought with the Salvemini donation.'

~

At this point we must go back to a new step in Salvemini's life. In 1940, after he had been teaching for six years at Harvard, he decided to apply for American citizenship and took the consequent oath of loyalty to the United States. He wrote later on:

> There is a wider area in this country of generosity than in any other—at least in Europe. It is the feeling that one is at home here that conquers one little by little. And one day one feels that one is no longer an exile, but a citizen in one's own country. When I took my oath I felt that I was really performing a great function. I was casting off not my intellectual or moral, but my juridical past. The formula of this oath is a wonderful one . . . You are only asked to sever with the government of your former country, not with its people and its civilisation. And you are asked to give allegiance to the Constitution of your adopted country, that is, to an ideal of life.

It was also in 1940 that Salvemini found a new windmill to tilt at. He took up the cudgels for an anarchist friend, Armando Borghi—a sincere, pugnacious and uncompromising *romagnolo* who, after a visit to Stalin's Russia, had ended by rejecting communism as fundamentally irreconcilable with anarchist values. After a short period in prison in Italy and a vain attempt to unite the anarchist and socialist parties, he emigrated in 1926 to New York and there conducted an active anti-fascist campaign, which led to his friendship with Salvemini. But in the autumn of 1940, after the passing of the Aliens Registration Act, he was arrested, to be deported to Italy, and Salvemini wrote on his behalf to the Attorney General of the United States, Francis Biddle, begging him 'to correct a mishap which has come about through some New York officials of the Immigration Service.'

> . . . I am far from sharing Borghi's political opinions. However, I have known him for many years through his activities in Italy, and in these last two years I have come to know him in this country by personal acquaintance. He has always been an uncompromising anti-fascist fighter. If he were to fall into Mussolini's hands, he would be sentenced to death without further ado by the blackshirt tribunal, because of his many anti-fascist crimes which I have not been able to equal during twenty years of anti-fascist activities.

Salvemini went on to point out that Borghi was not at all dangerous to America, since the anarchists did not approve of war, but that he would become dangerous to Italy when he returned there after the war:

> But the United States do not need to concern themselves with what Borghi will do in Italy when the war is over. By arresting Borghi in this moment, while so many notorious fascist agents are left at large for the sole reason that they were shrewd enough to

become naturalized, a disastrous effect has been created among large sections of anti-fascist working people of Italian extraction . . . Some petty officials of the New York Immigration Service have in the past shown too great proclivity towards their fascist friends. In this case they have gone too far. I begin to wonder whether at Ellis Island, in order to drive him crazy, they will not put him together with the fascists who have been rounded up in recent days. I am afraid that the investigation of Borghi will drag on for months and months in order to keep him locked up as long as possible, while the fascists will be quickly examined and released with many apologies. This already happened last summer in the case of two anti-fascists belonging to the Mazzini Society.

Last year, when the problem of registering for illegal entry into the United States arose, I instantly urged Borghi to register and by so doing to heal his illegal status. I told him he must trust the fair-mindedness and generosity of the present administration, and that if he registered, he would be safe under the protection of the American law. I beg you with all my heart to put an end to his detention which I dare to say is a dangerous scandal. G. S.[66]

Salvemini's efforts, together with those of Toscanini, succeeded in freeing Borghi from Ellis Island after four months. But Borghi himself wanted to return to Italy and finally succeeded in 1945, after a meeting in New York of his friends and supporters. Salvemini, owing to an attack of asthma, was unable to be there, but sent Borghi an affectionate letter of farewell.

. . . If I believed humanity to be very intelligent and less indifferent to its own troubles than it is, I would be an anarchist myself. But unfortunately humanity around me, as I see it, is only interested in eating, making children and horse-racing. To these people the small fragments of anarchy that a democratic government guarantees, or should guarantee, are too inconvenient . . .

You, dear Armando, belong to the minority of one in a thousand which occupies itself not only with its own affairs but also with those of other people. And this minority is divided into little groups who prefer to break each others' bones rather than to unite against their common enemies . . . Consequently you are an anarchist and I am a poor, unfortunate democrat of the antediluvian school. But while I do not mean to minimize either for you or for myself all that divides us politically, I do intend to affirm publicly my respect for your moral integrity, for your coherence and capacity for self-abnegation and sacrifice. I consider it a piece of great good fortune in my life to have known, appreciated and loved you in these last years of your American life.

Bon voyage, dear Armando. When you are back there in our beautiful Italy, remember sometimes this American democracy which you have so often attacked, and which has certainly given you slight headaches, but which let you live and breathe in peace. With all its immense defects, it is preferable to any other political régime, except that of your anarchy.[67]

Salvemini's friendship and esteem for Borghi lasted all his life. Only a few days before his death in Sorrento, Borghi came to see him and after embracing him Salvemini said that he still had 'the candid expression of a child.'[68]

It was during his time at Harvard that Salvemini received the second greatest blow of his life: his stepson, Jean Luchaire, was shot as a traitor for having worked under the Pétain government and collaborated with the Germans in France. This was the cruel consequence that Salvemini had vaguely foreseen many years before, when he warned Jean as a schoolboy that his intransigent opinions would get him into trouble.

The whole subject is one which it is difficult to tell without bias. After Jean's death his mother wrote: 'I shall not live long enough to see the real truth told about Jean, but I have put together all the documents, notes and memorials and the advocate who was an incomparable support to him lives in the hope of seeing this real truth recognized, but the moment has not yet come.'[69]

The 'real truth' is still difficult to find, for one would have to steep oneself in the climate of the time—one of very complicated ideological conflicts and of much violence and hatred—and then to step aside from it enough to see the picture with detachment. However, it is possible, from the verbatim account of the trial[70] and Luchaire's own pamphlet, published shortly after the Franco-German armistice and entitled *Les Anglais et Nous*, to summarise the facts.

Before the war, as a young journalist with left-wing views who had founded a monthly paper called *Notre Temps*, he had made friends with a young German professor, Otto Abetz. This led to their joint formation of an 'Alliance of Franco-German Youth.' At this time Luchaire was still suspicious of Hitler and disagreed with Nazi doctrine, but believed that a collaboration between France and Germany was the only way in which Europe could be united against the common enemy of England. After the establishment of the Vichy Government in France, Luchaire got into touch with Pierre Laval, the Vichy leader. He maintained that this move was dictated by his desire to collaborate with Abetz, intensely francophile and by this time German Ambassador in Paris, in order to obtain 'a milder occupation' for France. Luchaire became President of the French Press Corporation, and did indeed obtain many privileges for his employees at every level. He said that these were due to the fact that the German authorities trusted him because of his political pronouncements and articles. He also received great financial support from the Germans, including a large part of the capital for his paper *Les Nouveaux Temps.* In August 1944 he fled with the Germans to Sigmaringen, where he became Minister of Information in a puppet government, and was one of those who signed a note demanding 'a merciless struggle' against the Frenchmen who had helped the Allies after their landing in France. In 1945, when the Allies reached Germany, Luchaire fled to Merano and attempted unsuccessfully to obtain immunity from arrest[71] through American and Italian support.

The prosecution at his trial alleged that Luchaire's action had not been inspired by his belief in fascism, but by 'corruption and rottenness'; and that his motive had been 'nothing but money.' He had received 100,000 francs a month for his own expenses (which included the lavish entertainment of German officers and officials) and 7 or 8 million francs for his journalistic enterprises. His paper had published articles against de Gaulle, against England, and against the Jews, but in praise of the new Germany and of Hitler. The defence advocates maintained that Luchaire had always fought for a single ideal—not of collaboration, but of reconciliation. He had believed that he could use his influence with Abetz to obtain better terms for France if Germany had won the war, and during the occupation, he had been able to do much to alleviate the lot of his compatriots.

Witnesses testified that he had saved 50,000 men from being sent to labour camps in Germany, had saved many Jews from arrest or deportation and had obtained a better status for the members of the Press Corporation. He had only been able to do this by publishing pro-German, anti-English and anti-Semitic articles which threw dust into the eyes of the Nazis, and concealed his real motives.

In spite of their praiseworthy efforts, the defence could not prevent Jean Luchaire from being condemned to death, to 'la dégradation nationale' and to the confiscation of all he had. An appeal to the Higher Court was refused and one for pardon was not accepted. Jean Luchaire was executed on 22 February 1946.

Jean had never relinquished his religious beliefs, and on the night before his execution he wrote, at his chaplain's request, the following prayer:

> Dieu de l'infini des espaces et des temps, mon âme est à vous,
> Dieu de toutes puissance, ma volonté est la vôtre.
> Dieu d'amour, je vous donne mon coeur.
> Daignez vous pencher sur moi et guider mes pas vers la vie éternelle.
> Pardonnez-moi les péchés qu j'ai commis et ceux que j'ai fait commettre.
> Aidez-moi à protéger, sur cette terre comme du ciel, ceux que vous m'avez fait aimer.[72]

As soon as the tragic news reached Salvemini, he flew over from America to be with Fernande, but only for a very short time. 'Gaetano,' wrote his wife, 'didn't understand. He suffered, without understanding. I told him nothing. For him, too, it was too soon.'[73]

Fernande herself felt that her life had come to an end. She was totally isolated; she wrote:

I have no life left of my own. I am alone from morning to night in a little room which seems like a nun's cell, only rather more cluttered. Two or three friends come to see me, and after twenty years we still call each other 'Madame.' *O douce France*! My family? Everyone is busy getting themselves out of trouble. Gaetano was blind to all this—inevitably perhaps, since he was only here for two days. Why tell him what he never tried to find out? Everything went with Jean . . . During the war I was the wife of Salvemini. Since the Liberation I have become the mother of Jean Luchaire.[74]

So far I have written about Salvemini's life at Harvard as his American friends saw it, and as he himself felt it to be —one of freedom, study and friendship. But beside all this there was a darker aspect, of his American life—his nostalgia for his friends in Italy, his anxiety about those who were participating in the Resistance, his increasing longing to be with them. It was only to people arriving from Italy, as I did every year to visit my family, that he allowed this longing to transpire. 'Salvemini,' we would say, 'is coming today.' We would hear his heavy step in the hall and laughter exploding like great guns—and then he was there, enfolding one in a great hug. He would settle his heavy form in an armchair and then, with a sharp glance of his kind, bright eyes, 'E gli amici? Mi parli degli amici.'* There was great nostalgia in his voice.

I could tell him only about a few of them, who were my friends, too. But now, reading his correspondence in those years, I realise more clearly how close his links still were with the combative members of the Resistance in Europe. A

*'And my friends? Tell me about my friends.'

letter to him from Ernesto Rossi after a long time in prison or in banishment, shows the depth of the devotion that his old friends still felt for him, but must have torn his heart by the insistent pleas that he should come home again.

> It is with indescribable emotion that I am writing to you. How often in all these years I have thought about you and spoken of you to my fellow gaol-birds! When in my solitary cell I thought about the people whom I would really have wished to embrace again ... I thought first of all of my mother and of you. Your example has prevented me from sinking into a sterile scepticism. You have given a meaning to my life, you have taught me to see things in a concrete way, you have introduced me to the people I esteem most highly; you have been my guide, not only in politics but in life itself. Let me thank you at last with my whole heart, without holding anything back.
>
> You cannot imagine how much good it does me to let myself go, for at least once, to the fullness of my feelings. I have lived for so many months alone in my cell ... that I feel as dried up as a pumice stone. Books, books, only books. A nourishment without vitamins for the spirit ... I have become old, so old that I'm afraid you would not recognise me. But now your invisible presence seems to be near me as I write—you have given my youth back to me ...

The letter goes on to a detailed account of Rossi's own experiences during their separation—his various prisons, the friends he had made there, his hunger strike, and his nine years of banishment in the island of Ventotene. It is written in a minute script only legible with a magnifying glass, on a single sheet of tissue paper—like the clandestine political pamphlets which Rossi sent to his wife from prison, and it ends with a passionate appeal to Salvemini to come home again:

> Your having taken American citizenship makes me fear that you may find some obstacles to taking up your activities in Italy—but if you can, go at once to the South. I think that your place is there, even if it is an uncomfortable one, which will cause you much trouble. Remember that we no longer have Carlo with us. He was a recognised leader. We need you, we need you terribly . . . [75]

It is easy to imagine how deeply disturbing such a letter must have been to Salvemini, who at that time still felt that he had no right, as an American, to take part in Italian politics.

In Florence, another close friend, Professor Piero Calamandrei,* spoke in 1944 in Salvemini's praise to the students of his University, expressing an ardent wish that he should come home. When Salvemini read Calamandrei's remarks, far away in Massachusetts, he was overcome by emotion: 'I began to cry like a child, and had to lean against a chair to hold me up. This had not happened to me since December, 1908† . . . I am writing not only to tell you that

---

*Piero Calamandrei, one of the most tenacious and able anti-fascists, was also a distinguished lawyer and writer, and a man of exceptional ability and charm. This speech is printed in *Uomini e fatti della Resistenza* (Laterza, 1977, pp. 149–61.) Later on, in an article dated 1955 and entitled 'Il nostro Salvemini,' Calamandrei again addressed his old friend who had by then returned to Italy: 'We thank you for the lesson you have given us in the art of living, for having taught us that the love of one's country must be identified with a patient study of its political and social progress, and for your serene and active perseverance in doing your duty, without hoping for paradise, either on earth or in heaven.'
†The date of the Messina earthquake.

your words have reached the depths of my heart, but also to say what I think about your idea that I should go back and teach in Florence . . .'

His doubts were on two grounds. First, that, as an American citizen, he had lost, not his love for his own country, but the right to exercise political activities there. 'I could come as an exchange professor, but no politics.' And secondly, he pointed out that even if he could come back as a teacher he was already seventy-one. 'My intellectual life cannot last more than three or four years . . . So what is the use of my taking his bread away from a young man?' And then he wondered whether any of the young would really want him. 'My name has been wiped out in Italy for twenty years. Why should the resurrection of the dead begin with me?'

Yet his deep attachment to Florence is shown in the last part of the letter, which is concerned with raising money for rebuilding the houses on the Ponte Vecchio (destroyed by the Germans before departing) and perhaps, later, also reconstructing the most beautiful bridge in Florence, the Ponte Santa Trinità, designed by Michelangelo. 'The Americans would give the money, and the Mayor of Florence appoint a commission of architects and archaeologists . . .'[76]

Calamandrei replied that the rebuilding of Ponte Santa Trinità would cost about 60,000 dollars, and with regard to Salvemini's return to Italy, repeated what Rossi had said: 'We have thought of you every single day for twenty years. We want to have you here as soon as possible.'

Letters from friends continued to reach him, all urging him to return. One of them, Egidio Reale,* had a concrete

---

*Egidio Reale was a lawyer and a jurist, and a *fuoruscito* from fascist persecution in 1926. He taught in Switzerland, and became Ambassador to Switzerland and President of the Italian Committee of Unesco.

suggestion to make, after Italy had become a Republic: 'I continue to believe that you should not return to play the part of a grumbling mother-in-law to your friends, and to rot your guts. If you come back, it should be to direct a daily paper of the Opposition, against the privileges of the rich and the better organised factions, against the bureaucrats who are eating Italy up, against the priests . . . No-one could awaken the healthy part of the country better than you, to defend the values of our dying civilisation.'[77]

Finally in 1947 Salvemini did come, but this time only for a short visit of four months. During this time he observed, with passionate interest, what had happened to his country during his absence. Some of his impressions he described during a brief visit to his old friends in Harvard, but set down more fully in an article in Italian entitled 'Ottimismo.' They were mostly impressions he had gathered during his first short visit to the north of the country, ending up in Florence and Rome. The first thing that struck him was the amazing speed with which his country had recovered from the war: 'The land has gone back to being the most beautiful garden in the world. The Italian peasants have once again shown themselves to be a marvellous antheap, swifter to rebuild than others had been to destroy . . . Vines, olive trees, fields, cattle, bridges, roads, trains, buses, those are realities, even if the government money is an illusion and a fraud.'

And the women! His breath was taken away, now that none of them wore hats any more: 'They all look, as they walk in the streets, as if they had come out of the pictures of the 15th and 16th centuries, "a miracolo mostrare."* And how many of them, even dressed very simply, have some-

---

*'To reveal a miracle.' The words are Dante's about Beatrice in *La Vita Nova.*

thing distinguished, refined and personal in their dress and their bearing; they seem queens dressed up as peasants or working women.'

Of course Salvemini also saw and admitted the other side of the picture: the tuberculosis and rickets of so many children, the struggles of all the people with fixed incomes: teachers, magistrates, state employees, pensioners. 'You have only to see their clothes, their drawn faces. I have been told that some of them "si arrangiano."* But those who have their souls—and there are many, many—sell their furniture, bit by bit, to fight against hunger.' He would not admit, all the same, that the political situation was alarming.

He spoke to the young about a new Italian republic, which would courageously admit its defeat and form a ten-year plan to substitute the Republican régime for the Monarchist one of the priests. 'Wherever I made this speech and outlined the plan, I saw eyes shining with faith and enthusiasm.'

And what about the atom bomb, people asked, and World War III? Here Salvemini fell back on Italian fatalism—based, in this case, on impotence. 'The Italians can neither provoke a war nor avoid one'—and therefore, not being responsible, they could go on quietly with their daily work: 'The bricklayer places his bricks just where a bomb has fallen, without asking anyone where and how another bomb will fall . . . From this kind of fatalism, optimism—at least a modest optimism—can spring up in their hearts.'[78]

Alessandro Galante Garrone has drawn a most vivid portrait of him as he was at that time. What struck him most, was the vigour and freshness of Salvemini's enthusiasms. Garrone first met him one evening in Turin, at a gathering

*'manage (by fair means or foul).'

of some of his old friends—scholars and politicians—but especially of young men, partisans of the Piedmontese Resistance.

> The old professor turned from one to the other, asked questions, listened eagerly; occasionally he laughed, showing his fine row of white teeth, scolded us for what we had not done, or had done wrong, after the Liberation . . . incited all those who were still hesitant, and outlined a programme for the immediate future: ten years of hard, obstinate work, without illusions, without hope of immediate success, without false reverence ('rebel against your bishops!') matter of fact, keeping one's feet on the ground, taking care not to let oneself be confused by fine generalisations or by philosophical follies. Was that the famous old Salvemini? It was we who seemed old, tired, devoured by scepticism . . .[79]

After his first lecture in his old chair in Florence, Salvemini spent the whole winter in a cold and frugal pension—Pensione Leoncini in Via Sangallo—with frequent attacks of bronchitis and asthma. His wife, Fernande, who was still in Paris but very anxious about him, wrote to Elsa Dallolio—a faithful friend to them both—to ask her whether, in her opinion, she should join him in Florence: 'Speak to me about Gaetano . . . and this is confidential—do you believe, you, that if my health allowed it, he would like me to go back to Florence to be with him. He won't ask me to, but do you think he wishes it, or would my presence sadden him? I need to know this so much.'[80]

In a subsequent letter she added, however, that she had become very deaf, suffered from fatigue, fevers and rheumatism and was becoming blind: 'You will wonder how, being in such a state, I can think of joining Gaetano. I have often asked myself this too. But if I was convinced that he would be pleased, I would begin to want it myself.'[81] As gently as she could, Elsa advised Fernande not to come. Soon after, without seeing her husband again, Fernande died in Paris.

Meanwhile Salvemini went on coughing and wheezing, and at last in the Spring of 1951, he wrote to Donna Titina Ruffini,* to ask whether he might come to spend Easter with her and her daughter Giuliana† in the warmth and beauty of Sorrento. He went there for four days and stayed for the rest of his life.

Many years before, during an evening in Marion Rawson's house, where he and Don Sturzo were talking about their longing to get back to Italy, Don Sturzo said that he would die happy if he could only see Sicily once again; Salvemini, that he would give anything in the world to see the wonderful stretch of coast to the south of Naples. Now, in La Rufola, this wish was granted.[82]

It was an enchanting place—a secluded villa on a little peninsula at Capo di Sorrento, looking down over silvery

---

*Donna Titina Ruffini, by birth a Tuscan and daughter of the distinguished man of letters Ferdinando Martini, had first been married to Giuliana's father, Marchese Benzoni, and after his death to Carlo Ruffini, with whom she spent her later years in their villa at Sorrento, La Rufola.

†Giuliana Benzoni had been engaged in her youth to a hero of the Czechoslovak struggle for independence, Milan Stephanic—a close friend of Benes and Masaryk—and after his death in 1919 in an air crash dedicated the rest of her life to Italian causes similar to his. An ardent anti-fascist and a friend of Umberto Zanotti-Bianco, she took an active part in the work of the Associazione per gli Interessi del Mezzogiorno and became an 'interventista' in World War II and a secret and fearless link between the world of anti-fascism, and that of the Court and the Vatican. During Salvemini's last years at La Rufola, the house became a meeting place for the most important anti-fascists, who were also Giuliana's close friends.

olive groves to the sea. Indoors, space and quiet and a fine library. Here Salvemini, after his long, combative life, at last found peace. He delighted in the dry humour and caustic comments of Donna Titina's conversation, as they exchanged reminiscences about Florence in the days of their youth. Her daughter Giuliana—a fearless leader of the Resistance and for many years a close friend of Salvemini's and of all his friends—nursed him devotedly, and loved him like a daughter. Concetta—Donna Titina's maid—looked after him in his last months and reminded him of the simple, innocent devotion of the southern women he had known in his youth. And up to the day of his death, an unending stream of visitors flocked to the house—old friends, young disciples, eminent politicians, scholars, foreigners from America, England, France, and even, almost daily, a young priest from Sorrento, Don Rosario Scarpati. And talk, talk, talk—discussion and laughter. No differences of opinion chilled Salvemini—on the contrary, they only stimulated him to even more stringent arguments, or to the *boutades* of a naughty child.

In the first Spring after his arrival, he wrote to Ruth Draper that he was now fully recovered and that the preceding winter had been the first in which he had not wished to die. 'Moreover my brain has begun to work like the engines of an airplane, so that I keep pace with it with difficulty.'[83] This was certainly true. Every day he read innumerable daily papers and wrote or dictated articles for the Press as well as letters to his friends. He wrote to B. B. in Florence about a forecast of Cattaneo's, and to Professor Higham in Oxford, where he had been invited to receive an honorary doctorate.[84] He insisted on playing some records of Ruth's monologues which she had sent him, and the whole house resounded with his laughter. He even found time to read twice—first in manuscript and then in book form—a long book of mine called *The Merchant of Prato*, and then to write to me two letters with higher praise than I could ever have hoped for—or perhaps deserved.

In 1955, two years before his death, his old friend from Harvard days, Isaiah Berlin, came to La Rufola to see him and asked him how he was. He admitted that he did not feel well, and added, looking puzzled, 'I can't understand it. Mussolini is dead, Croce is dead: I should be flourishing! Instead . . .'

He wrote Major Gordon Lett, an English leader of the Resistance in Liguria, a letter which bears witness to his admiration for the fighters of the Resistance, which he had not been able to share. Lett had sent him his book entitled *Rossano**—the name of the village in the Garfagnana in which Lett had built up a force of former Allied prisoners, young Italian partisans, and fugitives of many nations, forming an International Brigade (of Poles, Russians, French, Dutch, Yugoslavs, and even a Peruvian and a Somali), until they were able to cooperate with the Fifth Army in freeing La Spezia from the fascist rule. So impressed was Salvemini by this book that he warmly invited Lett to Sorrento to tell him about the Resistance and offered to help him, if the book was translated into Italian. 'As soon as I received your book I began to read it and for two days I could not leave it, until I had devoured the whole. You, dear friend, have understood the charm of the Italian People . . . When I reached the point in your story in which you sacked the secretary because she spoke scornfully about the peasants in the Governor's waiting-room, I sprang to my feet, thinking that I would have done the same.'[85]

Towards the end of his life, between 1949 and 1953, he dreamed of returning to the historical works which for

---

*Rossano by Gordon Lett, London, Hodder & Stoughton, 1955.

twenty-five years had lain in abeyance owing to his political activities—and in particular of writing a fuller study of Mazzini's youth and of the formation of his thought. But the wheels of time's chariot were turning fast. 'I am old!' he wrote, 'I am 76! I have been gathering notes, documents and ideas for at least a dozen books. I should like to get rid of it all before I die . . . What a pity it is to be old!'[86]

But what really prevented him from writing these books was not his age, but his passionate interest in current affairs. 'When I am seized by an epileptic fit about the troubles of today, I go out of my mind. I forget the past in the present.'[87] Day after day, he read the Italian papers and then denounced, with all the vigour of his moral indignation, every scandal, every instance of inefficiency, corruption or injustice that met his eyes. He described the sale at Benevento of boys offered up for auction by their own parents as shepherds, stable boys or farm labourers[88]; the arrest of women accused of having travelled in search for work or to join their families without a travel permit[89]; the scandal of pensions for war damages indefinitely delayed; the failure to rebuild or modernise school buildings[90]; the trial of an old peasant woman in Piacenza who had hidden, in 1943, a Croatian prisoner of war[91]; the overcrowding of prisons, owing to the long delay between arrest and trial[92]; miscarriages of justice and examples of gross superstition.[93] So the long list goes on—minute incidents, mostly concerning the poor and humble, but all part of his lifelong struggle for justice and freedom, and all related with his usual scrupulous determination to ascertain the exact truth of what he was saying. So, until his last breath, he went on fighting and hoping.

But time began to take its toll, in spite of all the care of his friends and the mild climate of Sorrento. Salvemini never stopped receiving the ever-increasing stream of friends and disciples (Ada Rossi has described to me how, only a few weeks before his death, she was obliged to 'behave like a policeman' to give him a moment's breathing space). But his cough became more persistent, his voice fainter. When Roberto and Maritza Bolaffio came to stay—having been warned by Giuliana that the end was not far off—he asked Maritza, who was well accustomed to his asthmatic attacks, whether she would interpret for him: 'Maritza, stay close to me,' he said, 'you are accustomed to my weak voice. Repeat what I say: If I see that you did not hear properly, I will shake my head, and nod if you have got it right. Speak slowly and clearly.'

During the following days, Maritza faithfully obeyed him. The first time Don Rosario turned up without warning, both she and her husband were startled, but Salvemini said, 'don't be afraid.' And turning towards him, 'I am glad to see you, but you must not go on coming to me, you'll get in trouble with your bishop.' Don Rosario replied, 'No, I won't have any trouble. I am an honest man.' 'Yes,' said Salvemini, 'you are, but the priests are not.' The Bolaffios, too, admitted Don Rosario to be an honest man:[94] 'He did not speak of religion or philosophy, but let Salvemini talk, listening respectfully. Finally Salvemini said, "Don Rosario, in a couple of days my young friends will carry me to the cemetery. You may come too, but dressed like a man."'*[95]

Don Rosario remained until the end one of Salvemini's most assiduous visitors. 'You bring in cheerfulness,' he would say, 'your friendship has been a great comfort to me in my last years.'

Don Rosario set down a detailed account of Salvemini's last days, from which I will quote a few passages:

*He meant, of course, dressed in the dark grey parson's suit that Don Rosario habitually wore, not in priest's vestments.

My most vivid impression, which nothing will ever wipe out, is that of his smile. The smile of both a child and a peasant, for no special reason, as gratuitous and spontaneous as innocence ... Perhaps in his last months, preparing for death, his smile seemed more gentle, lighter, as if it had secretly been pared down by death, which he did not feel to be waiting to pounce on him but to be a spiritual experience ...

Some people may think that the most serious problem for a priest beside a dying man is to make him accept the Last Sacraments. It would have been a joy for me to give the Last Sacraments to Professor Salvemini, but the indispensable condition was his faith in them and in the Church. This Salvemini did not have ... We often spoke about the problem, and about religious feeling. His was certainly a religious nature; it was shown in his attitude to death, and to justice and truth: all realities in which he believed for they were the only ones which had for him an absolute value. Truth and justice were not centred in a personal, revealed God, they could not be classified in decalogues or in theoretical discussions ... Truth and justice could only be verified in facts, in men's love, in their capacity for action, renunciation, suffering and indignation.[96]

Salvemini told Don Rosario that with regard to metaphysical truths, God, the soul and the other world, his attitude was that of Pascal's old woman: he behaved as if all of it were true, but did not know if it really was. Even the 'specialists,' he said, could not agree with each other. His moral beliefs were summed up in Plato's *Crito* and in the Sermon on the Mount.

Some of Salvemini's friends feared that Don Rosario wished to persuade Salvemini to be converted on his deathbed. But Salvemini had already expressed his own attitude very clearly. He had been shocked by the deaths of Toscanini, for whom religious services had been held in Rome and Milan, of Marchesi, and of Malaparte—considering the deathbed of the third to have been 'the writer's last comedy,' and he had told Don Rosario that he had no intention whatever of being converted in his last hours. Three days before his death he wrote to him a scribbled note: 'To Don Rosario—I haven't changed my mind. I trust you not to allow any mystification.'[97]

In the handwritten testament that he set down on the same day, he was even more explicit:

> This is my Testament. I should be grieved if in the last moments of my life a clouded mind should make it seem that I had returned to any kind of religious faith. If to admire and try to follow the moral teachings of Jesus Christ, without caring whether or not he was the Son of God, is being a Christian, I mean to die as a Christian as I tried to live—without success unfortunately. But I ceased to be a Catholic at the age of eighteen and I mean to die out of the Catholic Church, without any ambiguity. I wish to have neither funeral speeches, nor any other ceremony . . .[98]

But still Salvemini was uneasy, not for himself, but for Don Rosario. He was afraid that his visitor would get into trouble with 'the priests'; he was convinced that they would attack Don Rosario for his failure to convert him: 'You will come to a bad end, dear Don Rosario, you will see what they are capable of doing. They will take every thing away from you—teaching, freedom to write and other things besides. I am sorry that you have to suffer because you have been my friend.'

Salvemini, moreover, had another reason to be troubled.

Concetta, the old maid who was nursing him devotedly. He called her 'angel' and at bedtime said every night to her, 'God bless you.' But she was very religious—with the uncompromising piety of the simple and the poor—and could not bear to think that her dear professor would not receive the Last Sacraments. This was what was now troubling Salvemini, and one day he sent for Don Rosario in a hurry. 'You see,' he said, 'Concetta cannot understand why I want to die without the Sacraments, and this causes her great pain. She is an angel and does not deserve this grief on my account.' A tear rolled down his cheek. 'But I can't betray my convictions. See if you can explain it to her, if you can spare her at least a part of her grief.'

What Don Rosario said to Concetta we do not know, but perhaps he told her that her professor was dying like a Christian even without the Sacraments. That evening, when Don Rosario came back to see him, Salvemini was a little more cheerful. 'Do you really want to leave us?' Don Rosario asked. 'You have done so much good, and goodness bears fruit.' 'Don Rosario, you are intelligent, don't talk nonsense . . . My friends, my real friends will remember me; for everyone else, I am already a dead log.'[99]

A few days before, in August, Salvemini's pupil and friend, Ernesto Rossi, had come to visit him and was horrified by his emaciated condition and waxen face. 'He could no longer sit up in bed and spoke in a faint whisper: "This pitiless heart," he said, "won't give way. The doctor's care is prolonging my agony, not my life. I only wish they would put me to sleep, for good."'[100]

The last days had come. Many of the people he loved were in his small room, Giuliana, Concetta, his sister-in-law Lidia Minervini, Ernesto Rossi, Don Rosario, Roberto and Maritza Bolaffio, Egidio Reale, Ebe Flamini, Enzo Tagliacozzo. He had great difficulty in breathing. On 3 September, he asked Don Rosario:

'But why are people so afraid of death that they delay those who want to die?'

Don Rosario replied, 'For the simple reason that no-one considers himself the master of another man's life. It is a form of respect and affection.'

'Mistaken respect and affection, dear Don Rosario. If I could, I would hasten my last sleep, for death is perhaps like a sleep, a rest that will never end. Can't you hasten it? Can't you give me a pill? Pray the Almighty to make me die soon, you would really do me a great favour.'

'Will you allow me to pray for you, dear professor?'

'Why not, why should I prevent you from praying?'[101]

Two days later he dictated a last short note of gratitude to Bernard Berenson—his 'cock to Asclepius,' in payment of a debt:* 'An affectionate greeting before sending you my last farewell. You have always shown an unfailing generosity to me and I think of you with affection and gratitude . . . G.S.'[102]

On the last day—he died at 11.30 on 6 September—he spent a few hours in coma. Don Rosario tried to call him, but received no answer. Don Rosario raised his voice, 'Professore!' He slowly opened his eyes and smiled. 'Still alive,' he muttered. 'Goodbye, for good.' And he fell back again into his coma. Just before dying he returned to consciousness for a while, and spoke to the friends beside him.

'I have been so happy in my life, so many faithful friends. Thank you for everything.'

'How glad I am to die like this.'

(To the women around him) 'My dears, my dears, my dears, how much I have loved you! I have not been in love with you.'

'To pass like this into death, death. I don't understand why people are afraid of death. One should spread the news

*Plato, *Phaedo*.

about this way of coming to an end, so that people would not be afraid . . .'

'It is worthwhile to die like this.'

For a moment the historian in him appeared again.

'It would interest me to know the precise moment in which I shall be dead. To have a clear conscience is really interesting. It is not easy to solve life's problems, they are difficult problems . . .'

'I have been fortunate in life, and also in death. I could not have died better than this . . . I should like to embrace you all . . .'

'And to think that I could have done this a month ago . . .'

'Death is slow to come.'

'Thank you for everything. Concetta, how kind you have been.'

'Giuliana, my kind friend up to the end.'

'How difficult it is to distinguish between life and death.'

'I am still strong enough to clasp a hand.'

'One cannot fix the passage; it is all one.'*

A moment later he breathed his last breath.

'The hour of death has arrived,' said Socrates to his friends, 'and we go our ways—I to die, and you to live. Which is better only God knows.'†

Salvemini was buried, as he had wished, in the *terra dei poveri*‡ at Sorrento, the coffin borne by some of his young friends and by Don Rosario. But a few years later his remains were transferred to the cemetery of Trespiano above

---

*These words were written down in shorthand as he spoke and afterwards put together by his friends. They have recently been published in the *Soritti Vari*, 1900–57, op. cit. p. 959–60, with the title 'Parole di Commiato' (Last Words), but I have only quoted them in part.
†Plato, *Phaedo*.
‡'The poor man's grave.' In Italy, the bodies buried in such cemeteries are removed from their resting places after thirty years to make room for others.

Florence, beside those of his closest friends who had fought for the same cause, Italy's freedom and regeneration: Ernesto Rossi, Carlo and Nello Rosselli, Nello Tarchiani and, nearby, Piero Calamandrei. They lie in a little closed court lined with cypresses, above the city in which he had made his friends, and where he had studied and taught.

Ignazio Silone in the Abruzzi

V

Ignazio Silone

A Study in Integrity

'I don't know where to go . . .'
'Neither do I . . .'
'Then let's go together . . .'*
—IGNAZIO SILONE

On 23 August 1978 Ignazio Silone—one of the most remarkable Italian writers of our time—'a Socialist without a Party, a Christian without a Church'[1]—died in a nursing home in Geneva, at the age of seventy-six, while trying to finish his last book. 'If my literary work has any meaning,' he had written, 'it consists just in this: at a certain moment writing has meant for me an absolute need to bear witness.'[2] This need, in various forms, pervades every aspect of his work.

On the last occasion on which I saw Silone in his own house, he was sitting, as he often did, in front of the dominant feature of his little sitting-room: a very large photo-

---

*From Silone's drama, 'He Did Hide Himself,' from the words of the Gospels.

graph of Pescina de' Marsi, the village that was his birth-place, which he described as 'about a hundred shapeless one-storeyed houses, on either side of a long, steep street, battered by wind and rain.' On one side of the village square was the seminary, the only school available, standing on a bleak hillside above the drained lake of Fucino in the Abruzzi. The plain below is surrounded by an amphitheatre of mountains, 'a barrier with no way out . . . a village, in short, like many others, but for those who are born and die there, the world.'

> For twenty years, the same earth, the same rain, wind, the same feast days, the same food, the same poverty—a poverty inherited from our fathers, who had received it from their grandfathers, and against which honest work was of no avail. The life of men and beasts, and of the land itself, revolved in a closed circle . . . There has never been a way out. At that time, a man could perhaps save twenty or thirty *soldi* a month, and in summer perhaps even a hundred, so that by the autumn he had thirty *lire*. They disap-peared at once—in interest on some loan, or to the doctor, the chemist or the priest. And so one began again, the next day. Twenty *soldi*, a hundred soldi . . .[3]

In the same book, he has given an ironic picture of the hi-erarchy of the region—of which the greater part was owned by Prince Torlonia:

> At the head of everything there's God, the master of
>   Heaven.
> That everyone knows.
> Then comes Prince Torlonia, the master of the land.
> Then come the Prince's dogs.
> Then come the Prince's guards.
> Then, nothing.

Then, still nothing.
Then come the *cafoni* (the peasants).
And that's about all.

An official from the city who enquired where the local officials were placed, received the reply: 'Between the guards and the dogs.'[4]

Silone's recollections, in *Uscita di Sicurezza*,* open with a description of the day when, as a boy, he saw a handcuffed man limping down the road, between two guards. 'How funny he looks!' the boy cried. But his father took him by the ear and dragged him indoors, to be shut up in his own room.

> 'What have I done wrong?' he asked, and received the reply:
> 'You must never laugh at a convict.'
> 'Why not?'
> 'Because he can't defend himself. And then because perhaps he's innocent. And in any case, he's an unhappy man.'[5]

Silone's father was a small landowner, and his mother, a weaver. He speaks of her and of his grandmother as 'two grave, remarkable women, *series e straordinarie*,' the predominant influences of his childhood. Once I dared to ask him if he had a photograph of either of them, but the idea clearly surprised him. Photographs, he said (before emigration was forbidden), were taken only for passports, anything else was pure frivolity.

His childhood was, on the whole, a happy one, deeply influenced by these two women and their unquestioning faith. While he was a child, it was still the custom that on

*See end of notes for list of Silone's books and English titles when an English translation has been published.

Christmas Eve the house door should be left open, the fire lit and the table laid, in case the Holy Family, pursued by Herod's thugs, should need a hiding place or food.

During the long winter nights the boy would sit beside his grandmother's knee, helping her and eagerly listening to her stories. One can almost hear him following the rhythm of the loom's pedal and the beat of the shuttle. These tales have a dry yet almost childlike humour, characteristic of a side of Silone which was only well-known to his close friends, and are, as he wrote later on, 'not lacking in freedom of thought and even irreverence towards the Apostles, and especially towards Peter, not to mention civil authorities and their police spies.'[6]

Here, for instance, is the story of San Giuseppe da Copertino, the *cafone*, who became skilful like the juggler in 'Notre Dame' at amusing his Madonna. When he went to Heaven he was asked by the Lord (who had heard about him from the Virgin and therefore loved him) to express his greatest wish. In the Marsica the cafoni, like their donkeys, live on rough coarse food, and have never in their life tasted white bread.

> 'May I ask for anything?' San Giuseppe timidly asked.
>
> 'Anything,' said God the Father, encouragingly. 'Up here, in the sky, it is I who give orders, and I truly love you. Whatever you ask for, you will receive.'
>
> Only after a good deal of persuasion did San Giuseppe gather up his courage:
>
> 'Lord, a great piece of white bread.'
>
> God kept His word and was not angered, but embraced the *cafone* Saint and wept together with him. Then He called twelve angels and told them to give San Giuseppe da Copertino every day *in saecula saeculorum* the best white bread in Paradise.[7]

Silone explained that in the church in Fontamara there was a picture of Jesus Christ holding in His hands a small loaf of white bread, saying 'This is my body.' The congregation therefore concluded that white bread, and only white, could be the Son of God, the truth and the life. The man who had got no white bread but only brown bread, made with Indian corn, 'is deprived of God's grace . . . And the request in our daily prayer, "Give us this day our daily bread," refers only to bread made with wheat.'[8]

In a very different vein, but still centred on bread, the main necessity of life, the father of Luigi Murica—tortured and killed by the fascists—welcomed his friends beside the coffin of his dead son, and offered them bread and wine:

> 'It was he who helped me to sow, to hoe, to thresh and to grind the grain of which this bread is made. Take it and eat, this is his bread.'
>
> 'It was he who helped me to prune, to spray, to hoe and to pick the vineyard from which this wine comes. Drink it, it is his wine.'
>
> 'The bread is made from many grains of wheat,' said Pietro Spina, 'therefore it means unity. The wine is made of many seeds of grapes, and also signifies unity. Unity of things like each other, equal and useful.'
>
> 'The bread and wine of Communion,' said an old man, 'the wheat and the grapes pressed down, the body and the blood.'
>
> He added, 'And to make bread and wine you need nine months, as you do to make a man.'[9]

And here is another description:

> Have you ever met on the mountain roads, or on pilgrimages, or in the fields, strange men dressed in rags, dusty, sweaty, obviously underfed, but who in their

bearing, expression, smile and sadness, are real kings?
. . . Mastro Raffaele was one of these . . . Before starting work or a meal—the sign of the Cross.[10]

One day, on Silone's return to his village to gather material for *L'Avventura d'un Povero Cristiano*, he met on a hill
an old peasant looking for medicinal herbs.

> He told us that in his youth he used to make the pil-
> grimage to the Santa Casa di Loreto* and also to the
> Santuario della Trinità† above Subiaco. Once, he said,
> these two pilgrimages were an obligation to every
> good Christian. But as to San Piero Celestino, or
> whatever you call him, (he said that he, of course, took
> off his hat to him), he had never succeeded in under-
> standing what his special qualifications were, in other
> words, for what graces or favours one should turn to
> him. 'He can help you,' I explained, 'to overcome the
> temptations of power.' But this advice merely caused
> an attack of immoderate laughter. Then he said
> gravely: 'Then he is Saint not for poor men like me,
> but for the priests.'[11]

In local usage, the word Collemaggio does not indicate
the church in Aquila where Pope Celestino had been
crowned, but the lunatic asylum. On one occasion Silone
and a friend called in to pay a visit:

> In the porter's lodge we found a rough old man who,
> on hearing my name, said: 'At last, at last.' When I
> was about to leave, he called to me, 'Do you have a
> permit?' As we went down, the friend who was with
> me said: 'Your old friend confided to me that he had

---

*Holy House of Loreto.
†Sanctuary of the Trinity.

been waiting for you for a long time.' 'Does he think me mad?' 'If Silone isn't, who is? He's always been against the Government!' My friend added at once, 'But he is fond of you and expected your arrival to have someone he trusts to play cards with him. According to him, one Sunday when you were nine or ten you played cards in his house, and promised to come back on every feast-day. But you haven't kept your promise.'[12]

Silone was very young when he first became conscious of what he has called 'the strident, incomprehensible contrast between private life, which was generally decent and honest, and formal relationships—very often rough, odious and false.' One day, he saw an arrogant local grandee egging on his dog to attack a poor little seamstress, as she was coming out of church. The dog knocked her down, bit her, tore her clothes to pieces; several people saw it happen. But when the case came to court—for the seamstress sued the young man—no single witness came forward on her behalf. The only articulate voice was that of the official prosecutor who claimed that the woman had provoked the dog—whereupon the judge had little choice but to decide against her.

'I did it very unwillingly,' the judge said later to his friends, 'I was really very sorry. But a good judge must learn to silence his own personal feelings.'

'Yes, to be sure,' Silone's mother commented, 'but what a dreadful profession! Better mind one's own business at home.' And to her son she added: 'When you are grown-up, be whatever you like, but not a judge.'[13] But Silone has never been good at minding his own business.

By then he had moved for his secondary education to the big Seminary in the square, but I remember his saying that his four years there were not entirely wasted. Latin was well taught and Italian also, but no books except school textbooks could enter the building. Rising at five in the bitter cold, the boys led an austere and narrow life, and also a confusing one, owing to its double standard. Silone has given a vivid account of the narrow and sectarian atmosphere in a district where political organisations had not yet been formed. When the first Peasant Leagues were formed in 1911 and 1912, the parish priests would order the church bells to be rung so loud during their meetings as to drown the speakers' voices. The Bishop himself would address the boys on the theme of private property as a divine institution and on the sacrilegious attempt of the Peasants' Leagues to break up some of the neglected and untilled properties. History was taught with a similar bias, but also with a double standard, rendered necessary by the fact that while the teachers were all priests, the pupils had to pass State exams. 'It was inevitable that most pupils came to regard their diplomas and their future jobs as the true realities of life. All my prayers as a schoolboy ended with the words: "Help me, God, to live without turning into a traitor."'[14]

It is the accusation that his enemies have most often levelled against him, from both sides. One should add, however, that Silone firmly refused to make use of the errors of his education to defend his own subsequent conduct. 'The use of the word "If,'" he declared, 'is almost always misleading . . . I cannot guarantee that I would have behaved any less foolishly if my teachers had been more enlightened. These are plays of fancy that get one nowhere.'[15]

At this point I think I must be allowed a personal digression. We had taken Silone and his wife, Darina, to see the little Pieve of Corsignano, below Pienza, the beautiful 12th-century church where Pius II was baptised, and when we came out we saw on the rough grass beside the church a group of cold, scrubby seminarians who had tucked their soutanes into their knickerbockers and were kicking a football about. Silone stood still in silence, with his hands in his pockets. The sun went down, it grew colder and colder, and Darina suggested repeatedly that we would all like to go home. When at last we got Silone to the car, I said to him, 'Were you looking at the sunset?' 'No,' he replied, 'I was watching my youth.'

When he was fourteen and was still in the Seminary, a severe earthquake destroyed the greater part of his native town. Like some of his companions, he saved his life by straddling across one of the windows on the main outer wall. Looking out, all he could see of the town was a cloud of dust, and when at last he could get home, he found nothing but rubble. Five days later, his brother was found—still alive—in a sort of hollow beneath the stones, but his mother had been killed instantly. Yet perhaps he received an even greater shock from something he witnessed one night during the earthquake when he was believed to be asleep: a gross and cowardly theft committed by one of his own relations. This was a story that he told in veiled terms later on in a novel—attributing the crime to Pietro Spina's uncle, whom Pietro, as a boy of fourteen, saw stealing a pocket book beside his mother's corpse ... The next day, Pietro said, he realised that he had changed. 'To grow up needs a whole life, but to become old one night like that is enough.'[16]

To the people of Pescina the earthquake afforded at least one satisfaction. 'The earthquake killed rich and poor, educated and ignorant men, officials and subjects. In the earthquake nature brought about what the law promised in words, but did not keep: equality.'

But this euphoria did not last. It was followed by a state of things worse than the previous one. 'Thefts, frauds, embezzlement of every kind. This gave rise to the conviction of the people "that if one day the human race is destroyed, it will not be by an earthquake or a war, but afterwards."'[17]

～

It was only a few days after the earthquake that Silone saw a curious scene. Many of the corpses were still lying under the ruins, and the terrified survivors were living near their former homes, in shacks. The cold was bitter, for it was midwinter. All the animals—donkeys, cows, mules, goats and sheep—had been put into pens, since their stables were destroyed, and at nightfall the ravenous wolves would come down from the mountains, attracted by the animals' smell, and great bonfires were lit to keep them away. Among the ruins, Silone saw a little shabby, unshaven priest wandering about with a group of homeless children, looking—since the railway was no longer running—for some way of taking them to Rome. Just then a procession of five or six cars drove up, and the King, who had come to inspect the scene of the disaster, got out with his suite. Without asking anyone for permission, the little priest began to lift his children into the cars and, when the police protested, told the King firmly why he needed the transport and drove away. 'Who's that extraordinary man?,' Silone asked. 'He's a rather strange priest, called Don Orione.'[18]

A year later, under very different circumstances, Silone met Don Orione again. At the age of fifteen, to continue his classical studies, he had been sent to a grim school in Rome, in the most dreary part of the city, near the Roman cemetery, Il Verano. The Director of the Institute was severe and cold, his own tutor even more so, and he found it impossible to make friends with the town boys who seemed to him 'cynical, stupid and noisy.'

Then one day, shortly before Christmas, he ran away, without premeditation, without anywhere to go, just because he found the gate open to admit a lorry full of coal. He wandered about the city, aimlessly, and became conscious of his inexplicable behaviour. He had only a few lire in his pocket and of course, no luggage. He took a small attic room in a little hotel near the station, and here passed three interminable days—watching the trams and carriages pass. 'I wished to die. I even recited an Ave Maria to ask to be run over by a tram.'

The scandal in the college was naturally very great and when he was found by a policeman and brought back to the school, the Director would not listen to any explanation:

> 'I will not hear your nonsense,' he cried and made me kneel at his feet . . . [His feet, Silone remembers, were long and thin and he wore very soft shoes with a silver buckle.] I was at his mercy like a beaten dog. How was it possible?' he wanted to know. 'I don't know, Monsignore,' I replied. 'Why did you not ask your confessor to give you advice or help? Or your guardian angel?' 'I don't know, Monsignore, really I don't know.'[19]

Ignominiously expelled, he then heard from his grandmother that Don Orione would receive him in one of his schools. 'Have you ever heard of Don Orione?' the Director asked. 'Oh, yes,' he replied enthusiastically.

He was told that Don Orione would meet him at the railway station. The sulky schoolboy, too self-absorbed even to recognise the little priest he had seen after the earthquake, was asked whether he would like a paper and replied, 'Yes, the *Avanti*'—the anti-clerical socialist paper—and when Don Orione meekly bought it for him, he also gave him his suitcase to carry. Don Orione smiled and said he enjoyed carrying burdens for cheeky little schoolboys, 'like a small donkey,' he added. Silone began to thaw and confided that donkeys were his favourite animals, too. 'Not the absurd donkeys in public gardens, but the real ones, those the peasants have. They seem apathetic, because they're very old, but they know everything—like the peasants!'

It was then that a friendship began. Don Orione started by talking to the boy on equal terms, discussing matters of general interest, and even reading aloud to him the draft of a letter which he had sent to the Pope. He told Silone about his own poor and unhappy childhood, and—when the boy asked him if he knew that he had run away from his previous school, and asked whether the priest could understand what had made him do it—was it possible for an old man to understand a boy? 'Yes,' Don Orione replied, 'of course I understand.'

They talked through the night, while the train rumbled up the coast towards Genoa. Silone describes this journey. 'I heard in the darkness the sound of the sea, which was new to me, and the unfamiliar names of the stations. I felt as if I were discovering the world.' What he remembered best, many years later, about Don Orione, was: ' . . the quiet tenderness of his expression. His eyes had the kindness and clearsightedness which one sometimes sees in some old peasant women, who have endured all sorts of trials in their lives and therefore can know or guess one's most secret troubles.' During the whole night, Don Orione only once referred to religion:

> 'Remember,' he suddenly said, 'God isn't only to be found in church. In the future you will certainly encounter periods of despair; but even if you think you are alone and abandoned, you will not be. Don't forget it.' He spoke in the same voice and with the same simplicity as when he was speaking about other things, but I noticed that his eyes were shining with

tears ... 'Are you tired?' asked Don Orione at one moment. 'I should like the journey never to end,' I stammered.[20]

He stayed with Don Orione in San Remo for one year, studying in a second liceo. One is tempted to speculate whether his life would have taken a different course if he had remained longer under Don Orione's influence. But instead he was sent to finish the liceo in a school at Reggio, Calabria and only during the holidays went back to visit his grandmother at Pescina. There he came to believe that only one choice was open to him: 'Are we on the side of the men condemned to hard labour or of their keepers?'

On the village square the parish priest tried to drown the sound of the peasants' voices by the constant ringing of the church bells. A young socialist friend of his, Lazzaro, never set foot in the church again. 'Once,' he said to the priest, 'I used to think of the bells as God's voice—but you have made it that of the owners of the land. May God forgive you.'[21]

It was with such a background filling his mind, that Silone wrote his early novels: first *Fontamara*, *Bread and Wine* and *The Seed Beneath the Snow*, and then the autobiographical book which first brought him fame and recognition in Italy, *Uscita di Sicurezza (Emergency Exit)*.

In *Fontamara* he described the world of the cafoni—a world without hope. *Cafone*, the author explains, means 'Flesh accustomed to suffer.'[22] His symbol is the donkey, his daily companion, but more fortunate than he. Silone was well aware that the name cafone, in Italy, was an insult. 'But I use it in this book in the certainty that when in my country suffering is no longer something to be ashamed of, it will become a title of respect, perhaps also of honour.'[23]

The men of Fontamara distrust everyone: the priest, their master, their advocate, but cannot do without them.

They engage in interminable lawsuits. 'Centuries of resignation weigh upon them, founded on violence and deceit.'[24] 'My poor boy,' an old woman said to Silone, 'tell me what use it is not to resign oneself.'[25] 'But to these same men a guest was always sacred, and for an honourable man the first "act of mercy" was to help the persecuted.'[26]

Silone's novel about his village is not merely the story of bitter injustice suffered by the peasants of the Marsica at the hands of the landowners, but that of every rebel who has come to see the inevitable limitations of revolutionary movements and the recurring cycle by which, sooner or later, all revolutions turn into tyrannies. Indeed, he claims that his picture of his little world has a universal validity. All the world over, men such as these—fellahin, coolies, mujiks, peons, cafoni, 'men who cause the earth to bear fruit and go hungry themselves'—are alike. 'They are a nation, a race, a church of their own.'[27]

Indeed in a sense it is true, as Silone said himself, that all his books have the same theme:

> I should have liked to spend my whole life in writing and rewriting the same story, in the hope of ending by understanding it and being understood—as in the Middle Ages there were monks who spent their whole life in painting the self-same image of Christ, which was yet never quite the same. It is now clear to me what interests me is the fate of a certain kind of man, a certain kind of Christian, in the world's framework, and that I would not know how to write about anything else.[28]
>
> The Maiella is, for us, our Lebanon . . . In the same places where once innumerable hermits lived, as in the Thebaid, more recently hundreds of outlaws have been hidden as well as fugitive prisoners of war and partisans, helped by most of the population.[29]

Later on, Silone was deeply moved by a story to which his wife drew his attention—an incident described in a book entitled *The Long Walk* by a Polish author, Slawomir Rawicz—as being a close parallel to what occurred in the Abruzzi. It happened in January 1941, when Rawicz and other Poles deported to Siberia were transferred from one forced labour camp to another. A snowstorm obliged them to take refuge in the forest and there their leader turned for help to a group of Ostyaks—a Mongol people living in that region, with their reindeer and their sleighs.

> The little men [Rawicz wrote] arrived with sacks of food and sat with us around the fire, while we received our ration of bread and tea. They looked at us with compassion. With one of them I could speak in Russian. He was perhaps sixty years old. Like the other Ostyaks he called us the 'Unfortunate Ones' ... forced workers, obliged to extract the riches of Siberia without a salary. 'We have always been friends of the "Unfortunate Ones,"' he said. 'Since a long time ago, as far as my memory reaches ... we have had the habit of leaving a little food outside our door at night for any of them who had run away and did not know where to go.'

Silone comments: 'The poor, dear little Ostyaks. It is probable that they have never heard the names of our countries, but what does it matter? They are as much like us as brothers.'[30]

One of the dominant themes of Silone's writings is that of the need for brotherhood, of the destruction of human loneliness. 'Revolution,' says his young student, Murica, 'is the need to cease to be alone. It is an attempt to remain together, and not to be afraid anymore.' And a similar need is described in Silone's third novel, *Il Seme Sotto la Neve*

(*The Seed Beneath the Snow*), in the friendship that the protagonist, Pietro Spina, feels for a deaf and dumb workman, Infante, whose food and stable he shares, and who becomes for him, as he painfully teaches him to speak, a symbol of human companionship.

> *Compagnia* [says Pietro Spina], was the first new word that Infante learned from me. He could already say bread, *pane*, which he pronounced *paan*; and I explained to him with gestures, that two men who ate the same bread became *compagni*, companions. The next day . . . Infante showed me some mice burrowing in the straw for crumbs, muttering '*compagni*.' From that day he began to give a piece of bread every day to our donkey, so that he, too, should belong to our company.[31]

In Bread and Wine, or rather in the later, revised Italian version, *Wine and Bread*, as well as in *The Seed Beneath the Snow*, Pietro Spina is pictured as a socialist lay saint. 'Socialism is his way of serving God . . . Pietro Spina is not so much seeking God, as pursued by Him.' We even find Silone quoting the English poem:

> I fled Him, down the nights and down the days,
> I fled Him, down the arches of the years,
> I fled Him, down the labyrinthine ways
> Of my own mind . . .[32]

The theme—already expressed with unequalled eloquence by St Bernard—has many centuries of Christian tradition behind it.

⌒

It was during his early adolescence that Silone took an important step. How it occurred, he described many years later in his essay 'A Change of Comrades.'

It has happened to many of us to give up going to Mass one Sunday morning, not because its doctrines suddenly seemed untrue, but because we were weary of the other people who went there, and attracted by those who stayed away . . . Outside our village church stood the workmen. It wasn't their psychology that attracted us, but their condition . . . In other words, we first decided to be conservatives or rebels according to the motives we bore within us, sometimes very confusedly. Before choosing, we were chosen unawares. But we cannot give up trying to fathom it. What could the workmen of his own village represent, in the eyes of a young student during the years just before the First World War, so that he should take up their cause?

The young man was certainly not yet thinking of a political career. But it was then that in his region, partly owing to the influence of workers who had come back from America, the first Peasant Leagues had sprung up, 'awakening unspeakable fear and dismay.' 'It is not surprising,' Silone wrote, 'that this new, unexpected upheaval, observed by a young man already disgusted by his local environment should have brought about in his heart a deep change, that is, a conviction that in a society as old, tired, exhausted and bored as that one, the poor represented the last resource—a reality which it was salutary to share.'[33]

He went to Rome in 1917 to join the Junior Branch of the Socialist party, of which he soon became a leader. But at a stormy meeting in Livorno in 1921, which ended with the secession of the left wing of his party to the Communist party, he decided to go with them. He, too, would become a Communist.

It was a far more decisive step, he knew, than just joining a political party: 'For me as for many others it was a com-

plete dedication which implied a certain way of life . . . That
was still a time when to declare oneself a Socialist or a Communist implied burning all one's boats, breaking with one's
relations and friends, finding oneself without a job.'

And the spiritual experience was even more disruptive.

> It was at the moment of the break that I felt I was
> bound to Christ in the deepest fibre of my being. Yet
> I would not allow myself any mental restrictions. The
> little lamp which had been kept alight before the
> shrine of the intuitions which were dearest to me, was
> blown out by an icy draught. Life, death, love, good,
> evil, truth all changed their meaning . . . And how can
> one describe the inner dismay of an ill-nourished pro-
> vincial boy, in a squalid city room, at having definitely
> renounced his faith in his immortal soul? It was far
> too serious a matter to talk about with anyone. My
> comrades in the Party would perhaps have laughed at
> me, and I had no other friends left.[34]

During his first years as a communist, Silone's life was
entirely identified with that of the Party. It became, as he
wrote, 'his family, school, church and barracks.' After
working in Trieste for a communist paper, he was sent to the
Moscow of Lenin and then, in 1923, to Spain—then under
the rule of Primo de Rivera—to strengthen the communist
position there. He soon found himself in prison, first in Ma-
drid and then in Barcelona—a period of which he once said
to me that it was one of the happiest times he had ever
known. 'Why?' I asked him. 'Because of the company.'

The company, as might be expected, consisted largely
of dedicated anarchists or communists like himself. It was
a world in which he at once felt at home. In looks, Silone
might well have been a Spaniard: his natural reserve and
dignity and his dark, sunken eyes were very Spanish, and

indeed for some years this was the nationality he adopted. It was in Spain, too, that instead of his real name, Secondo Tranquilli,* he first made use of the pen-name Ignazio Silone, which he then used for all his books. It had been suggested to him by the story of Quintus Pompaedius Silo, a man of his own region whose victorious battle against Rome in 90 BC had helped to lead to the *Lex Julia*, a granting freedom and civil rights to all the allies of Rome.

Owing to the influence of a Spanish professor whom he scarcely knew, Silone was set to work in the prison library. At night he slept in the Infirmary, where—since all the other inmates were seriously ill—his presence surprised the beautiful young nun in charge of the ward. Gradually, a platonic friendship sprang up between them; she lent him her devotional books (in particular the Life of St Teresa), but she also began to listen, no doubt with some dismay, to his opinions. When the time came for him to be moved to Barcelona, to be embarked on a ship sailing for fascist Italy, she somehow heard of the danger beforehand and managed to delay his departure long enough for him and his guards to miss the ship. His recollection of her has a special flavour of tenderness and nostalgia of emotions never entirely fulfilled. What became of her later on, during the Spanish

---

*The name Secondo had always been distasteful to him (a 'secondino,' in Italian, is a gaol warden) and had only been given to him by accident, when his father, Paolo Tranquilli, went to register his birth in the office of the Commune. His father wished to give him the Republican names of Mameli or Cairoli, but the Mayor objected, saying that no-one had ever had these Christian names. Tranquilli then suggested the Mayor's own name, Severino, but the secretary intervened, saying 'Give him *my* name'—and so Silone was registered as Secondino. Later on, in his clandestine activities, he assumed several different names (especially 'Pasquini' in Russia) and it was not until 1946 that his name was legalised as 'Ignazio.' See Darina Silone, *History of a Manuscript*, in *Severina*, p. 135.

Civil War, he was never able to discover. He must surely have caused a deep upheaval in her monastic life.

After a further period of imprisonment in Spain—again 'in excellent company'—he was finally extradited, but this time via Marseilles to Ventimiglia, and was easily able to make his way to Paris, where he had many friends of his way of thinking.

The main theme of Silone's next book, *Emergency Exit*, which at last brought him full recognition in his own country, was his break with the Communist Party. He has left us a vivid account of the Session in Moscow in May 1927 of the Soviet Executive Committee, as well as of the Communist International (Comintern), which caused the break to occur. It was a decisive moment in his life, and a decisive moment for Stalin, too. The alliance of the Chinese Communists with the Comintern had ended in a bloodbath and Trotsky had violently criticised it.

Silone describes how he and Togliatti arrived at the first meeting together. He at once had the impression that they had come too late. They were received in a little office, the headquarters of the Communist International, by Ernst Thälmann, the leader of the German Communist Party, who at once read a resolution to be presented at the full session, expelling Trotsky from the Party—'an old lion,' Silone wrote later on, 'waiting to be killed or captured'—on the basis of a document which many of those who sentenced him had not even read.

Silone pointed this out:

> 'As for that,' said Thälmann candidly, 'we haven't read it either, except the Russian delegates' ... At this point Stalin intervened. He was standing at the side of the room, and appeared to be the only man present who was calm and serene. 'The political office of the Party [Politburo],' said Stalin, 'considered that it was

not desirable to translate and distribute Trotsky's document . . . because it contains some allusions to the policy of the Soviet State in China.'

'He lied,' Silone wrote. The document, which was published by Trotsky abroad later on, contained 'no State secret, but an attack on the policy of Stalin and of the Communist International towards China.'

Silone then said: 'We do not contest the right of the political office of the Russian Communist Party to keep a document secret, but I do not understand why others should be asked to condemn a document unknown to them.'

Stalin said: 'If a single delegate is against the resolution, it must not be presented.'[35] The meeting was closed without a decision, but after the Italian delegation had left Moscow for Paris, they learned that, as soon as they were out of the way, the Comintern had signed Trotsky's expulsion.

It was then that Silone was overcome by discouragement. He asked himself: 'Is this the true face of Communism? Is this the ideal for which working men have risked their lives or died in prison? Is it for this that we are leading our wandering, dangerous, solitary lives?'[36]

Silone's own turn came two years later, in the Spring of 1929, when he was in Switzerland on leave on account of his ill health. Three Italian members of the Comintern—Leonetti, Tresso and Ravassori, whom Silone respected and liked—were accused of being Trotskyites, and the rumour spread that Silone had been their inspirer. It was not so. He had simply refused, as in the meeting of the International in Moscow, to take Stalin's anathemas seriously, and to consider the three Italians as dangerous enemies. Togliatti wrote to Silone from Paris: 'The success we have obtained in fighting against that little group of traitors does not free you from giving the Party the declaration you owe them.' Silone did not answer. Togliatti then followed him to Zürich, explained his own position 'clearly and loyally,' and again tried to persuade him to come back. 'Listen, Ercole,' Silone said, 'I'm not coming back to any political office, I'm not meant for that sort of job. You can use me as a proof reader if you like.' Togliatti replied that even for that Silone would have to declare his condemnation of the three men who had been expelled. 'Even to accept coercion,' he said, 'is a homage to the Party.'[37]

The truth was that this was a genuine but most unhappy friendship. Togliatti stood for all that was most orthodox in the Comintern, accepted its decisions and expected his colleagues to do the same. He then returned to Moscow. It was the end to what had been a close friendship. When asked what he felt about Togliatti some years later, Silone replied, 'First admiration—and now compassion.'

One explanation of this change is perhaps connected with an episode which Silone relates in the essay entitled 'La Lezione di Budapest.' In it he said that for some time he had been surprised by the fact that while in the Communist Party in Italy there was a real cult of the writings of Gramsci, and Togliatti himself had spoken of him as 'certainly the greatest modern thinker of Western Europe,' these works had never been translated into another language. The explanation was simple. In Moscow the works of Gramsci had been found to contain certain grave heresies. It was only with difficulty that Togliatti was able to obtain permission to admire Gramsci in Italy, but they were not to be translated or spoken of abroad. 'Truth on this side of the Alps, a lie on the other.'[38]

Two years more passed before Silone finally left the Party. A member of a Communist Commission before which he appeared pointed out to him what his future position would be: 'Under the fascist régime, you can't go home to Italy. Without any papers, you can't stay abroad. You have no means of support and very poor health. Your brother is in prison on account of the Party. All your friends are in the Party and would break with you as soon as you have left. Against fascism, there is no power except ours. If you have any common sense at all, if you can behave like a normal man . . .' At this point, Silone interrupted him: 'Listen, I don't know if you can understand me; but in the sense that you mean I have never been and perhaps never will be a politically normal man.'[39]

The remark enabled his former comrades to state in the decree of his expulsion, that he himself had admitted that he was politically abnormal, a pathological case.

⌒

Ignominiously expelled from the Party, on the grounds of having played a double game, Silone wrote: 'I could have defended myself, I could have proved my good faith . . . I did not wish to do so. In a flash, I clearly perceived the uselessness of any tactics, of any delay or compromise. After a month, or after two years, it would all have begun again. It was better to be done with it, once for all.'[40]

Before his expulsion, Silone had already obtained leave from Russia to live in Switzerland, on account of his ill-health. This was also a refuge then for many others in a similar position, men without a passport, 'yet who could not call themselves No-one, like Ulysses'—whose break with Communism had often been a confused, reluctant process, and in whose good faith practically no-one believed. Former communists, he said, 'constitute a category of their own, like former priests and former army officers—and their number is legion.' 'The final struggle,' he once remarked to Togliatti, 'will be between communists and former communists'—meaning that it would be the communist experience itself that would in the end destroy its doctrine.

In summing up his own experience, he affirmed that the original mistake was certainly his own, in demanding from political action something that it could not give. He added:

> I do not mind admitting that I go on thinking about it ... If I have written some books, it is to try to understand, and to try to make others understand ... The truth is this: the day I left the Communist Party was a very sad day for me, a day of deep mourning, of mourning for my youth. And I come from a region where mourning is worn longer than elsewhere. One does not free oneself easily, as I have already said, from an experience as intense as that of the Communist organization. Something is always left, which marks one's character for the rest of one's life ... What is left to me after the long and sad adventure? A secret affection for a few men whom I have known and the taste of the ashes of a wasted youth.[41]

Silone lived on in exile during the rise of fascism in Europe and the uneasy years before the outbreak of war in 1939.

It was in December 1941 that Ignazio Silone first met the beautiful Irish girl, Darina, who was to become his wife. He was then in Zürich, and had become—without the knowledge of the Swiss authorities—Secretary of the Foreign Centre of the Italian Socialist Party, and had been warned to be on his guard against Darina, as a spy of the OVRA, the Russian secret service. (This calumny had been circulated by a man who was working in the British Intelligence Service, whose advances she had repelled.) Silone first caught sight of her in a private library in Zürich, the Museum Gewaltschaft, where she was preparing some articles about Italy by reading Mussolini's works. Silone's interest was awakened, and he asked her to tea.

Several years before, when Darina was still at school, she had seen a copy, in the Penguin edition, of *Fontamara*—written, according to the back page, by an anti-fascist Italian in exile. 'Is it a good book?' she asked her father. 'Very good, but it's not for you.'

The next day, Darina found the book on a high shelf in her father's library and devoured it in one gulp. In June 1941, after a long sequence of events, she found herself in exile in Switzerland—and, after four months in Bern set to work in the Zurich library where Silone caught sight of her. It is hardly necessary to say that she accepted his invitation, and found herself in the house of one of his friends, in a room with many beautiful modern pictures and a fierce dog. While she was waiting for her host, she made friends with the dog and sat on the floor, playing with him.

At last Silone came in, wearing a greyish blue velvet jacket. But the conversation languished. 'I did not know what to say, and he did not help me. So I said the only thing I really wanted to say. I have read three of your books (in the interval *Wine and Bread* and *The School for Dictators* had appeared in English) and naturally I realize that in a moment like this one, you must certainly be involved in some way with the Italian Resistance. It's the only thing I care about; if I can be of any use, I am at your disposal!'

Not unnaturally, Silone lied. 'He said he did not know what I was talking about; he was only busy writing and studying. I must get rid of my romantic notions. I did not believe him, but could not insist . . . Silence fell. He must have thought that if I was a spy, I was a very bad one. A maid brought in the tea. "Sugar?" "No, thank you." Soon after I went away.'[42]

It was not until three years later, on 28 December 1944—after Silone's return to Italy for good*—that he and Darina were married in the registry office of the Campidoglio in Rome, with Saragat and Nina Ruffini as their witnesses.

In December 1942, while Silone was still in Switzerland, he wrote an appeal for civil resistance in Italy, and later on was approached by the head of the American Intelligence Service in Geneva, Allen Dulles, but replied that only one kind of struggle against fascism had any validity: 'that which takes place *within* each country, without foreign propaganda or aid . . . Our interest is not in victory, but in freedom.' He considered himself and his friends to be waging 'a private war against Fascism, which started long before the war between different countries, and will go on much longer, since the struggle against the danger of totalitarianism will certainly not end with the War.'[43]

However, it appears that, owing to a mislaid letter, his remarks did somehow come to be relayed to the BBC, and at the end of 1942 Silone was imprisoned by the police of Zürich, on the charge of illicit political activities. His *Memoriale dal Carcere Svizzero* was written on December 17 in a single night, and has only recently been published. At the time, he was Secretary of the Foreign Centre of The Italian Socialist Party, which was in close touch with the Resistance movements in France, Germany, Austria and the Balkans. His appeal to the police authorities in Bern is of great interest and in some parts very moving.

He began by saying that he was willing to suffer any penalty for the cause of freedom, but hoped that 'the Swiss

---

*In 1966 Silone went to the U.S.A. to give lectures in several universities and in the same year was invited by the Italian Institute in London. In 1966 he returned to the U.S. for a meeting of the PEN Club. But his home was henceforth in Italy.

authorities, whom I respect, should not condemn or punish me for reasons that are not connected with me or for events which have been misunderstood.'

He repeated that he took full responsibility for any action in Switzerland of the Foreign Centre of the Italian Socialist Party. All the papers that had been sequestrated by the Swiss police, he maintained, testified 'that "the crime" of which I am held responsible is not of Communism or Anarchism, but purely and simply, of love for democracy and freedom . . .' Twelve years before, he wrote, in December 1930, he had been a guest of the same prison in which he now found himself—on the previous occasion merely for entering Switzerland without a passport. He was then thirty years old, and had just left the Communist Party.

> I was seriously ill and penniless, I had no family; I had been expelled from France and Spain; I could not return to Italy; in other words, I was on the brink of suicide . . . In Switzerland I became a writer, but what is of greater value, I became a man. Not only has my conception of society grown clearer, but I have discovered, in the daily spectacle of a free, democratic and peace-loving people, the possibility of a kind of human existence which I had considered impossible, and, what is more, I have acquired the sense of significance of man's existence on earth . . . My books bear witness to this inner struggle and ripening. They are the story of the uncertainties, the difficulties, the successes of this victory . . . There are some pages in them that are written with blood . . . My moral debt towards this country is so great that I cannot hope ever to be able to repay it . . .

He added that his time in Switzerland could not be interpreted as tied to a political activity in Italy, since his detachment from political work had been complete until the middle of 1941.

Silone then went on to explain how, following the news brought to him by Italian friends who were horrified by the turn that fascism had taken in Italy and the alliance with Germany, he felt that a grave political crisis was impending and that it was necessary 'to inspire a small pioneer-group of working men with courageous ideas of freedom, to awaken their enthusiasm for ideas superior to the crude ones of Communism, so that they might become leaders of our unhappy country . . .'

He proceeded to quote a summary of his correspondence with these men, the text of which was already in the hands of the Swiss authorities, and added that 'to guide the Italian Socialist Movement along these lines was my only preoccupation . . . My arrest and that of other friends implicated in this work has brought that activity to a definite end . . . I don't think it indispensable to the life of the Italian Socialist Party . . . I am not, and do not want to be, a political man . . . I want to remain a writer, tied to no discipline but that of my own thoughts and conscience . . .'

The document ends with a passionate appeal to the Swiss authorities to realise how tragic the consequence would be to anti-fascists still living in Italy:

> If, through the negligence or indiscretion of some functionary the Italian police should enter into possession of the news that concerns these men . . . Their lives are in danger! These are brave men, convinced idealists, in whom the passion of freedom burns, as in the purest heroes of the democratic revolutions . . . Their lives deserve to be defended, safeguarded with every precaution . . . I implore, beg, entreat the Federal Attorney-General who will have to examine and keep in his custody the sequestered papers of the For-

eign Centre of the Italian Socialist Party, to take every measure to defend the lives of the anti-fascists who are still in Italy.

I have finished ... I have expressed myself with complete sincerity. I hope to be read, not by a policeman, but by a Christian. May he receive this message of mine as a Christmas present. If he does not understand it, perhaps it will be understood by the men who in a hundred or two hundred years will look among these poor papers to catch a spark of the great struggle of our time.[44] Secondo Tranquilli

It was at this point that Silone had to make up his mind what he was going to do with the rest of his life. His first duty, he felt, was to tell the story of his own experiences so that others should not make the same mistakes. 'It is not agreeable to speak about oneself, about one's own blunders, one's follies, one's hysteria. It is not amusing to live again, even only in one's memory, those years of nightmare, but it is our duty to testify. Many have entered the Party through our fault. Our first duty is to them, and then towards young people still looking for a banner and an army. What shall we tell them? Simply the truth. The truth is not scandalous revelations for the Press, but the tragic reality which lies behind the façade of Communism.'[45]

A particular bitterness was added to Silone's state of mind by the knowledge that his young brother, Romolo—a handsome, simple Catholic boy, with no interest in anything but sport—had happened by bad luck to find himself in Milan (hoping to expatriate and join Silone in Switzerland, to study in the Polytechnic of Zürich) on the very day in which an attempt was made on the King's life.* He had been arrested, without a trace of proof, as a Communist,

---

*12 April 1928.

and had been tortured and sent to the island of Procida, where he died four years later, his lungs destroyed by tuberculosis, the effect of cold, hunger and the internal lesions received during his interrogation. The bitter irony of this tragedy lay in the fact that Romolo was not a communist, and, apart from his courage, had nothing to reveal, but, when questioned, felt that he must say, from a sense of loyalty to his brother, that he too belonged to the Party. 'I tried to behave,' he wrote to Silone from prison, 'as I imagined you would have in my place.'[46] It is easy to see, after this, how peculiarly painful it was to Silone to deny the convictions that had cost his brother his life. He wrote: 'What can a man do, under such circumstances, to feel that he may still be of some use? Only one weapon was still available to me: one that then caused a certain sensation, but was, nevertheless, a crude piece of work.* I still needed help, and this had been given to me in a correspondence with an exile like myself, for whom I had the greatest respect.'

From this letter† it would appear that Salvemini had written to Silone a very frank criticism of his first novel. Silone's answer is very modest—the letter of a young man to an old one.

> 2 November 1937
> Germaniastr. 53
> Zürich 6
>
> Dear Salvemini,
>   Many thanks for your most welcome letter. You will believe me that criticism as frank as yours gives me greater pleasure than the usual vague compliments, and also I am still young and can still learn.

---

*He was referring, of course, to his first novel, *Fontamara*.
†Now published for the first time, by kind permission of Darina Silone.

Your comment that my picture of the peasants of *Fontamara* is not quite real and almost a caricature has been pointed out to me by others but having been said by you, has caused me to give fresh thought to the matter. Two years ago, in a paper on emigration, I already explained what I have now said in the preface of the novel, that *Fontamara* corresponds to a backward type of village of the Marsica. The same things could be said of Pietra Secca, Rocca, Fossa, Orta and other villages I mention in *Pane e Vino*. In the Italian edition of this last book, while correcting the proofs, I made a few brief additions, which most readers would not even notice, but which are important for people like you, who are justly preoccupied by the truth . . . On page 230, for instance, I have added nine lines to the description of the crowd which was awaiting the broadcast from Rome announcing the beginning of the African War.

In the crowd, Don Paolo noticed only one or two peasants who, by their disconcerted, lost and confused glances at each other, and also by the cleanliness and soberness of their clothing, reminded him of the kind of *contadino* who used to prevail in the countryside of the Abruzzi: churchmen rather than sacristans, dignified, reserved in their gestures and their speech, honest, proud, accustomed to serious matters and conscientious work. There are still some left here and there, and they seem the survivors of a vanished race.

These are the peasants that you must have known before the war. As far as the Marsica is concerned, this kind of peasant has been, if not destroyed, at least decimated, by the following plagues which have taken place one after the other in the course of the last ten years: the earthquake, the war, Fascism and the closing of emigration to America. Each of these plagues would deserve a comment of its own. For instance, the damage of the earthquake would have been slighter if the sappers of the 'Genio Civile' were not by their racketeering and Mafioso methods, after twenty-two years, still raking in their gold. These sappers have produced, among other things, several thousand shoddy and dishonest workmen from Northern Italy and Rome, who have now settled down in the Marsica. (For many contadini of our region Fascism is nothing more than the offspring of the sappers.) What I am trying to say is that with us, in the last twenty years, there has been a terrifying lowering of morals. It was preceded by Fascism and became worse under it. There may be some peasants who have kept some of their old decorum and honesty and are capable of thinking with their own minds; I hope so. In *Pane e Vino* . . . these peasants are represented by Cardile (who gives a temporary shelter to Spina in Chapter II) and by the family of Murica and the boys who wrote on the walls. I must, however, frankly tell you that some of these are creations of my own imagination. I have personally known several thousand peasants, but I do not know if there is a single one who would shelter me in his stable, if the Fascist police were looking for me. I try to believe it. I am not 'justifying' Fascism on these grounds, but seeing things like this helps one to realize how Fascism became possible, how it has been able to keep going, how it has been able to carry through the war in Abyssinia, how it has been able to send 40,000 or 100,000 volunteers to Spain. There were certainly in Italy before Fascism many thousand peasants who were quite advanced, and whom Fascism has subdued, disorganized, demoralized, humiliated and taken back to the level of the more backward *cafoni*—and it is a very great pity that nobody has written something legible and alive about Andria, Marinella and Colle Val d'Elsa. It is not my fault that foreigners and even Italians, believe Fontamara and Pietra Secca to be average Italian villages.

P. S. I am writing now a continuation of *Pane e Vino*, and I think you will like it better than the first volume.*[47]

How right Silone was in thinking that Salvemini would greatly prefer his second book, *Bread and Wine*, is shown in the following letter—not addressed to Silone, but to his editor at Harper's, Mr Aswell.

7 December 1936
321 West 24th Street
New York

Dear Mr. Aswell,

I am deeply indebted to you for giving me the opportunity of reading in galley Silone's new novel, *Bread and Wine*. I have read, or rather devoured, it with increasing interest and delight.

There is between *Fontamara* and *Bread and Wine* a tremendous progress. Silone's genius is rapidly maturing. *Fontamara* was no doubt a fine piece of work. Several parts attained a high pitch of artistic power. Its direct, virile and economical style left nothing to be desired in the Italian text and the English translation was a masterpiece of skill, although like all translations it could not render the entire strength and flavour of the original. But *Fontamara* contained too much 'propaganda.' Its peasants were at times too stupid or insufficiently human. Silone was looking at

_____

*By kind permission of Darina Silone.

them from above, as befits a Communist by whom the peasantry needs to be rescued from its degradation by Marxist industrial workers, the chosen people of the new era.

Bread and Wine is much less tainted with propaganda. It is, in almost all its pages, a distinguished work of art, that is to say, a true and great work of art. The characters of *Bread and Wine* are human beings who live on their own account because they have their own peculiar reasons to exist. They have seized upon the imagination of the author, who follows them oblivious of all else. No doubt, here and there, he does take advantage of their thoughts and actions to unfold his theories. But these theories have now become less dogmatic, more realistic, more human than those of *Fontamara*, and therefore creep into the novel with greater discretion. Only in a few spots is artistic emotion disturbed by the interference of political propaganda.

I, too, come from Southern Italy. I have known a few priests like Don Benedetto and, as one would expect, many more like Don Cipriano. I have known families as vulgar as that of Don Pasquale Colamartini, from which sprang marvellous women like Cristina, flowers upon a dung heap. I have known men who have made a sacrifice of their own ideas, like Don Zobaide, and men who have heroically stood up against the tide, like Paolo Spina. To each of the men and women who live in *Bread and Wine* I might give a name.

For people who have never experienced what life has become in countries like Italy and Germany today, Silone's picture may sometimes seem overdrawn.

I myself, fifteen years ago, would not have dreamed that the conditions described by Silone might develop in my country. It requires a great effort of imagination to realize that men like Pietro Spina do exist, that newcomers swell their ranks every day, that out of prisons and penal islands, other men are working underground and facing martyrdom.

Novels like *Bread and Wine* are more historical than history. History only gives crude reality. Works of art give more than crude reality. They give the spirit of reality.

Very truly yours, Gaetano Salvemini[48]

I am not sure that I agreed with Salvemini about the superiority of *Bread and Wine* to Silone's first novel, *Fontamara*, but how seriously Silone took Salvemini's criticism is shown by the differences between the first edition of *Fontamara*, published in German in Zürich in 1933, and the revised edition, published by Mondadori in Italy in 1952. The first edition, which brought fame to Silone in every country but his own, was at once translated into English, and subsequently into twenty-seven other languages, and was also published in Braille.

The later version is certainly more finished and more measured than the first version. Silone has transferred into his preface many of his early descriptions of the village of Fontamara, of which he says that he has given this name to 'an ancient and obscure home of poor peasants, north of the dried up lake of Fucino.' It was his own village, Pescina de'Marsi. He adds a few details that were lacking in the earlier book—for instance, that most of the houses had only a single opening, which served as a door, window and chimney:

> Inside, generally without flooring, men and animals lived together ... The higher part of Fontamara is dominated by the church with its bell-tower ... If one looks at it from a distance, the village seems like a

flock of dark sheep, with the bell-tower as its shepherd.[49]

The relation between the land and the peasants in our region, and perhaps also elsewhere, is a hard and serious one, as between husband and wife. It is a kind of sacrament. It is not enough to buy a piece of land, for it to be yours. It will become yours in the course of years, with hard work, sweat, tears, sighs. If you have some land, on stormy nights you cannot sleep for you do not know what is happening to it, and in the morning you hurry there to see . . . Even when it is sold, it keeps for a long time the name of its old owner.[50]

The so-called princes Torlonia, who in dialect were called *Torlognes*, were men who, while possessing many thousand of hectares, even for fun, had never touched the earth. 'They had, however, speculated on the war, later on the peace, then on the state monopoly of salt, then on the turmoils of '48, the war of '59, the Bourbon Kingdom of Naples, later on the Royal Family of Savoy, the Democracy and the Dictatorship. Thus, without even taking off their gloves, they had made millions.'[51]

Silone then gave his reader two warnings. First, he admitted that his picture was very unlike that of Southern Italy which is often found in literature for tourists. There:

The peasants go to work singing with joy, dressed in traditional costumes, while in the woods the nightingales are trilling. Unfortunately, in Fontamara these wonders have never taken place. Its inhabitants dress like the poor of every country, and there is no wood in Fontamara, the mountain is arid and barren. The birds are few and timid, owing to the pitiless shooting. There are no nightingales, there is not even a word for them in the local dialect. The peasants do not sing, either in chorus or alone . . . Instead of singing they often swear . . . The only person in my youth who sang rather often was a cobbler. He often sang a song which dated from our first war in Africa, and went like this:

Non ti fidar della gente nera
O Baldissera.*

Finally he remarked that he had often asked himself in what language he should tell his story:

Let no-one think that the inhabitants of Fontamara spoke Italian. The Italian language is one learnt by us at school, like Latin, French or Esperanto . . . [It] cannot but deform the *cafone's* speech, make it look like a translation. But since I have no other means of making myself understood (and to express myself is now an absolute necessity) I have tried to translate into the language I have learnt what I want everyone to know: the truth about Fontamara.[52]

He put his tale into the mouths of three cafoni of Fontamara who visited him in Rome when he was feeling a great nostalgia for the Abruzzi, and who told him their story. He identified himself with them, but more detachedly than in the first version and with a certain irony. Yet once again his unchanging solidarity with the poor and oppressed was allowed to appear in the book's last words, the same as in the first edition: '*Che fare?*' 'After so much suffering and despair, what is to be done?'[53]

⟨⟩

It is not possible to separate Silone's position as a political rebel and as a writer: both spring from the same patient,

*'Do not trust the blacks
O Baldissera.'

persistent preoccupation with the condition of human suffering. He is a moralist who began to write novels because, in exile, that was his only way of bearing witness to what he had seen. The controversial echoes that his work has awakened have sometimes obscured, at least until recently, a full realisation of his gifts as a writer, yet they cannot and should not be separated. He himself compared his style to the weaver's craft he practised as a boy: 'the old art of placing one thread after another, one colour after another, tidily, persistently, clearly.' He is weaving a pattern; and the pattern, whether in his novels, his political essays, or his recent recollections, is always the same: it has always been concerned with men's suffering, and with their need for brotherhood and freedom.

Silone has defined his own attitude most clearly in 'The Choice of One's Comrades.' In this remarkable essay he speaks of the horror awakened in him by the number of writers who had committed suicide in the preceding ten years:

> Under the most diverse régimes, in Russia, in America and in Europe (among them Esenin, Mayakovsky, Ernst Toller, Kurt Tucholsky, Stefan Zweig, Klaus Mann, Drieux la Rochelle, F. O. Matthiesen, Cesare Pavese and many others). To mention them all together, what a crowd of terrifying shades! . . .
>
> Apart from the external circumstances invoked at the time to explain the desperate end of each one of these men of talent (persecution, exile, loneliness, poverty, illness, abnormality) it is enough to know what they themselves wrote before dying or confided to friends, to find, in final analysis, an identical confession of anguish and despair, about the painful effort of living and its uselessness.
>
> Nietzsche was the first to define this decadence,

calling it nihilism and giving to this word a sense that has remained with it, different to that given it by Turgenev in his celebrated novel . . .

In its most common moral aspect, nihilism is the identification of what is good, what is right, what is true, with one's own advantage. It is the intimate conviction that basically there is nothing real behind all faith and doctrine and that therefore only success is of any importance. It is sacrificing oneself for a cause in which one does not believe, while pretending to believe in it . . .

From the higher classes nihilism has spread over the whole social surface. The nihilist cult of power and success has become universal. It is nihilist to identify history with the victorious, the ignoble cowardice that led so many intellectuals towards Communism or towards MacCarthy . . . The dead, the weak, then, are always in the wrong? Was Mazzini wrong? Was Trotsky in the wrong only because he was defeated? Gobetti, Matteotti, were mistaken? And Gramsci only began to be right after the Spring of 1945? How monotonous is human stupidity! . . . Each group or institution cries out in defense of an ideal, but on the way identifies itself with it, placing above all ideals its own interests. 'Whoever harms the party is against History.'

Fascism in its various forms meant the taking over of power by nihilism . . . Fascism, in short, had the illusion of curing the Italians of their scepticism by means of orthopedic measures . . . Thus a public life was established which expressed heroic sentiments without profound roots in men's consciences, and out of it came a noisy and gesticulating expression of passion, which was ambiguous or fictitious or superficial.[54]

Silone proceeds to describe instances of writers who, starting out as nihilists, gradually came to take on a more humane attitude, giving a meaning to life: Ernst Jünger, Albert Camus, André Malraux.

He looked back once again, too, on the path that he himself had followed in his youth, which he believed to be that of many others, too. And finally he drew the attention of his readers to what he called 'the terrible letter' which Simone Weil wrote to Georges Bernanos in 1938, after reading his book about the Spanish Civil War, *Les grands cimetières sous la lune.*

Bernanos, although a Catholic and a Monarchist, had been appalled by the fascist executions in Majorca—a revulsion very similar to that which Simone Weil, too, had felt against what she had seen in Spain.

> I have never seen [wrote Simone Weil], among the Frenchmen who have come either to fight or to look on, a single one who expressed even in private, repulsion, disgust or disapproval for the blood shed in vain. Yes, it is true that fear played some part in the butchery, but where I was, it did not seem to play the large part you assigned to it. Men who seemed to be brave . . . would relate with cheery fraternal chuckles how many priests they had killed, or how many 'Fascists'—the latter being a very elastic term. My own feeling was that when a certain class of people has been placed by the spiritual and temporal authorities outside the ranks of those whose life has value, then nothing comes more naturally to men than to kill. As soon as men know that they can kill without punishment or blame, they kill, or at least they encourage the killer with approving smiles . . . In this there is an impulse, an intoxication which it is impossible to re-

sist, without a strength of character that I can only consider exceptional, since I have found it in no-one . . . The very purpose of the fight is soon lost in such an atmosphere. For the purpose can only be defined in terms of the public good, of human welfare—and men have become valueless . . . [And the letter ended] One goes as a volunteer believing in self-sacrifice, and one falls into a war of mercenaries, with much cruelty besides.[55]

Silone comments: 'In this universal moral shipwreck, to what flotsam can one cling in order not to sink?' Among Simone Weil's letters there is the following indirect reply: 'One must always be ready to change sides, like justice, who flees from the field of the victorious.'[56]

Silone goes on to say that in order to know what a man is like, it is enough to look at him. 'The expression of Cain is unmistakeable . . . This, then, is the central problem of existence, the chief characteristic of our responsibility, as men of today . . . Our number is an ever-increasing legion, that of the refugees from the International. They are really very many, outside any party or church, who secretly bear within them these burning stigmata.'[57]

Yet Silone himself did not return to Orthodox Catholicism, though he agreed that the Church of the Second Council was a very different one from that of his old school days. He was fond of quoting another passage of Simone Weil's:

I cannot but ask myself whether, at this time when so great a part of humanity is submerged by materialism, God does not want to have men and women who have given themselves to Him and to Christ and who yet have remained outside the Church . . .

At all events, when I take into positive considera-

tion, as something which could take place in the near
future, the act by which I would enter the Church, no
thought pains me more deeply than that of being
parted from the immense and unhappy mass of un-
believers. I feel the essential need, I might even say
the vocation, to pass among men and different human
settings mingling with them, taking on their same
colour, in so far at least as conscience allows it, disap-
pearing among them, in order that they may reveal
themselves as they are and without any disguise for
me.[58]

One is reminded of Péguy's phrase: 'What would He say,
if one of us came to Him, without all the rest?'

It was only after leaving the Communist Party that Silone felt able to form true friendships with other men again.
'The real human solitude is the one produced by falsehood,
envy and selfishness . . . To save ourselves from the wolves,
some of us have been obliged to overcome our petit-bour-
geois, nineteenth century limitations, and to rediscover our
Early Christian affinities.'[59]

On his return to Italy after the war, Silone became a Deputy for his region and a member of the Parliament which
compiled the new Italian Constitution. He had said in 1949
that they hoped to be able to renew the old parties from
within and to prevent their division into two camps, one on
the side of the United States and one of Russia. 'Our hopes
have failed.'

He was probably never meant, by temperament, to be a
professional politician, and was at one time, like Salvemini,
a very unpopular one, since his fellow-citizens found it impossible to believe that, if he really chose to exert his influence as a member of parliament, he would not be able to
achieve as much as his fascist predecessor by writing 'lettere di raccomandazione.' He wrote very scornfully about

the letters he received from his parish priest who, in return for some eggs, a basket of fruit, or a small cheese, asked him to find a soft job as a porter or doorman, for young peasants tired of farming. 'In my mind I can hear them saying the misleading phrase, "If he wants to, he can do it."' [60]

The tradition of using this kind of influence goes back very far into Italian politics—only Silone did not care to make use of it. On the other hand, he spent a great deal of his failing strength and breath (he suffered from asthma) in coaching young country students who were preparing their school theses—for this he did gladly, feeling that he was giving them something that he genuinely knew about.

For many years Silone was undervalued in Italy both as a thinker and writer. All his first books necessarily appeared abroad in translation[61] and had already earned for him there a great reputation. 'Silone's name,' wrote Guido Piovene, 'has often been mentioned to me during my travels in places where I least expected it. For instance, I remember, in the Reserve of the Navajo Indians—a sterile and splendid region of red and black canyons, of pastureland and shepherds, lost in Arizona—the official who went with us, as soon as he knew that I was an Italian, at once asked, "Do you know Silone? What is he doing?"' Piovene went on to say it was then that he first realized how much celebrity and moral prestige Silone enjoyed abroad: 'An idealized image has been formed of him, to prove that there was still a real democracy in Italy, too . . .'[62]

Silone himself was well aware of the discrepancy between his reputation abroad and the indifference shown to his work in Italy, especially by intellectuals.

> Writing has not been and never could be, for me, a serene aesthetic pleasure, but the painful continuation

of a struggle, after having separated myself from very dear companions . . . The difficulty I sometimes find in expressing myself does not come from a lack of knowledge of the rules of 'fine writing,' but from an awareness that finds it difficult to heal certain hidden wounds, perhaps unhealable.[63] *Non ci si pensa quanto sangue costa.**

When he first wrote *Fontamara*, according to himself, even his command of his own language was very rough. He had always spoken dialect at home and had only learned Italian, like Latin and French, at school 'like the peasants of my region', he wrote, 'who have learned in the city to wear shoes, a collar and a tie.' It was only, as we have said, after the publication in 1963 of his *Emergency Exit*, that he won the sympathy of Italians of almost every class.

In this change there was also, I think, an element of political opportunism: to admire his work became not only the fashion, but almost a certificate of integrity. But there was also a very genuine admiration for a man who had covered such controversial ground, and yet laid the blame on no one but himself. 'Here,' a recent reviewer justly remarked, 'there is only one man on trial, Silone. And only one judge, his own conscience.'

In a review written by his friend, the critic Geno Pampaloni, on the day after his death, Pampaloni traces the course of Silone's long but always consistent struggle towards justice and truth. He had read Silone's first two novels—*Fontamara* and *Wine and Bread*—during World War II, when his regiment (fighting with the Allies) was marching from the Abruzzi to the Adriatic coast. 'His books, in the regiment, passed from hand to hand, like a secret taste

*'One does not think how great the cost in blood,' Dante, *Paradiso* XXIX, 91. Silone has used this quotation as his heading to *Emergency Exit*.

of the freedom that seemed to be awaiting us beyond the War and the Apennines, as a first example of a "new world" . . . and even now, when I have taken up these novels . . . to speak about them critically, I cannot free myself from this impression, and from the romantic impression that those novels by an unknown exile brought with them.'[64] Pampaloni confirmed, however, that—with the exception of Piovene, Cecchi and himself—the Italian literary world had not recognised the value of Silone's work, considering him as merely a writer of political propaganda. 'This gave rise to what was called *il caso Silone*. He was a writer who caused us to be regarded with envy abroad, but was considered by us with superciliousness and mistrust.'

He described, too, the controversy which arose when *Emergency Exit* was first presented in 1965 for the Premio Viareggio because the majority of the judges did not feel inclined to give an award to a book in which Palmiro Togliatti appeared in a bad light. Such a scandal followed that it aroused the interest of the general public.

Pampaloni considers *Emergency Exit* 'the best of Silone's books' and believes it to be: 'One of the most important documents of political literature after the War. Its specific theme is the renouncement by Silone of the Party in which he has played a very important part, as soon as he became aware of Stalin's methods. But the true theme is the incurable struggle between freedom and deceit . . . He has defended religiously the honour of heresy. Our debt to him is incalculable. Our gratitude is a land-mark in our life.'[65]

I don't think Silone attached any undue value to his sudden popularity. His yardstick was a different one, and he remained as he started out, a solitary and questioning man, who had suffered a double ideological bankruptcy. Yet the strongest impression when one talked to him was not one of pessimism. Beneath the mistrust which life had taught him of political frameworks and clichés, of human hypocrisy, cruelty and opportunism, there remained a stubborn, un-quenchable strain of hope. To the more general question whether he still had faith in mankind, he answered: 'I feel a certain confidence. I feel it in the men who accept the inevitable suffering of existence and find some certainties within it. And in the same way I believe that out of the forced labour camps and the prisons of the totalitarian countries, some may yet come forth, who will cause the blind to see.'[66]

Silone's next public appearance in Italy was at a meeting held in his honour by the Jesuit Fathers of San Fedele in Milan in 1968, at which many of his friends and other literary critics were present, to celebrate the publication of *L' Avventura di Un Povero Cristiano* (*The Story of a Humble Christian*).

This was a book in two parts: a long Preface, entitled 'What is Left,' which describes Silone's return to the Abruzzi, the course of his research and the reflections to which it gave rise, followed by the drama which tells the story of Pope Celestino V, the humble Franciscan hermit known to history, owing to Dante's misleading phrase, as the Pope of the 'great refusal.'* It is a tale of total and deliberate renouncement—a tale that goes back very far. Already in the time of the Apostles, according to Silone, when the Abruzzi were still a Roman province called Valeria and long before the days of St. Benedict, the Gospel had arrived there, but the beginning was then temporarily crushed by the violence of the invading Lombards. 'But the ascetic flame of Christianity in the Abruzzi was not put out in the dark time that ensued, it became for many Christians the most acces-

---

*'Moved by cowardice, made the great refusal,' Dante, *Inferno*, III, v. 59.

sible form of salvation and of rising above a human condition that was often very hard and close to despair.'[67]

The next man to reawaken with his prophecies a new era of Christianity in the Abruzzi was, in 1202, Gioacchino da Fiore. After a youth spent in the East following the austere rule of the Basilians, he was inspired by a vision to return to Italy in the high upland of the Calabrian Sila, to restore the ideals and manner of life of primitive monastic Christianity. It was then that many groups of hermitages were founded, like those of the 'Desert Fathers,' in the mountains of the Abruzzi. 'While avoiding open heresy, this stream of ascetic life remained out of the official life of the Church . . . Receiving inspirations similar to those of the Benedictine, Joachimite and Franciscan spirituals . . . Some hermits following the strictest Benedictine rule, the *Celestini*, were founded into a congregation on the Maiella in 1204 by Pietro Angelerio, the future Pope Celestino V . . .'[68]

Later on, arose the 'poor hermits of Celestino' (subsequently suppressed), who were joined by some of the 'Franciscan spirituals.' They followed the strictest rule of Franciscan poverty, and were also expecting the realisation of the forecasts of the Calabrian Abbot Gioacchino da Fiora, 'granted the gift of prophesy.* The prophesy that influenced them most was the one predicting the advent of an 'angelic Pope,' and it seemed about to be realised in 1292, when Pietro da Morone was elected by the College of Cardinals and, against his own wishes, but hoping to bring back peace to the Church, left his humble hermit's cave. Mounting on his little grey donkey, he set forth—escorted by the King of Anjou and his son, Charles Martel—for his coronation in the Church of Collemaggio. He was then seventy-seven, having been born in 1215.

A contemporary chronicler has described Celestino as

---

*'Di spirito profetico dotato,' Dante, *Paradiso*, XII, v. 141.

'tall in stature, strong in body, cheerful and most vivacious in appearance, gentle and attractive in his speech.'[69] 'One cannot understand certain aspects of the Abruzzi,' Silone wrote, 'without understanding him.'[70]

After only five months of great spiritual conflict, during which the new Pope found himself involved in the bitter feud between the Orsini, Colonna and Caetani Cardinals, he declared his renunciation of the Pontificate, fled back to his hermit's cell, was captured and, it is said, later on paid for his decision with his life.[71,72]

'We must not try to understand,' said one of the humble Fraticelli. 'The destiny of certain Saints, in their lifetime, is among the most obscure mysteries of the Church.'[73]

It was not Cardinal Caetani's cruel whispers at night, through a speaking-tube installed secretly behind the Pope's bed, telling him to renounce a power for which he was not fit,[74] but his own inner turmoil, that determined Pope Celestino's decision. He refused to sign documents until he had ascertained the underlying facts, and then became unwilling to do so. He discovered, in talking to Cardinal Caetani, how scanty his knowledge of theology was: he longed for the peace of his hermit's cave. He rebelled against the constant strife between the Cardinals, and their display of luxury and power.

> If I began to prefer a horse to a donkey, fine silk garments instead of rough cloth, and a richly appointed table, I should begin to think and feel like those who ride on horses, live in great halls and hold banquets . . . Even in my new state of life, I do not intend to separate myself from the way of life of the poor to whom I belong.[75]

'I thought,' Celestino said to the Little Brothers who accompany him throughout this drama like a Greek chorus, 'that I might be able to use the King for a good purpose.'* But, my dear sons, do not forget it, there is no such thing as a good purpose, there is just plain goodness . . . There is nothing more ridiculous than a simpleton who tries to be clever . . .

'Now I am consumed by remorse and shame for all that I tried to do in the name of good intentions. To make use of powers: what a pernicious illusion! This is power making use of us. Power is a difficult horse to guide; it goes where it wishes or rather, where it can go and where it is natural that it should go . . . The aspiration to rule, the obsession of power, at any level, is a form of madness. It devours the soul, it engulfs and falsifies it.'[76]

Silone has chosen to write this story in the form of a drama—reminiscent, indeed, of a medieval mystery play—in which each of the characters takes on a symbolic meaning. This does not make, in the conventional modern sense, a good play. There is not enough action or diversity in the dialogue, except in the conversations between Cardinal Caetani, the implacable defender of the Church's power, and Celestino himself, the man who dreamed of 'the restoration of an ascetic church . . . a pastoral and apostolic community of the faithful, awaiting the advent of the Kingdom of God.'

What interested Silone most in the story of Pope Celestino was 'the painful wound to Christianity' caused by the disappointment that the Reign of God which had been announced by Christ had not yet come.

> If this Utopia has not yet died out . . . it is because it corresponds to a need deeply rooted in mankind. There is in the human conscience an unrest which no reform and no prosperity can soothe. The history of

*'A fin di bene.'

this Utopia is therefore the history of a hope that is always disappointed, but a tenacious hope . . .[77] When and how will the Reign be established? . . . When and how will charity take the place of the law? No one can know . . . And in our daily prayers the invocation remains: 'Thy Kingdom come.'[78]

The monastic life in the Abruzzi did not prevent the survival of many pagan myths and customs so deeply rooted that some of them still survived in Silone's time. For instance, the popular legends, especially in the mountain villages, contain strange identifications with Biblical events and characters, in which Herod and Pilate, Pilate's maid and other characters in the story are declared to be of Abruzzese origin. And among the local miracle plays there is a dramatic dialogue between the body and the soul, entitled *Verbum Caro*, 'The tale of the conflict that has existed in all times and places between the religious spirit and the overbearing instinctive life. But in the Abruzzi this conflict has taken on an extreme form. To be a true Christian meant to escape entirely from the world.'[79]

When Silone arrived at the meeting in his honour that was being held by the Jesuit fathers at San Fedele he had an annoying surprise. He had believed that his invitation required only his presence, but found that an announcement had been made that, after the speeches of his friends and admirers, he would reply.

He did speak, but no-one could accuse him of attempting to ingratiate himself with his audience. After thanking the previous speakers for all that they had said about his work, he added somewhat acidly that when he realised that he was expected to reply he had said to his friends, 'These Jesuits are like the Communists. Offer them your finger and they will take the whole arm.'

This remark—published by Father Scurani who was present—was hardly conciliatory, but is characteristic of one aspect of Silone. He went on to say that though he did not like speaking in public, he would have been equally prepared to do so at a Communist meeting, 'If they would guarantee me the same freedom of speech that I enjoy here tonight.'

> Someone said to me 'You began with Fontamara and now you have reached the Jesuits of San Fedele.' That is not accurate. The Jesuits were at the beginning of my long journey. The small amount I know of Latin and Greek was learnt from them and other religious orders. My work . . . is the story of my journey . . . I will not comment [he added about favourable remarks of Piovene, Pampaloni, Fabbri and Father Scurani] for I know myself from within, and what I see there is much more painful and sad than the critics, judging from my books, can imagine.

Silone then said that he would speak about the link between his books and the men of his region. Some Abruzzesi felt that he had given a false picture of their landscape—to them the most beautiful in God's creation—while he had described it as arid and austere. But that landscape was a necessary background.

> It would honestly be impossible for me to place Pietro Spina in an idyllic and attractive setting . . . I should like to tell you about an incident which helped me to explain it to myself. In Palestine in December 1961 I had a strange experience. I was riding through the bare waste lands that lead to Jericho and before me

there was a woman with a black shawl over her head, riding on a little grey donkey. My wife, who saw that I was much moved, said 'This is the landscape and these are the people of your Marsica'—and it was true. Then suddenly, it was plain to me that I had carried within me for years this landscape which I was seeing for the first time, the spiritual landscape in which Pietro Spina and the others moved. So the Abruzzesi must not be sad if my books lack the sweet shores, the mountain lakes, the rocky heights of which they are so proud! . . . In its own way, my landscape, too, is beautiful.[80]

Those present that day at San Fedele realised that the true character of the Marsica was not to be found in the creation of works of art or churches, but in the structure of its mountains, and the effect that this produced on the inner life of its inhabitants.

Silone had already written, twenty years earlier:

The mountains are the most over-bearing characters of the life of the Abruzzi. Life there still takes on a severe, humble, hard, bare aspect . . . and the essential facts of human existence (to be born, to live, to suffer and to die), constitute almost 'all that happens.' In the severe frame of the mountains and in the difficult conditions of life produced by them, the spiritual portrait of the Abruzzi has been shaped by Christianity. It is only necessary to look at a map of the great uplands of the Maiella to realize the isolation and hard conditions of life of the men who live there. But to understand the life produced by such conditions of hardship and poverty, it is necessary to get to know not only the outer structure of the Abruzzi, but its inner life . . . After having understood its outer structure, which is its body, one must discover the inner life which has been shaped by Christendom—the life of Saints and working men.[81]

It is interesting, after all this, to see what Father Domenico Grasso, S. J., wrote about *The Adventure of a Humble Christian* in the most important Catholic review, *Civiltà Cattolica.* He called the book, 'one of the works of greatest value that has appeared in Italy for the last twenty years.'

What interests this Abruzzese writer is not so much the historical figure of Pope Celestino, as his universal significance. In Pietro Angelerio a problem takes shape which belongs to the whole human race, that of the relation between spirit and institution, between authority and freedom . . .

The greatness of Pope Celestino lies in this: to have understood that, not being able to serve the institution of which he was the head, all he could do was to put it into more capable hands . . . We might say that the whole history of the Church has been a tension between Christian freedom and the institution which, having originated to guarantee and develop it, may run a risk of suffocation.

Christian reality has a double dimension. The Reign of God as preached by Jesus Christ holds, as well as a heavenly phase, an earthly one . . . It is a fact that every Christian tends to undervalue in his spiritual life one element rather than another. Therefore all experiences are possible in the Church, that of the Stylites living at the top of pillars, and that of Thomas More, Chancellor of the King of England . . . Unfortunately, the Stylites are inclined to condemn the Chancellors of the Kings of England, and the Chancellors, to consider the Stylites mad.[82]

Though I have written about Silone's earlier novels, I have not referred to his later ones. Among them, two stand out as particularly significant: *Una Manciata di more* (*A Handful of Blackberries*) and *Il Segreto di Luca* (*The Secret of Luca*).

The first of these, Silone told me, was a novel for which he had a special affection—perhaps because it was the first to be published directly in Italy, and not in Zürich or Paris. Certainly it is a book with an autobiographical vein. Its protagonist, Rocco de Donati, is closely akin to Pietro Spina—and to Ignazio Silone. His Don Nicola says: 'Rocco was born with an obvious vocation for the religious life . . . He did not follow it owing to one of those mysteries that only God can explain or judge. But he asked of secular life what only a convent could have given him. That is why he is in a tragic and absurd situation.'[83]

Rocco had abandoned conventional Christianity to become a better Christian, and was on the point of defecting from the Communist Party, so as not to betray his socialist ideal of human brotherhood. 'It may happen one night,' said his friend Lazzaro, 'that when you go to sleep, the wall is there, grey and insurmountable . . . You don't know how to go forward, and refuse to go back. In the morning you wake up and find yourself outside the wall.'[84]

But Silone's pessimism still shows through: 'The changes that had occurred during the war brought surprises and illusions even to this remote valley; but in the end it rained and snowed as in other years, and the poor remained poor.'[85]

The Secret of Luca—according to many critics and in Silone's own opinion—is his best novel, and is in some ways different from his other books: A merchant is killed one night in the countryside, and a sum of money is stolen from him. Luca, a *cafone* who has spent the night away from home, is accused of the crime, tried, and given a life sentence—since he will offer no explanation. Forty years later another man, on his deathbed, confesses his guilt, and Luca returns home. Andrea, a young socialist who, as a child, had written to Luca in prison on behalf of his mother, is determined to find out the truth about the man whom the whole village knows to be innocent, but who has spent his whole life in jail. The villagers, however, do not like Luca: they feel him to be a stranger, and besides, they feel guilty of having been responsible for his sentence by their silence—the *omerta** of the South, which still exists today. It was Luca himself who had compelled them to keep silent—even the parish priest, even his own mother—although they all knew where he really was that night. Andrea compels them, one by one, to break their silence, and is helped by the old parish priest. The second part of the book is given up to the story, told with great restraint and all the more moving, of Luca's secret love affair, which accounts for his silence. He prefers life imprisonment to betraying the person with whom he was that night.[86]

Here, as Geno Pampaloni has remarked, Silone has put aside his political opinions, to reveal more freely the strength of a man's fidelity towards another person and to his own word. It is a book that has kept the flavour of popular country stories, with a background of melodrama: 'The prison, the convent, the old deserted villa, the evening by the fireside where the fiancé must repeat his promise in the presence of his friends. I am prepared to say that Silone has courageously faced the dangers of such a setting and that his story has gained simplicity and clearness from it.'[87]

The author has given his characters free rein; he does no moralising. But there are things he does not say, which permeate this work, like all his others: his love of justice and of truth.

---

*'A conspiracy of silence,' as practiced in Southern Italy, particularly by the Mafia.

Many of Silone's later articles appeared for some years in *Tempo Presente*, a magazine which he edited jointly with Nicola Chiaromonte. One of them, 'The Children of the Party,' is an account of a book which had recently appeared in Italy by one of the children (already grown up) whose communist fathers had died or been imprisoned in other countries on account of their political faith—Spaniards, Austrians, Poles, Hungarians, Germans, Greeks, etc.—before or during World War II, and who were then taken off in trainloads to Russia and brought up in communist institutions there; they knew, until they grew up, no father but Stalin. Silone remarks that, in a sense, their fate was not dissimilar to that of orphans brought up in religious institutions, but with one great difference. When, in Russia, the Father became angry, the repercussions of his anger penetrated even within the school walls. 'The Father,' the wretched children said in whispers, 'has gone mad.' And an even more complex crisis awaited those children whose real father was released from prison after many years; they then discovered that the Party to whom he had given up his whole life and his children, had shown him little gratitude.[88]

At that time—the period of the 'thaw'—Silone was much concerned about the problems of coexistence with Russia.

It is not necessary to offer the Russians our own pattern of society as a model, especially as it does not awaken unmitigated enthusiasm even in all of us, but it is desirable that we should remain constantly aware of the changing elements in that country—just as a countryman standing on the edge of a landslide would watch each crack in the shifting soil. In the 'difficult dialogue' with the Communist world which many intellectuals and left-wing Catholics are now attempting, we should not consider 'the other' as a remote symbol or potential instrument, but rather as 'a neighbour,' with whom a mutual and sympathetic relationship (in spite of all difficulties) can be established.

'However unforeseen,' he added, 'the future developments in Russia may still be, it is now plain that they are not going to take the paranoid form foreseen by George Orwell in *1984*.' 'The face of Russia,' he wrote, 'is no longer that of Medusa: it is a human face.'[89]

⌒

It was during his last years in Italy, before moving to the clinic in Switzerland in which he died, that I began to see Silone more frequently.

I had always admired his work and purpose and felt very grateful when, in 1968, after the translation into Italian of my unpretentious war-diary *War in Val d'Orcia*, he spontaneously offered to come to our house in Tuscany, La Foce, where all the events described had taken place, to talk about the book for a television programme. On that occasion, I got into touch with one of the leaders of our local Resistance, Dario Bianchi, who had been living with his brother and his men in one of our farmhouses in the hills, Pietraporciana—beside a gushing spring and surrounded by woods, which formed an ideal hiding place. (At one moment, when the fascist paper of Siena, *La Republica Fascista*, had written a venomous article asking for my arrest, the partisans invited me to join them there.) After Dario's capture by the fascists, he was tortured to find out whether my husband and I had indeed hidden ammunition and arms for the Resistance in the little castle near by, and had helped the escape of the British prisoners of war who had come there to work on the land. Dario answered Silone's questions very simply and convincingly, and so did Vera Berrettini, the directress of the children's home which we opened after the bombing of Turin and Genoa, for twenty refugee children who had lost their homes, and were living in railway tunnels. They stayed with us until we were able to return them to their parents, safe and sound after the liberation. Silone, in spite of the breathlessness caused by the high altitude of La Foce, spoke at some length and with great humanity. But I only began to see him often after an act of generosity which perhaps only another writer can fully appreciate.

We had both been dining with a mutual friend and afterwards, in a quiet moment, I had confided to him that I was distressed by not having found any suitable material for my next book. I would prefer to write, I said, about a medieval figure with a spiritual and moral significance, but was baffled by the fact that, except St Francis, so few medieval figures had left us echoes of their own voice. We only had the records of bare facts, or the comments of chronicles or of later historians. 'I will send you something tomorrow to look at,' was Silone's reply, and we rejoined the rest of the party.

Next morning a great pile of manuscripts arrived for me: the material for his *The Story of a Humble Christian*. 'Use it, if you want to,' he wrote, 'if not, return it to me.' For days I pored over it with fascinated interest, but realised almost at once that I must give it back to Silone. Only he, with his intimate knowledge of the whole background of the Abruzzi, and his preoccupation with the struggle between faith and power, could write this book. But my gratitude to him remained, and set a seal upon our friendship.

After this, he would come often to spend a couple of hours with me—talking freely, as he would never do in the company of strangers. Once, when he had offered to bring to me one of the Little Sisters of Charles de Foucauld, whom he greatly admired, I confessed to feeling uncomfortable about receiving her in my Roman house, with its unmistakeable atmosphere of luxury. 'Could we not meet on neutral ground?' 'No-one,' he replied, 'is satisfied with his own state in life.'

We hardly ever spoke about politics, but one day, when I was thinking of writing a Life of Mussolini, I asked him his personal opinion of Mussolini's character and policy. 'The key,' he replied, 'is inconsistency, both of character and ideas, combined with an extraordinary intuitive capacity for improvisation. In every crisis of his career, he swung over completely from his previous attitude, and always successfully. The only constant was his desire for power ... You should always bear in mind,' he added, 'the *suddenness* of Mussolini's emergence as a leader: the result of one successful political speech at a Congress of the Socialist Party. He sprang into a sudden prominence, for which he was completely unprepared.'

I asked him whether he considered the theory of fascism to be a serious political doctrine, or one which had been patched up later on. 'The latter, undoubtedly. Mussolini had very few and very confused ideas. Even in his early Socialist days, he did not adhere to orthodox Socialist doctrines ... You must resist the temptation of creating a consistent figure. It would always be a falsification.'

With regard to Nazism, Silone said: 'The great difference between Nazism and Fascism was this, that whereas Nazism absorbed *every* aspect of German life and thought, in Italy two other institutions went on existing side by side with the Fascist Party: the Church and the Family. This was true to such an extent that the Germans used to say that Fascism in Italy was not a totalitarian régime at all. This was a matter of national temperament—which Mussolini himself understood.'

If we compare what Silone said that day with what he wrote in his *School for Dictators* (published in Zürich in

German in 1938, but in Italy only twenty-four years later) we find that it has no comments similar to those he made to me, but it contains some prophetic passages: 'The whole of humanity has entered on a crisis of its civilisation and we are probably only at the beginning of a long series of revolutions, counter-revolutions and disasters of every kind . . . The people may again become barbarians . . .'[90]

The title page bears the quotation *Quam parva sapientia regit mundum.**

Silone remarks, 'Mussolini founded the first *fascio*, but it was Fascism that afterwards created the *Duce*, seeing in him the image of the ideal self of millions of Italians. To attack him was like saying to a church-mouse: "Haven't you noticed, my good woman, that the statue of San Antonio before which you are kneeling has no artistic value and is made of papier-mâché?" The good woman would scratch your eyes out.'[91]

More often, however, when I saw Silone, the conversation would turn to religion or morals, or to recollections of his life as a child. Of this he spoke with much nostalgia, and also—though not unmixed with irritation or sadness—of his summers in the Abruzzi.

The day came, in 1976, when he was no longer well enough to come to my house, and reluctantly asked me to go to his instead—a very dreary flat in an anonymous apartment house in a modern part of Rome. It was a very hot summer's day and after I heard his slow footsteps approaching to open the door, I saw to my surprise that he was wearing his best suit, of thick black cloth, with a collar and a tie. Before he could speak, I asked him, 'If I had not come, what would you be wearing?' He admitted that it would have been cool pyjamas. I told him that I would wait until he

*'How little wisdom rules the world.'

had changed, but if he did not, I would go away again. He granted my request, and looked more comfortable. But his voice was very faint—he had just had an attack of asthma—and his breathing was difficult. I asked him how he spent his days now. Sometimes, he said, but rarely, an old friend would come to see him. But he still occasionally wrote an article for a paper, or helped some young student with his thesis. Did he have anyone to look after him? I asked (his wife was away at the time). He replied that a maid came every day, and left in the evening leaving his dinner, and he pointed to a table with an Indian tablecloth laid with a covered plate, a piece of bread, a bottle of water and a small one of wine. What would he do when I left? I asked. He smiled, 'Watch the news on the television, read a few papers, and go to bed.'

Sometimes in the mornings he would walk down the road to the dusk of the half-empty church at its end, and there resume the habit of his youth of meditation. 'The results are not always very clear, but it's a habit one cannot lose,' and he added, 'I still find that the best position is on one's knees.'

I realise that I have not attempted to describe his looks and manner, beyond saying that he was more like a Spaniard than an Italian. In his slow tread and measured speech, he was unmistakeably a countryman, with a countryman's reserve, and—having learned, when he came to a big city, to wear a dark suit—he never wore anything else. His figure was stocky; his expression, which a friend has described as 'both cordial and impenetrable,' was always sad in repose, but would light up in the presence of an old friend or of young people whom he liked. He would sometimes quote the phrase from Seneca which he had already set down in *Emergency Exit*. 'There is no art more difficult than that of living.' His voice—partly owing to his asthma—was always quiet and, in late years, faint. He would make no compromises for the sake of conventional usage. If the company bored or displeased him, he showed it by lapsing into total silence. But with his friends he could be very talkative, and would show a dry, ironic humour, which he kept only for them and for some of his later books.

What else? He was a faithful friend, but never made any demands—and, in his later years, had very few illusions. And he carried within him wounds which he knew to be unhealable.

In his last months, which he spent in a Swiss nursing home, Silone was trying to finish a novel of which, on the last day I saw him in Rome, he had already written a small part. Indeed Darina thought that it was only the desire to finish this book that later on, in Switzerland, kept him alive. It was, he said to me, the first book he had written about a woman, and its original title was to have been *La Testimonianza* (The Testimony), but this he changed later on to *La Speranza di Suor Severina* (Sister Severina's Hope). He only told me a small part of the story, that of a young nun, a teacher in a convent-school, who had happened to be present during a street riot in which a young workman called Renato was mercilessly beaten up by some angry policemen. Sister Severina was the only eyewitness and was called upon the next day by the Mother Superior to be instructed as to what form her testimony should take. It was a question of vital importance to the convent, at a moment when its standing as a scholastic institute was at stake, and the Mother Superior required the nun to sign an inaccurate statement which had already been drawn up, or else to hold her peace. Sister Severina refused to bear witness, and the Mother Superior having heard of her refusal made her kneel down at her feet and accused her of 'pride, arrogance and exhibitionism.'* In the end Sister Severina was obliged to leave the convent and was unable to find work in any other school, but what happened to her afterwards, Silone did not tell me—perhaps because it had not yet taken shape in his mind. I can only remember Severina's words when an old nun, Sister Gemma, asked her on her deathbed, whether she had still kept her faith: 'I hope, Sister Gemma, I hope—hope is still left to me.' These were her last words.

This is all I remember of what Silone told me that afternoon, but now the whole story has been published—partly in Silone's own words, partly in those which Darina used, during his illness, to bind together disconnected or incomplete passages.[92] It is, for anyone who is interested in Silone's work, a book—even if fragmentary—of intense interest. At the end of the story of Severina, Darina has added some pages. 'The History of a Manuscript,' which enable the reader to follow its whole difficult progress. Silone wrote it, Darina says, in three months, two at Fiuggi, before leaving Italy, and one in Geneva. He wanted desperately to finish it and fortunately did not realise in his nursing home that he was suffering from *agrafia*—a disease described in a medical dictionary consulted by Darina as 'an incapacity to express one's thoughts in writing, caused by a lesion of the cerebral cortex. The patient retains or recovers the capacity to form single letters or words, but—though he is not aware of this—their combination is meaningless.' 'In his last afternoon,' Darina wrote, 'he began to write in a great hurry, looking very happy. When, later on, I gathered up my courage and looked at those last pages, I found that he had recovered his own handwriting and that the words were

---

*This phrase is taken from the fuller version of the story, set down by Darina Silone.

all legible . . . It was almost possible to catch their meaning. Unfortunately, only *almost*.'[93]

The manner in which Darina has reconstructed these fragments from his notes, together with other earlier and more complete passages, shows a most remarkable patience and tenacity, as well as a knowledge of the workings of her husband's mind. For each chapter she has set down which passages were written by Silone himself, and which she was obliged to reconstruct. In two chapters (4 and 8) she even inserted some passages from the first Italian edition of Silone's *The Seed Beneath the Snow*. What is remarkable is that the whole of Darina's patchwork holds together. For Chapter 11 she invented—perhaps unnecessarily—a whole scene, but for the last one everything was to be found in Silone's notes, and the final sentence is exactly as he first wrote it at Fiuggi.

Under the title 'Ignazio Silone's last hours,' Darina has described his end.[94] It is very poignant. Five days before, during a walk in the nursing-home's big garden, he said that he felt like talking, and asked Darina about her health and about the payment of the hospital bills, and then tried to find out when the doctors were going to operate on him. This had indeed been envisaged some time before, and he felt very hopeful about it. 'It's odd, the surgeon's knife always alarmed me, but now I am not afraid. I want to get well.' Darina well knew that the operation had been rendered impossible by a spasm of his cerebral arteries in the preceding autumn, but since the doctor had not told him about it, she kept up the pretence. (He would feel nothing under the anaesthetic, would get rid of his pains, would be made much of in his convalescence.) 'I'm not afraid of dying,' he repeated, 'as long as I am conscious. It is the last moment of life, the most solemn, that I don't want to lose.'

It was then that his thoughts went back to his dead brother, Romolo, and he talked to Darina about him, more fully than he had ever done before. He told her that when he returned to Italy in 1944, he had not wanted to go back to the Abruzzi without bringing Romolo's ashes with him, but he was then told that his body had been buried in a 'common grave' in 1941. 'There was nothing left to recover.' He had thought of writing something about Romolo, but the memory was so painful to him that he went on putting it off. After he had finished *Celestino* he was not able to face writing another book. 'They told me it was arteriosclerosis of the brain, that I ought to resign myself but I had had five or six other books in mind.'[95] He made Darina promise to put together all his literary material, however fragmentary—a promise which she said it was unfortunately impossible to fulfill. Physically, Silone seemed much better; he slept well, his bronchitis—in a room filled with oxygen—no longer troubled him, his kidneys were working again. He was fond of his doctor. This was his last long talk. Darina did not believe that he had any presentiment.

On the following morning he was already working at seven o'clock and enjoyed the croissants for his breakfast. He was annoyed because his pedicure, followed by his physiotherapist, took up so much of his morning, and in the afternoon refused to take his siesta: he wanted to work on *Severina*. He wrote busily, happily, Darina writing letters beside him. When his supper came, he at first refused to take it until Darina's, too, was brought. But by then, something had happened. He pushed his table away, and, turning round, sat up very straight in his armchair. 'In a loud voice, very clearly, he said: "*Maintenant c'est fini. Tout est fini. Je meurs.*"* He put his hands to his temples and moaned four times. Then he fell back in his chair and closed his eyes. I called him desperately, but he did not answer. It was then

*'Now it's over—everything is over. I am dying.'

about 18:30 on August 18, and he passed into a deep coma. He only once opened his eyes, when the doctor called his name. At 4:15 on August 22, his heart ceased to beat. Remembering a promise made many years before, I said an "Our Father."'

Many years before (probably between 1963 and 1966) Silone had written a document entitled 'Et in hora mortis nostrae' which Darina found in his writing desk addressed to her, and with it an even earlier drawing, on the back of an old photograph of the church of San Berardo in Pescina (cut out of a French magazine), showing the place where he wished to be buried.

In the first document he stated that, though he hoped he was not 'wounding or disappointing anyone who loves me,' he wished to be buried 'without any religious ceremony, either at the moment of my death or afterwards. To return [to the Church] has not been possible, even after the modernizations of the recent Council . . . It seems to me that in the course of the centuries a theological and liturgical elaboration has been superimposed over the essential Christian truths, so as to make these unrecognisable. Official Christianity has become merely an ideology. Only by forcing myself, could I declare that I accept it; but I should not be in good faith.'[96]

The inscription beside the drawing said: 'I should like to be buried like this, at the foot of the old bell-tower of San Berardo at Pescina, with an iron cross leaning against the wall, and the view over the Fucino in the distance.'[97]

A few steps away from Silone's present tombstone there is an almond tree, from which it is possible to look over the older houses of Pescina and the empty spaces left, half a century ago, by the earthquake. Here Silone came one evening at twilight and looked down at the whole village life— 'a long row of carts coming back from the fields . . . a few women and children coming out of church . . . a man at the inn's door.' Only no sound came up to him, as the wind was blowing the other way. 'It was as if I were looking at an old silent film, rather worn out and dim.'

> In this narrow frame [he wrote] I used to know every alley, every house, every fountain, and which girls would come at a certain time to draw up water, and who would come out at certain moments from every door and window. For fifteen years this was the closed circuit of my adolescence, the world I have known and its barriers, the stage of my secret anguish . . .
>
> I try to understand. This reality which I am seeing new has been carried within me for many years, an integral part of myself . . . But now that I have it before me, it appears to me like a foreign world, going on living without me . . . with naturalness and indifference. It seems to me no different from an ant heap. It is thus, I think, that a dead man would watch the continuing process of human life . . . if he was able to see.

From this Silone passed to an awareness of 'the irrevocable solitude and precariousness' of every man's existence.[98]

Silone's last wishes were granted. His tombstone was hewn out of rough rocks of the hills above Pescina, and around it some paths and steps were made, shaded by cypresses and pines. There was no religious service, only the recital by his wife of the words he himself had wanted, the Lord's Prayer.

In the long, narrow street, crowded with friends from Rome and his fellow-citizens, those who felt inclined to do so joined in the prayer. His ashes will remain, as he wished, in a casket looking down over the Fucino. 'In spite of everything, then, is something still left?' Silone had asked himself:

> Yes, there are some inescapable certainties. These certainties are, to my feeling, Christian certainties. They

seem to me so deeply built into human reality as to identify themselves with man himself.

This is too little to constitute a profession of faith, but enough for a statement of confidence. It is a confidence that rests on something more stable and more universal than simple compassion. In the end it rests upon the intimate knowledge that men are free and responsible beings; on the certainty that man has an absolute need of remaining open to the reality of other human beings; it rests on the certainty of the ability to communicate of human souls. Is that not an irrefutable proof of the fraternity of men? This certainty also contains a rule of life. Love for the oppressed is born from it, as a corollary that no historical delusion can question, being disinterested love. Its validity does not depend on success . . .

This must not be understood, naturally, in the sense of political power or tyranny. To use the oppressed as a step toward power and then betray them is undoubtedly the most iniquitous of sacrileges, for they are the most undefended of men. We must frankly admit that we do not possess any panacea. A panacea for social wrongs does not exist. We are forced to proceed under a dark ideological heaven; the ancient and serene Mediterranean sky once filled with shining constellations is now overcast. But this little light which is left can at least show us where to place our feet.

The spiritual situation described by me does not permit any apology or arrogance. Frankly it is a second-best. It is like a camp of refugees in no-man's land, in an open, haphazard camp. What would you expect these refugees to do from morning till night? They spend most of their time in telling each other their stories. They are certainly not amusing stories, but they tell them to each other, more than for any other reason, to try to understand.

Now, while this obstinate determination to understand and to explain what one has understood still survives, perhaps we need not entirely despair.[99]

'La foi que j'aime le mieux, dit Dieu, c'est l'éspérance.'*

*'The faith I value most, said God, is hope': Charles Péguy, *Le Porche du Mystère de la deuxième vertu*. Geno Pampaloni, in quoting this remarks that, for Silone, hope is the last relic of Christianity in a world that has lost faith and denied charity.

Appendix I

The Story of My Death

The Story of my Death, originally written in French, was translated into almost every European language, the first English translation being by Ruth Draper, and the first Italian one by Salvemini (de Silva, Torino, 1948) with a preface of his own. The French text was released to the press, according to Lauro de Bosis's wishes, by his friend Francesco Luigi Ferrari on 6 October 1931.

Articles about de Bosis by Neville Rogers also appeared in the *Times Literary Supplement* of 5 February 1948, and *The Listener* of 19 October 1961, and Gilbert Murray provided a preface to Ruth Draper's translation of de Bosis's poetic drama, *Icaro* (Faber & Faber, 1933). Romain Rolland, in a foreword to the French edition, said, 'The sacrifice of de Bosis is not only valid for Italy, but for the whole world. For us, too, for you, young men of Europe and America, you who have lost your way and are looking for it in the darkness, Lauro has shown it to you. He has redeemed, with his death, your renunciation and your weakness.'

Appendix II

The Leaflets which
de Bosis Dropped on Rome

(1). *To the King of Italy*

Your Majesty,

Between the King and the people there is a sacred Covenant; this Covenant you have sworn to keep. When, in the name of this Covenant, You called upon us to defend the liberty of Italy and the principles to which You had sworn, six million men took up arms and six hundred thousand laid down their lives at Your command.

Today both in the name of those principles, trampled under foot as they never were before, and in the name of our dead, it is our duty to remind You of that Covenant.

At a sign from You these six hundred thousand Italians gave their lives to deliver the two cities of Trento and Trieste from the foreign yoke. Is it with Your consent that an infinitely more burdensome yoke has for years weighed down the whole of Italy? After Vittorio Veneto are You willing to break the oath to which, after Novara, Your grandfather kept faith?

For seven long years we have seen You signing with the

pen of Carlo Alberto decrees unworthy of any but Radet-sky. Yet we are loath to give up faith in You. You led us to victory and for twenty-four years You were the champion of our liberty. This we cannot forget. Your father handed down to us a free Italy. Is it for You, a victorious King, to be the one to hand it down enslaved to our children? Sire, we refuse to believe it.

Great is the number of those who have lost their faith in the Monarchy. Do not cause their numbers to increase. Do not compel the Italian people to regard You as responsible for this oppression, as has happened in the case of Spain. How can Your people continue to have faith in You, when the best of us are punished for that faith as if it were the worst of crimes, and all this in Your name? Italians who burn with shame at being branded before the world as a breed of servile men, ask themselves whether You are with them or with the stronghold of their oppressors.

Your majesty must make Your choice. There is no middle course.

From the depths of their despair, forty million Italians are looking to You.

THE NATIONAL ALLIANCE

(ii). *To the National Alliance*

ROME. 8th year since the murder of Matteotti.

Whoever you may be, you certainly curse Fascism and feel the disgrace of servitude to it. But you yourself by your own inertia have your share of responsibility for it. Do not attempt to excuse yourself by saying there is nothing to be done. This is not true. Men of courage and honour are all doing what they can silently to prepare for a liberated Italy. Even if you do not want to join our ranks, there are *ten things* you can do on your own account. You can, therefore you must.

1. Never be present at any Fascist ceremony.
2. Never buy a newspaper; they contain nothing but lies.
3. Never smoke. Tobacco brings in to Fascism more than 3,000 million lire annually, enough to pay all its assassins. Treat this present oppressor as the Milanese in the past treated Radetsky. No smoking was the beginning of the 'Five days of Milan.'
4. Never pay homage to the régime by word or deed.
5. Boycott or obstruct all Fascist enterprises. Where successful, they only serve to rivet your chains. Bottai, the Minister of Labour, declared: 'The Corporative State is the best police weapon ever invented.'
7. Accept nothing from Fascism. All that it can give you, is but the price of your prostitution.
8. Distribute Alliance tracts. Spread any true information you may happen to possess. The Truth is always anti-Fascist.
9. Gather round you a group of friends on whom you can rely in emergency.
10. Have faith in Italy, have faith in liberty. The real basis of the present régime is Italian defeatism. Make others share in your own faith and enthusiasm. They are living in the midst of our Risorgimento.

Our new oppressors are more corrupt and more barbarous than those of the past. And, like them, they are bound to fall.

They are held together only by a common guilt. We are united by the will to be free.

The Spaniards have delivered their country. Do not despair of your own.

THE DIRECTORS OF THE NATIONAL ALLIANCE

(III).

ROME. 8th year since the murder of Matteotti.

Italians,

You have raised an altar at the tomb of the 'Unknown Soldier,' the hero of liberty, but every day you witness its profanation by the oppressor who casts close by into prison anyone who still believes in freedom. The Hapsburg, clad in a blackshirt, has slipped into his old stronghold by a back door. His presence is an outrage on our dead. The liberty for which they gave their lives, is by him treated as a 'putrifying corpse' which he has trampled under foot with impunity for the last nine years.

Six hundred thousand Italians gave their lives to deliver a couple of cities. How long will you submit to the man who holds the whole of Italy enslaved?

For nine years you have been told that it is worth while to surrender your conscience and your liberty, so as to have a wise and powerful government. After nine years you realize that you have been under not only the most tyrannical and corrupt, but also the most bankrupt of governments. You gave up your freedom to be robbed of your daily bread into the bargain.

Entrenched among you like a foreign army, Fascism not only corrupts your souls but destroys your substance, paralyses the economic life of the country, squanders millions to prepare for war and hold you in submission, piles up public expenditure over which you have lost all control and abandons the country to the rapacity of its fortune-hunting leaders. While Fascism boasts of its 'prestige' in the world, the world views with horror a régime which, to reduce you to a gang of galley-slaves, has to laud the brutality of its hirelings and manhandle a Toscanini.

Italians, do not let yourselves be intimidated by the gangs who are paid out of your own purse, nor by this pocket edition of Radetsky. The second Risorgimento will be victorious, no less than the first. The National Alliance has launched a programme for the union of all forces against Fascism. The Bourbon ferocity of its sentences on our adherents betrays how greatly Fascism fears our programme. Join together in our Alliance. The Spaniards set their country free; do not play false to your own country.

THE DIRECTORS OF THE NATIONAL ALLIANCE

(iv). *To Militiamen, Avanguardisti, Balilla*

Be the first to carry out the Truce of Arms proposed at Geneva by your chiefs.

While today they are assuming abroad the mask of Peace they have transformed Italy into a vast barracks.

While the world clamours desperately for Peace, you cannot desire to be the followers of the Kaiser. Do not behave in such a way that Italy continues to be a powder magazine in the midst of Europe. Be the first to demand Peace, which can only exist where there is liberty.

Mothers of Italy, do not allow your sons to be torn from you at the age of eight years in order to be made into cannon fodder. Refuse Fascist education.

THE DIRECTORS OF THE NATIONAL ALLIANCE

NOTES

1. *Biography*

This essay is based on the Ann Radcliffe Lecture which I gave in Cambridge in the autumn of 1958, and which was subsequently printed in the *Cornhill* and in the *Atlantic Monthly*. It has now been revised and considerably enlarged.

I wish to acknowledge the help I have received from three books, all of which were originally given as lectures, and written by men who were also biographers themselves: *The Development of English Biography* (originally given in the *Hogarth Lectures on Literature* Series) by Sir Harold Nicolson, The Hogarth Press, London, 1927, *Literary Biography* (originally given at the University of Toronto, as five of the Alexandra Lectures) by Leon Edel, Rupert Hart-Davis, London, 1957, and *The Nature of Biography* (delivered in the University of Washington, Seattle, in the Jessie and John Dang Lectures) by Robert Gittings, Heinemann, London, 1978. For all three of these, from which I have quoted, I should like to express my gratitude.

1. Quoted from William Allingham's Diary by Logan Pearsall-Smith in *Reperusals and Recollections*, p. 210.

2. James Froude, *Thomas Carlyle, A History of his Life in London*, p. 1, quoting Carlyle's *Journal* of 10 October 1843.

3. *Malahide Papers*, Vol. VI, 'The Making of the Life of Dr Johnson,' introduction by Geoffrey Scott to 'The First Records,' p. 16.

4. Ibid, p. 17.

5. Ibid, p. 18.

6. Mrs Piozzi, *Anecdotes*, 1766 edition, p. 100.

7. Dr Johnson in *The Rambler*, No. 60, 3 October 1750.

8. Boswell's *Life of Dr Johnson*, Everyman edition, Vol. I, p. 509.

9. Dr Johnson, *Lives of the English Poets*, Everyman, p. 156.

10. Geoffrey Scott, Introduction to Vol. IV of the *Malahide Papers*, 'Boswell with Rousseau and Voltaire,' pp. 1–2.

11. Ibid.

12. Boswell, Letter to William John Temple, 28 December 1764. *Malahide Papers*, Vol. IV, p. 14.

13. Ibid, pp. 17–18.

14. Voltaire to Boswell, 11 February 1765. *Malahide Papers*, Vol. IV, p. 29.

15. Boswell to William John Temple, 28 December 1764. *Malahide Papers*.

16. Quoted by Geoffrey Scott in Vol. VI of the *Malahide Papers*, 'The writing of the Life of Dr Johnson,' p. 19.

17. Ibid, quoting Dr Burney's *Memoirs*, II, 194.

18. Quoted by Leon Edel, in *Literary Biography*, p. 17.

19. Harold Nicolson, *The Development of English Biography* (Hogarth Press, London, 1927), p. 107.

20. Ibid, p. 105.

21. Geoffrey Scott, Introduction to 'The First Records' in the *Malahide Papers*, Vol. VI, pp. 15–16.

22. Conclusion of Vol. VI of the *Malahide Papers*, pp. 289–91.

23. From Carlyle's review of Lockhart's biography of Sir Walter Scott.

24. Carlyle himself wrote to this neighbour: 'We have the misfortune to be people of weak health in this house, bad sleepers particularly, and exceeding sensitive in the night hours to disturbance from sound. On your premises for some time past there is a cock . . . If you would have the goodness to remove that small animal or in any way render him inaudible from midnight to break-

fast time, said charity would work a notable relief to certain persons here.'

25. *Letters and Memorials* of Jane Welsh Carlyle, Vol. I, p. 26.

26. Jane's own spirited account of her 'domestic earthquake' is to be found in a letter to Mrs Stirling. *Letters and Memorials of Jane Welsh Carlyle*, Vol. I, pp. 217–18.

27. *Reminiscences by Thomas Carlyle*, ed. by J. A. Froude, Vol. II, p. 225. Carlyle called the room 'the least habitable and entirely despicable bit of human workmanship.' But he wrote almost the whole of *Frederick* there.

28. Ibid, Vol. II, p. 286.

29. J. A. Froude, *Thomas Carlyle, A History of his Life in London*, Vol. I, p. 197.

30. Op. cit. pp. 201–2, *Carlyle's Journal*, 26 December 1840.

31. Op. cit. p. 279, *Carlyle's Journal*, 20 October 1842.

32. Op. cit. p. 333. Letter from Carlyle to his mother, 31 December 1843.

33. Ibid, p. 339, *Carlyle's Journal*, 8 May 1844.

34. Ibid, p. 396, Letter from Carlyle to Jane, 23 August 1845.

35. J. A. Froude, op. cit. Vol. I, p. 356.

36. Ibid, Vol. II, p. 135.

37. Ibid, Vol. II, pp. 47–8, quoting *Carlyle's Journal*, 28 February 1854.

38. Ibid, Vol. II, p. 283, Quoting *Carlyle's Journal*.

39. Logan Pearsall-Smith, *The Rembrandt of English Prose* in *Reperusals and Recollections*, pp. 202–21.

40. Harold Nicolson, op. cit.

41. William Roper, *Life of Sir Thomas More* (written in 1626).

42. *Thomas Wolsey, late Cardinal, his Life and Death, written by George Cavendish, his gentleman-usher*. Reprinted by The Folio Society, London, 1972.

43. Ibid, pp. 46–9.

44. Ibid, pp. 111–17.

45. Ibid, pp. 197 and 204.

46. Harold Nicolson, op. cit.

47. Dryden, in Dr Johnson's *Lives of the English Poets*.

48. Ecclesiastes XLIV, 7.

49. Quoted from *The Compleat Angler* and *The Lives of Donne, Wotton, Hooker, Herbert and Sanders* (Macmillan, 1901). Walton's lives were written between 1640 and 1678.

50. Op. cit. p. 417.

51. Ibid, p. 219.

52. Aubrey's *Brief Lives*, edited from the Original Manuscripts and with a Life of John Aubrey by Oliver Lawson Dick (Secker and Warburg, London, 1949).

53. Lytton Strachey, Introduction to *Eminent Victorians*, p. VIII.

54. Robert Gittings, op. cit. pp. 3–4.

55. Mrs Gaskell, Preface to *The Life of Charlotte Brontë*.

56. Leon Edel, *Literary Biography* (Rupert Hart-Davis, London, 1957), p. 11.

57. So, too, Dickens, after lighting a similar bonfire at Gad's Hill, exclaimed, 'Would to God every letter I have written were on that pile!' Quoted by Leon Edel, op. cit. p. 30.

58. Quoted by Leon Edel, op. cit. pp. 31–2.

59. Ibid, pp. 33–40.

60. Lytton Strachey, Introduction to *Eminent Victorians*, p. IX.

61. Marc Bloch, *Métier d'Historien*, p. 70.

62. Ibid, p. 72.

63. Lytton Strachey, Preface to *Eminent Victorians*, p. IX.

64. I do not, of course, mean to underestimate the other recent admirable lives of Queen Victoria, especially Lady Longford's and Cecil Woodham-Smith's; but the purpose of these books was entirely different.

65. Virginia Woolf, 'The Art of Biography' in *The Death of a Moth and Other Essays*, 1952.

66. 'The New Biography,' first published in the *New York Herald Tribune*, 30 October 1927, and included in *Granite and Rainbow*, p. 149.

67. Ibid.

68. Dr Johnson in *The Rambler*, op. cit.

69. Kenneth Clark, *Another Part of the Wood*.

70. *A Writer's Diary*, pp. 88–93 and 94.

71. *The Land*, p. 106.

    'Down from the hill the slow oxen crawl,
    Dragging the purple waggon heaped with must,
    Raising on sundered hoofs small puffs of dust,
    With scarlet tassels on their milky brows,
    Gentle as evening moths . . .'

72. Virginia Woolf, *The Art of Biography*, first published in *The*

Atlantic Monthly, April 1939, and subsequently in *The Death of a Moth*.

73. Ibid.

74. Quoted by Leon Edel, op. cit. p. 11.

75. From Sir William Temple's essay, *Of Poetry*.

11. *Lauro de Bosis*

Abbreviations for the essays on Lauro de Bosis and Ruth Draper

A.C.S.	Archivio Centrale dello Stato.
A.G.S.	Archivio Gaetano Salvemini.
Esteri	Archivio Storico del Ministero degli Affari Esteri.
CB	Carte Bolaffio.
Houghton	Houghton Library, Harvard University.
I.A.S.	Italy-America Society.
Icaro	*Icaro* by Lauro de Bosis, translated by Ruth Draper with a preface by Gilbert Murray. OUP, 1933.
Minculpop	Ministero della Cultura Popolare.
N.A.I.R.	National Archives, Italian Records.
N.Y.H.S.	New York Historical Society.
Warren	Neilla Warren, *Collected Letters of Ruth Draper*, Scribner's.
Zabel	Morton Dauwen Zabel, *The Art of Ruth Draper, Her Dramas and Characters, with a Memoir*. OUP, 1960.

1. Arturo Vivante, 'The Visit,' in the *New Yorker*, 3 July 1965.

2. Arturo Vivante, 'The Rallye,' in the *New Yorker*, 29 July 1963.

3. Professor Gilbert Murray in his introduction to Ruth Draper's translation of *Icaro*.

4. Ibid.

5. G. M. Trevelyan, Foreword to Lauro de Bosis's anthology, *The Golden Book of Italian Poetry*.

6. Gaetano Salvemini, *Memorie di un Fuoruscito*, Feltrinelli, U.E., 296, 1973, p. 110.

7. Archivio Caetani, A 8–1, Gelasio Caetani, *Discorso agli Italiani di Detroit*, 14 March 1923, quoted in Gian Giacomo Migone,

Problemi di storia nei rapporti tra Italia e Stati Uniti, Torino, Rosenberg e Sellier, 1971.

8. ACS, Minculpop, b. 105, f. 18, Gelasio Caetani to Mussolini, 28 January 1923. Allegato 'E.'

9. Documenti Diplomatici Italiani (DDI), 7, IV, the President of the Italy-America Society, Lamont, to Commendatore Giovanni Fummi, New York, 25 March 1926.

10. Salvemini, op. cit. p. 114, quoting de Bosis's words to him.

11. Ibid, p. 113.

12. Ibid, p. 114.

13. Letter from Beniamino de Ritis to Ambassador Giacomo de Martino, 11 August 1931, ACS, and letter from Beniamino de Ritis to Piero Perini about the nomination of Lauro de Bosis as representative of the Ministry of Education, 2 December 1930, and Memorandum from Professor Bruno Roselli on de Bosis's activities, 17 March 1931.

14. Arturo Vivante, 'The Visit,' in the *New Yorker*, 3 July 1965.

15. Note in Ruth Draper's writing in the Houghton Library, Harvard University.

16. Lauro de Bosis to R.D., Spring, 1931.

17. de Bosis to R.D., June, 1930.

18. Such letters were called in Catholic circles 'St Antony's chain.'

19. These pamphlets are quoted in the special number of *Italy Today* devoted to Mario Vinciguerra and Renzo Rendi, 31 May 1931.

20. de Bosis to Ambassador de Martino, 16 October 1930. Minculpop, b. 164, R 7, Itam ACS.

21. Ambassador de Martino to the Foreign Minister in Rome, Dino Grandi, 24 October 1930. ACS, Minculpop, b. 164, R 79, Propaganda.

22. de Bosis to Ambassador de Martino, 15 June 1930. ACS, Minculpop, b. 166, p. 114.

23. Ambassador de Martino to de Bosis, 22 November 1930. ACS.

24. Irene de Robilant's warm recommendation of de Bosis described him as a scholar and a gentleman, and said that she would be able to help him in his work.

25. Ambassador de Martino to the Foreign Minister, Dino Grandi, 24 December 1930. 'Confidential.' ACS, Ministero Esteri.

26. de Bosis to Francesco Luigi Ferrari, 22 June 1931.

27. de Bosis from Europe to the Italian Consul General in New York, Emanuele Grazzi, December 1930, ACS. Commenting on this letter to Ambassador de Martino, Grazzi wrote: 'It is indisputable that at first the arrest of such persons as the widow de Bosis and Rendi produced a certain bewilderment in American public opinion. In the Italy-America Society, of which Lauro de Bosis had been a director until a few months ago, this was felt even more strongly. My first concern, together with the directors of the Italy-America Society and with the help of Morgan's bank, was to avoid the publication of disagreeable editorials in the local press.' Grazzi enclosed a copy of Lauro's letter to him, commenting that 'it was not only a proof of his irresponsibility, but an open confession of his anti-fascist activity in Italy last summer.' Console Emanuele Grazzi to Ambassador de Martino, New York, 28 December 1930, ACS, Ministero dell'Interno, 17 June 1931. Alleanza Nazionale Q.I. 816 025495.

28. de Bosis to R.D.

29. de Bosis to R.D. after the trial of Vinciguerra and Rendi.

30. Telegram from the Italian Embassy in Washington to the Foreign Minister in Rome, dated 6 December 1930. ACS.

31. Communiqué of Ambassador de Martino to the American Press. ACS.

32. Gaetano Salvemini, *Memorie di un Fuoruscito*, op. cit. p. 161.

33. From the number of *Italy Today* devoted to de Bosis, Nov.–Dec. 1931.

34. From the number of *Italy Today* devoted to the case of Mario Vinciguerra and Renzo Rendi, pp. 4–6.

35. One of them, an Avvocato Gemelli, wrote an appeal to be released to Mussolini, with fulsome protestations of loyalty.

36. Quoted from the *New York Times* of 23 December 1931.

37. From the number of *Italy Today* dedicated to Vinciguerra and Rendi, p. 7.

38. de Bosis to R.D., 7 January 1931.

39. Ibid.

40. Ibid.

41. de Bosis to R.D., 5 February 1931.

42. de Bosis to Gaetano Salvemini, undated.

43. Ibid.

44. Gaetano Salvemini, *Memorie di un Fuoruscito*, op. cit. pp. 75–9.

45. de Bosis to R.D. from Paris 14 March 1931.

46. Ibid, 1931.

47. Ibid, 1931.

48. Gaetano Salvemini, *Memorie de un Fuoruscito*, op. cit. p. 163.

49. de Bosis to Eric Wilmer Wood, 11 December 1930. In the Houghton Library, Harvard University.

50. de Bosis to Eric Wilmer Wood, 21 December 1930.

51. Eric Wilmer Wood to de Bosis, 28 December 1930.

52. de Bosis to Eric Wilmer Wood, 17 January 1931.

53. Ibid. Probably March 1931.

54. Ibid, 24 March 1931.

55. Eric Wilmer Wood to R.D., undated (1931 or 1932).

56. Franco Fucci, *Ali contro Mussolini*, Mursia, 1978, p. 174.

57. de Bosis to his mother from London, 26 June 1931.

58. de Bosis to Francesco Luigi Ferrari, written from London, 22 June 1931, but only posted from Marseilles on 2 October, together with *The Story of my Death*.

59. The German pilot, Max Rainer, to R.D., from Munich, 4 November 1931. In the Houghton Library, Harvard University. Quoted in part by Fucci, op. cit. p. 182.

60. Max Rainer to R.D., dated 6 May (1936). Houghton Library, Harvard University.

61. Quoted in translation in the double number of *Italy Today* (Nov.–Dec. 1931).

62. Account of Massimo Salvadori, who did not then know that the leaflets had been thrown by de Bosis. Quoted by Fucci, op. cit. p. 188.

63. Quoted from *Le Matin* of 6 October 1931, by Fucci, op. cit. p. 190.

64. Fucci, op. cit. p. 90, quoting an article in *Il Tevere* of 7 October, entitled 'Una carogna' (a skunk).

65. Quoted from the London *Times*, 4 October 1931.

66. Ambassador Antonio Bordonaro, telegram to the Italian Foreign Office of 14 October 1931, ACS, no. 7282 R.R.

67. Comment of the Italian Ministry of the Interior on the report of the examination of the German pilots, no. 320274, 24 October 1931.

68. Description of the course of events which led to Lauro's death, Fucci, op. cit. pp. 185–6.

69. Francesco Luigi Ferrari to R.D. (in French), 7 October 1931.

70. Transmission through the Ministry of the Interior, signed merely 'Hani,' 12 November 1931. ACS.

71. Vittorio de Bosis to Ruth Draper.

III. *Ruth Draper*

My most grateful thanks are due, first of all, to Miss Neilla Warren, the editor of Ruth Draper's letters, for her kind permission to quote from these, and for the accuracy and advice which has saved me from many blunders. I owe deep gratitude to William D. Carter, for permission to quote from the notes about his Aunt Ruth which he wrote for me, and for his account of his visit to Rome after Lauro de Bosis's death, as well as for his unfailing help in research work in the New York Historical Society and the Houghton Library in Cambridge. I am most grateful to his mother, the late Alice Carter, for permission to examine the letters received by her sister Ruth in England from her friends and admirers. My thanks go to Penelope Draper Buchanan, for the descriptions she has sent me both of Ruth's earlier days at Dark Harbor, and of her last days there, before her death, and to Joyce Grenfell, both for a long letter describing Ruth's performances and technique, and for permission to quote further details from her book *Joyce Grenfell Requests the Pleasure*.

1. Morton D. Zabel, *The Art of Ruth Draper, Her Dramas and Characters*, p. 21.

2. Ibid, pp. 13–16.

3. When Ruth's mother died in 1914, she left this house to all her children, but Ruth then bought it back from the others.

4. Letter from Penelope Draper Buchanan to Iris Origo.

5. Letter from Joyce Grenfell to Iris Origo.

6. Zabel, op. cit. p. 32.

7. Ibid, p. 22.

8. Most of them indulged in the facile melancholy of youth, but one at least reflected the first stirrings of her ambition,

'. . . My self-love and the vision
Of the great things I would be.'

9. Zabel, op. cit. pp. 34–9.

10. Ibid pp. 34 and 37–8.

11. Ibid, pp. 38–9.

12. Ibid, p. 47. Letter from Henry Adams to Elizabeth Cameron in 1911.

13. Ibid, p. 30.

14. Letter from Henry Adams to Anne Lodge, 15 May 1913. Quoted by Neilla Warren in the prologue to *The Letters of Ruth Draper*, p. 6.

15. Ruth Draper to Mrs Yates Thompson, 4 June 1915, Warren, op. cit. p. 9.

16. R.D. to Laura White from Bloomfield, N.J., 22 June 1918.

17. R.D. to Martha Draper, from Châtillon-sur-Seine, 6 June 1919.

18. Neilla Warren, prologue to *The Letters of Ruth Draper*, p. 12.

19. Ibid, p. 13.

20. Permission to do this was kindly granted to me by Ruth's sister, Alice Carter.

21. Letter to R.D. from Ellen Terry. Quoted by Zabel, p. 70.

22. Virginia Woolf, *The Moment*, pp. 169–70.

23. Part of the material in this letter was used or elaborated later in the book *Joyce Grenfell Requests the Pleasure*, but I am quoting from Joyce Grenfell's letter to me.

24. Zabel, op. cit., pp. 112–13.

25. R.D. to Martha Draper, 7 July 1920, Warren, op. cit. p. 18.

26. R.D. to Harriet Marple, 9 July 1920, ibid, p. 19.

27. R.D. to Harriet Marple, 1 September 1920, ibid, p. 24.

28. R.D. to Harriet Marple, 20 September 1920, ibid, p. 26.

29. Virginia Woolf, *The Moment*, p. 165.

30. Henry James to R.D., 4 December 1913. Quoted by Zabel, op. cit. pp. 49–50.

31. Zabel, op. cit.

32. Zabel, op. cit. p. 55. Neville Rogers gives a slightly different version, which he says Ruth gave to him herself, saying 'a magic carpet' instead of 'Persian.' *The Ohio Review*, Vol. XIX, no. 1, winter 1978, p. 19.

33. See *The Complete Plays of Henry James*, ed. by Leon Edel, J. B. Lippincott & Co., New York, 1949.

34. Zabel, op. cit. p. 48, quoting a holograph copy of Henry

James's letter among Ruth's papers, by permission of William James.

35. From the text of Ruth Draper's monologue 'Showing the Garden,' in Zabel, *The Art of Ruth Draper*, p. 296.

36. 'The Italian Lesson.' Recording issued by Spoken Arts entitled *The Art of Ruth Draper*, no. 779.

37. 'Three Generations,' the same recording.

38. Lugné-Poe, *Dernière Pirouette* (1940).

39. Warren, op. cit. p. 38.

40. Quoted by Zabel, op. cit. p. 65.

41. R.D. to Harriet Marple, 15 February 1928. Warren, op. cit. p. 95.

42. Professor Neville Rogers, in a brilliant article, *The Art of Ruth Draper* in *The Ohio Review*, Vol. XIX, no. 1, winter 1978, p. 22.

43. Zabel, op. cit. p. 72.

44. R.D. to Martha Draper, 18 December 1922. Warren, op. cit. p. 54.

45. R.D. to Harriet Marple, from the SS *Ile de France*, (c. 22 June 1928).

46. R.D. to Harriet Marple, 11 October 1928 from Avon, Connecticut, where Ruth was staying with Corinne Alsop, who had kindly suggested that Lauro should meet her there. Warren, op. cit. p. 100.

47. *Recollections of my aunt Ruth, for Iris Origo*, unpublished MSS. kindly set down for me by W. B. Carter.

48. R.D. to Harriet Marple, 'at sea,' 25 May 1929. Warren, op. cit. p. 102.

49. R.D. to Harriet Marple from Vienna, 18 June 1929. Warren, op. cit. p. 105.

50. R.D. to Harriet Marple, 27 June 1929. Warren, op. cit. p. 106.

51. Warren, op. cit. pp. 108–9, as written early in December 1929.

52. Warren, op. cit. p. 155.

53. Lauro de Bosis to R.D. from Paris, 1931.

54. It has been suggested that this news was sent to him by Ruth, but the matter remains uncertain.

55. Letters written by Lauro de Bosis to R.D. from his concierge's desk in Paris between February and April 1931, mostly

undated. They have been summarised by Neilla Warren on p. 113, op. cit.

56. Lauro de Bosis to R.D., 20 January 1931. Most of this letter is printed in the double number of November 1931, of *Italy Today* devoted to Lauro de Bosis.

57. Lauro de Bosis to his mother, 26 June 1931.

58. R.D. to Harriet Marple from Paris, 18 April 1931. Warren, op. cit. p. 114.

59. R.D. to Harriet Marple, 8 May 1931. Warren, op. cit. p. 115.

60. R.D. to Harriet Marple, 14 July 1931. Warren, op. cit. p. 120.

61. There has been some discussion as to whether Lauro flew the plane from Corsica himself, but there now seems to be no doubt that it was the English pilot who flew it all the way. See Franco Fucci, *Ali contro Mussolini*, pp. 173 and following pages.

62. R.D. to Harriet Marple from Starnberg (Bavaria), 4 September 1931. Warren, op. cit. p. 123.

63. R.D. to Harriet Marple, 2 August 1931. Warren, op. cit. p. 120.

64. R.D. to Harriet Marple, 10 September 1931. Warren, op. cit. p. 124.

65. Quoted in part in Warren, op. cit. p. 126.

66. Warren, op. cit. p. 122.

67. From William Carter's *Recollections of my visit to Rome.*

68. R.D. to Harriet Marple, 13 October 1931. Warren, op. cit. p. 127.

69. R.D. to Harriet Marple, 16 October 1931. Warren, op. cit. p. 128.

70. Ibid.

71. R.D. to Malvina Hoffman, 2 November 1931. Warren, op. cit. pp. 132–3.

72. Letter from William Carter to his mother, Mrs Edward Carter. Quoted in Warren, op. cit. p. 147.

73. The phrase was used by Ruth in her monologue *In County Kerry.*

74. Letter from Gaetano Salvemini to R.D., 1934.

75. Lillian de Bosis to R.D., 20 December 1931. In a postscript written an hour later he thanked Ruth for a letter written on 31 October (not preserved—perhaps it suggested a meeting) and said, 'I can only add that we are in such uncertainty and apprehen-

sion of very difficult times financially that all movement is arrested.'

76. Elena Vivante to R.D., 2 January 1932.

77. Vittorio de Bosis to R.D., late spring or summer, 1932.

78. Lillian de Bosis to R.D., May 1933.

79. R.D. to Harriet Marple, 17 May 1934. Warren, op. cit.
p. 180.

80. R.D. to Harriet Marple, 8 May 1934. Warren, op. cit.
p. 179.

81. Charis de Bosis to R.D., 17 May 1934.

82. Lillian de Bosis to R.D. from Florence, 13 October 1935.

83. Lillian de Bosis to R.D., 30 January 1936.

84. Arturo Vivante, 'The Visit,' *The New Yorker*, 3 July 1965.

85. Warren, op. cit. p. 166.

86. Warren, op. cit. pp. 165–6.

87. Ibid, p. 167. Letter from R.D. to her sister Dorothea, 19 December 1933.

88. Warren, op. cit. p. 187.

89. Ibid, p. 190–2.

90. Ibid, p. 224.

91. Ibid, pp. 225–6. Letter from R.D. to Mrs F. D. Roosevelt, 25
April 1941.

92. Ibid, pp. 218–19.

93. Ibid, p. 230. R.D. to Mrs David Terry Martin, 14 April
1943.

94. Letter from R.D. to her sister Dorothea James from La
Foce.

95. R.D. to Dorothea James, 13 March 1946. Warren, op. cit.
p. 241.

96. R.D. to Mary Sheldon MacArthur, 7 April 1946, Warren,
op. cit. p. 245 and to Dorothea James, 6 April 1946. Warren, op. cit.
p. 245.

97. The full text of the broadcast is quoted in Warren, op. cit.
pp. 241–2, 16 March 1946.

98. R.D. to her sister Alice Carter, 16 March 1946. Warren, op.
cit. pp. 242–3.

99. R.D. to the Mayors of the cities she had visited on her English tour, 28 July 1946. Warren, op. cit. p. 254.

100. R.D. to Dorothea James, 24 November (1951). Warren, op.
cit. p. 296.

101. R.D. to Dorothea James. Warren, op. cit. p. 292, 11 June 1954.

102. R.D. to Dorothea James, 14 June (1951). Warren, op. cit. p. 290.

103. R.D. to Dorothea James from Vallombrosa, 14 September (1946). Warren, op. cit. p. 258.

104. R.D. to Mrs David Terry Martin, 17 March 1950. Warren, op. cit. p. 278.

105. From two interviews quoted by Zabel, op. cit. pp. 99–100.

106. Zabel, op. cit. p. 112.

107. Letter from Penelope Draper Buchanan to Iris Origo.

108. Warren, op. cit. pp. 341–2.

IV. *Gaetano Salvemini*

1. From Salvemini's lecture on 16 November 1949, in the University of Florence. First published in *Il Ponte* and afterwards printed in *Scritti Vari*, p. 54.

2. Prof. Enzo Tagliacozzo, *Gaetano Salvemini, nel cinquantenario liberale*, ed. 'La Nuova Italia,' 1959.

3. Last words of Salvemini's essay *Che cos'è la cultura?* ('What is culture?').

4. Eugenio Garin, in *Gaetano Salvemini e la società italiana dei suoi tempi* (Gaetano Salvemini and the Italian society of his time) in the collection of essays about Salvemini published by Laterza, Bari, 1959, p. 209.

5. Ernesto Rossi, *Salvemini il non-conformista*, first published in *Il Mondo*, 17 September 1957.

6. Ibid, p. 10. Taken from nos. 2–3 of *Politica e Mezzogiorno*.

7. Ernesto Rossi, *L'Uomo Salvemini*.

8. Alessandro Galante Garrone, Introduction to *Scritti Vari* (1900–57) a cura di Giorgio Agosti e A. Galante Garrone, p. 10.

9. A. Galante Garrone, op. cit. *Scritti Vari*, p. 10.

10. Salvemini to Ernesta Bittanti, 19 October 1896, *Carteggio I*, pp. 34–5.

11. Salvemini, *Cesare Battisti*, first published in *L'Unità*, 27 July 1917, and reprinted in *Scritti Vari*, pp. 82–5.

12. Salvemini to Carlo Placci from Palermo, 1 November 1895. *Carteggio I*, pp. 7–8.

13. Salvemini to Carlo Placci, 6 April 1896. *Carteggio I*, p. 20.

14. Carlo Placci to Gaetano Salvemini, 20 April 1896, *Carteggio I*, pp. 23–4.

15. Salvemini to Carlo Placci from Palermo, 30 April 1896. *Carteggio I*, p. 25.

16. Salvemini to Carlo Placci, 25 February 1899, *Carteggio I*, pp. 82–3.

17. Unpublished letter from Salvemini to Bernard Berenson, Archivio I Tatti, now Harvard Cultural Centre of Renaissance Studies, 19 October 1912.

18. Salvemini to Carlo Placci from Faenza, 3 November 1897, *Carteggio I*, p. 67.

19. Lidia Minervini, *Amico e Maestro, Ricordi di Salvemini*, published in *Il Mondo*, 22 October 1942.

20. Salvemini to Prof. Giovanni Gentile, 1 April 1909. *Carteggio I*, p. 399.

21. From Giuliana Benzoni's unpublished recollections of Salvemini.

22. Salvemini to Giustino Fortunato, 14 February 1910. *Carteggio (1865–1911)* a cure di Emilio Gentile, Bari Laterza, 1978 Vol. I, p. 197.

23. Salvemini to Giustino Fortunato, same letter.

24. Unpublished letter from Fernande Luchaire to Elsa Dallolio, 18 November 1918.

25. Ernesto Rossi, *Salvemini il non-conformista*, pp. 14–17.

26. Unpublished letter from Fernande Luchaire to Elsa Dallolio, 12 April 1916.

27. Quoted by Salvemini, *Memorie di un Fuoruscito*, from the Florentine paper *La Nazione*, 4 October 1923.

28. Lidia Minervini, op. cit. A similar account by Piero Calamandrei is quoted by Salvemini, *Memorie di un Fuoruscito*, pp. 12–13.

29. Salvemini, *Memorie di un Fuoruscito*, pp. 14–15 and 17–18.

30. Lidia Minervini, op. cit.

31. Salvemini to Fernande Luchaire. Undated, but clearly written in 1925, when Salvemini was under arrest.

32. This story is told by Meryl Secrest in *Being Berenson*, and has been confirmed to me by Umberto Morra.

33. Gaetano Salvemini, *Memorie di un Fuoruscito*, p. 31–2.

34. Quoted by Salvemini from *Il Torchio*, *Memorie di un Fuoruscito*, p. 46.

35. Unpublished letter from Salvemini to Mary and Bernard Berenson, 4 November 1922. Archives of Villa I Tatti.

36. Salvemini to Mary Berenson, 8 September 1922. Archives of I Tatti.

37. Salvemini to Bernard Berenson from Brighton, 6 October 1922. Archives of I Tatti.

38. Salvemini to Mary Berenson from Paris, 2 October 1924. Archives of I Tatti. The Berensons at once responded by sending 2,000 lire.

39. Salvemini to Mary Berenson from Paris, 11 November 1925. Archives of I Tatti.

40. Salvemini, *Memorie di un Fuoruscito*, p. 54.

41. Marion Rawson, Account written for Iris Origo of Salvemini's life in England.

42. Salvemini, *Memorie di un Fuoruscito*, pp. 52–3.

43. Salvemini to Umberto Zanotti-Bianco. Undated.

44. From Marion Rawson's account of Salvemini's life in England.

45. Salvemini, *Memorie di un Fuoruscito*, pp. 88–9.

46. Ernesto Rossi, *Salvemini il non-conformista*, pp. 18–19.

47. Salvemini, *Memorie di un Fuoruscito*, p. 66.

48. Salvemini to Roberto and Maritza Bolaffio, 12 January 1930. Unpublished letter in the Archivo Salvemini. In a note Bolaffio wrote, 'We took him into our house and till he left the U.S. in 1951, it became, as he used to say, his home in New York.'

49. Salvemini, *Memorie di un Fuoruscito*, p. 169 and p. 116.

50. Ibid, p. 124 and pp. 116–18.

51. *Monthly Bulletin of the North American Association for Justice and Freedom*, 24 September 1932. Quoted in *Memorie di un Fuoruscito*, pp. 119–21.

52. Salvemini, *Memorie di un Fuoruscito*, p. 124, pp. 158–9, pp. 161–8, and pp. 116–17.

53. Salvemini to Roberto and Maritza Bolaffio, 10 January 1956. In thanking Salvemini for his generous gesture, President Pusey wrote: 'The new occupant of your chair will be fortunate if he can attain these high standards of scholarship and breadth of human sympathy which characterized your term of service.' Carte Bolaffio.

54. Roberto Bolaffio, *Salvemini and his Widener Library*. An unpublished account based on Bolaffio's recollections of his visits

to Salvemini at Harvard. This was intended to be part of a book about Salvemini which Bolaffio's ill-health and premature death did not allow him to finish.

55. Salvemini, *Memorie di un Fuoruscito*, pp. 137–8.

56. Ibid, p. 147.

57. From a speech by Louis M. Lyons, on Boston television, shortly after Salvemini's death.

58. The author of this letter was Professor Nicholas Risianowsky, of the University of California, 14 May 1965. Carte Bolaffio.

59. Professor Kenneth B. Murdoch to Roberto Bolaffio, 25 May 1965. Professor Murdoch was for many years Professor of English literature at Harvard and Master of Leverett House, where Salvemini lived.

60. Letter from Salvemini to Roberto and Maritza Bolaffio, just before leaving Harvard. Carte Bolaffio.

61. Professor Murdoch to Roberto Bolaffio, 10 January 1956. Carte Bolaffio.

62. Interview of Roberto Bolaffio with Professor Samuel E. Morison. Professor Morison, before writing *A History of the Discovery of America*, had followed Columbus's route across the Atlantic in a caravel like Columbus's *Nina*.

63. Interview of Roberto Bolaffio with Professor William Langer, March, 1965. Professor Langer was the Professor of European History at Harvard and President of the American Historical Association.

64. *Harvard University Gazette*, 18 January 1958.

65. Story told by Arthur M. Schlesinger senior, in an interview with Roberto Bolaffio, 29 May 1965.

66. I have only a typewritten copy of this letter (in English and signed G.S.) and have been unable to trace its source, but the style and sentiments are unmistakeably Salvemini's.

67. Salvemini to Armando Borghi, 13 September 1945, published by Merola, *Lettere dall'America*, I, pp. 170–1.

68. Ernesto Rossi, *Salvemini il non-conformista*, p. 27.

69. Fernande Salvemini to Elsa Dallolio, 9 May 1948. Carte Bolaffio.

70. I am indebted to Hallam Tennyson for a summary of this trial. It is only fair to point out that Luchaire never made use of his relationship with Salvemini—as he might well have done—to save his skin. On the only occasion in which the President of the

Court mentioned the Professor's name—erroneously, as 'Salveti'—Luchaire made no attempt to rectify the mistake.

71. Summary of the 'facts' by the Court's registrar, on p. 352 of the transcript of the trial.

72. 'God of infinite space and time, my soul is yours.

God of omnipotence, my soul is yours.

God of love, I give you my heart.

Deign to lean over me and guide my steps towards eternal life.

Forgive my sins, both those I have committed and those I have made others commit.

Help me to protect, on earth as well as in heaven, those whom you have made me love.'

73. Fernande Salvemini to Elsa Dallolio, 9 May 1948. Carte Dallolio.

74. Ibid, 15 January 1948. Carte Dallolio.

75. Ernesto Rossi to Salvemini, 24–5 March 1944. Original in the Archivio Salvemini. Printed by Merola, *Lettere dall'America 1944–46*, pp. 1–3 and 17.

76. Salvemini to Piero Calamandrei, 13 October 1944. Printed by Merola, op. cit. p. 294.

77. Egidio Reale to Salvemini, 10 June 1946. Printed by Merola, op. cit. p. 294.

78. From *Ottimismo*, by Gaetano Salvemini, first published in *Il Ponte*, Nov.–Dec. 1947, and reprinted in *Scritti Vari*, pp. 747–52.

79. A. Galante Garrone, *L'Ultimo Salvemini*, first published in *Il Ponte*, Nos. 8–9, 1957.

80. Fernande Salvemini to Elsa Dallolio, 1 November 1947. Carte Dallolio.

81. Ibid, 15 January 1948. Carte Dallolio.

82. From Marion Rawson's account of Salvemini's stay in England in 1926.

83. Salvemini to Ruth Draper, from La Rufola, 11 January 1952. In the same letter he thanked Ruth for going to see Fernande in Paris. 'In her loneliness, she feels deeply any kind of move from old friends. I am sure your letter cheered her up for days and days.'

84. Gaetano Salvemini to Thomas Higham, Public Orator of Oxford University. Since Salvemini was not well enough to attend, the degree was not conferred.

85. Salvemini to Gordon Lett, 2 January 1957. Gordon Lett was a Major in the East Surrey Regiment who, after being captured in the African desert and interned in Italy, formed after the armistice of 1943 the force I have described in the village of Rossano near the Ligurian coast, where he hoped for an Allied landing. The local population collaborated with him and his partisans until the whole district became a centre of the Resistance against the government of Salò. This information comes from a paper read by a friend of Lett's (whose health prevented him from attending) at a meeting of the 'Congress of Italy and Great Britain in the Struggle for Liberation,' held in Bagni di Lucca, 11–13 April 1975.

86. Salvemini to A. Galante Garrone, 24 May 1949.

87. Ibid, October 1953.

88. *Un mercato di schiavi* (a slave-market), in *Il Mondo*, 28 July 1953. The price of children aged 9 to 15 was 4,000 lire a year, and three bushels of wheat. The boys' teeth, chest and legs were examined as if they were animals.

89. *I servi della gleba* (the serfs), in *Critica Sociale*, 29 January 1954. 'This infamy,' Salvemini wrote, 'had its origins in a fascist law passed to dissuade countrywomen from moving from the land to the cities.'

90. Salvemini in *Critica Sociale*, 24 October 1953, quoting a report of Zanotti-Bianco about the hygienic conditions in Italian schools in the South.

91. Salvemini in *Il Ponte*, referring to hundreds of similar cases of giving shelter to 'enemy aliens.' The old woman did not know where Croatia was or that it had been an enemy country. Her defence was that her prisoner, too, was *'un figlio di mamma'*—some mother's son.

92. Salvemini in *Il Ponte*, January 1955.

93. *I miracoli del Kodak* (the camera's miracles), describing various alleged miracles recorded by photographs, including one of the occasion, in the election year of 1948, when hundreds of pilgrims saw the Madonna of the Basilica of Assisi nodding her head.

94. From Roberto Bolaffio's unpublished account of Salvemini's last days. Carte Bolaffio.

95. Umberto Morra, in speaking to me, has fully confirmed the Bolaffios' opinion about the correctness of Don Rosario's behaviour. His attitude, Morra said, was 'rather that of a devoted disci-

ple than that of a priest, always seeking for advice, rather than imparting instructions.'

96. From Don Rosario's *Recollections of the Death of Professor Gaetano Salvemini*.

97. Quoted by Roberto Bolaffio in his account of Salvemini's last days. Carte Bolaffio.

98. Will of Gaetano Salvemini in his own writing, Sorrento, 4 March 1957. Printed in *Scritti Vari*, p. 960.

99. From Don Rosario's *Recollections*.

100. Ernesto Rossi, *Salvemini il non-conformista*, p. 23.

101. From Don Rosario, *Recollections*.

102. Salvemini to Bernard Berenson, 5 September 1957. Archives of I Tatti.

v. *Ignazio Silone*

Books by Ignazio Silone referred to in the text, with English titles where there has been an English language edition even if now out of print. Italian editions published by Mondadori unless otherwise stated (see note 61):

Fontamara (Fontamara)
Il Seme Sotto la Neve (The Seed Beneath the Snow)
Una Manciata di More (A Handful of Blackberries)
Vino e Pane (Wine and Bread): a revised version of *Pane e Vino*
La Volpe e le Camelie (The Fox and the Camellias)
La Scuola dei Dittatori (The School for Dictators)
Uscita di Sicurezza (Emergency Exit) Longanesi 1965
Il Segreto di Luca (The Secret of Luca)
L'Avventura d'un Povero Cristiano (The Story of a Humble Christian)
Memoriale dal Carcere Svizzero, pub. Lerici, 1979
Severina (a cura di Darina Silone)

English and American editions in print:

Fontamara: New American Library, Journeyman Press and Manchester University Press
Wine and Bread: New American Library and (extract) Easy Readers edn. John Murray

1. The words are Silone's own, in an interview given to the Paris *Express*, 23 January 1961.

2. *Uscita di Sicurezza*, pocket ed., Longanesi, 1971, p. 62. This book incorporates many of Silone's other essays. The one which gives it its title first appeared in the periodical *Comunità* (1949) and was then translated into English. It was published in *The God That Failed* together with essays by Koestler, Gide, Stephen Spender and others.

3. *Fontamara*, ed. Mondadori, 1974, pp. 7–8.

4. Ibid, p. 29.

5. *Visita al Carcere*, incorporated into *Uscita di Sicurezza*, op. cit. p. 3.

6. *L'Avventura di un Povero Cristiano*, Mondadori, 1976, p. 32.

7. *Fontamara*, op. cit. p. 157–8.

8. Ibid, pp. 156–7.

9. *Vino e Pane*, Mondadori, 1979, the revised version of *Pane e Vino*, pp. 378–80.

10. *Il Seme Sotto la Neve*, Mondadori, 1977, p. 269.

11. *L'Avventura di un Povero Cristiano*, op. cit. pp. 19–20.

12. Ibid, pp. 16–17.

13. *Uscita di Sicurezza*, op. cit. pp. 63–4.

14. Ibid, pp. 79–80.

15. From an interview in a newspaper.

16. *Il Seme Sotto la Neve*, op. cit. p. 325.

17. 'Incontro con uno Strano Prete,' in *Uscita di Sicurezza*, op. cit. p. 76.

18. Ibid, pp. 29–30.

19. Ibid, pp. 24–9.

20. Ibid, pp. 29–40.

21. 'Polikusc'ka' in *Uscita di Sicurezza*, op. cit. p. 48.

22. *Fontamara*, op. cit. p. 43.

23. Ibid, p. 6.

24. *Uscita di Sicurezza*, op. cit. p. 72.

25. 'La Pena del Ritorno' in *Uscita di Sicurezza*, op. cit. p. 180.

26. *Pane e Vino*, op. cit. p. 79.

27. *Fontamara*, op. cit. p. 4.

28. *L'Avventura di un Povero Cristiano*, op. cit. p. 11.

29. Ibid, p. 18.

30. Ibid, pp. 34–5.

31. *Il Seme Sotto la Neve,* op. cit. p. 176.

32. Francis Thompson, *The Hound of Heaven.*

33. 'La Scelta dei Compagni' in *Uscita di Sicurezza,* op. cit. pp. 141–3.

34. *Uscita di Sicurezza,* op. cit. pp. 82–3.

35. Ibid, pp. 93–4.

36. Ibid, p. 100.

37. Ibid, pp. 111 and 113.

38. 'La Lezione di Budapest' in *Uscita di Sicurezza,* op. cit. pp. 165–6.

39. *Uscita di Sicurezza,* op. cit. p. 115.

40. Ibid, p. 114.

41. Ibid, pp. 116–17.

42. Darina Silone, *Primo Incontro con Ignazio Silone.* Printed here by kind permission of Darina Silone who owns the copyright.

43. *Uscita di Sicurezza,* op. cit. p. 125.

44. *Memoriale dal Carcere Svizzero,* only published after Silone's death by Lamberto Mercuri, on behalf of the 'Italian Federation of Partisans' Association' (partly summarised) pp. 4–36. Silone's Memoriale is signed with his real name: Secondo Tranquilli.

45. *Uscita di Sicurezza,* op. cit. p. 123.

46. Ibid, p. 112.

47. Unpublished letter from Silone to Salvemini, 2 November 1937.

48. Salvemini to Mr Aswell, 7 December (1936 or 1937).

49. *Fontamara,* op. cit. pp. 4–6.

50. Ibid, p. 76.

51. Ibid. p. 9.

52. Ibid, pp. 12–14.

53. Ibid, p. 226.

54. 'La Scelta dei Compagni' in *Uscita di Sicurezza,* pp. 136–7 and 146.

55. This letter, translated into Italian by Silone and quoted 'La Scelta dei Compagni' in *Uscita di Sicurezza,* op. cit. pp. 147–8, is here quoted in the English translation by Richard Leas in *Seventy Letters* (O.U.P.).

56. Simone Weil in *La Pesanteur et la Grâce,* quoted by Silone in *Uscita di Sicurezza,* op. cit. p. 148.

57. 'La Scelta dei Compagni' in *Uscita di Sicurezza*, op. cit. pp. 149 and 151.

58. Simone Weil, *Lettres à Père Perrin*.

59. *Uscita di Sicurezza*, op. cit. pp. 128–9.

60. Ibid, p. 173.

61. Silone's first books, *Fontamara* (1933), *Pane e Vino* (1936), *La Scuola dei Dittatori* (1938) and *Il Seme Sotto la Neve* (1941), were all first published in Zürich in German. The first edition of *Fontamara* in Italian appeared in Paris in 1934, and then in England and almost every European country, as well as in America, Japan and Africa, but was not published in Italy until 1949 (ed. Mondadori). *Pane e Vino* was also translated and published in almost every European country, but only appeared in Italy in a much revised edition, entitled *Vino e Pane*, in 1955. *Il Seme Sotto la Neve* only reached Italy in 1950 and *La Scuola dei Dittatori* not until 1962. The first of Silone's books to be published in Italian was *Una Manciata di More* (1952) (which he particularly liked, perhaps for this reason). It was followed by his other novels: *Il Segreto di Luca* (1956), *La Volpe e le Camelie* (1960), and then by his autobiographical essay, *Uscita di Sicurezza*. This incorporated many of his earlier essays (The Lesson of Budapest, The Sadness of Going Back, The Choice of Comrades, The Situation of Former Communists, among the most important) (Longanesi, 1965). *The Situation of Former Communists* is the Italian edition, previously unpublished, of a lecture by the author in German, held in Zürich in 1942, before an audience consisting mostly of German former Communists. 'The Lesson of Budapest' is the Italian version of an article in the Paris *Express* of 7 December 1956, previously unpublished in Italy.

62. Guido Piovene, in an article in *La Fiera Letteraria*, 4 August 1954.

63. *Uscita di Sicurezza*, op. cit. p. 62.

64. Geno Pampaloni, in a review entitled 'L'Opera Narrativa di Ignazio Silone.'

65. Geno Pampaloni, in an article entitled *Parabola di un Dissenso*, written after Silone's death and published in *Il Giornale*, 24 August 1978.

66. From an interview with Silone entitled 'Confiteor' in *La Fiera Letteraria*, 31 March 1956.

67. *L'Avventura di un Povero Cristiano*, op. cit. p. 27.

68. Ibid, p. 28.

69. From Silone's historical notes in the Appendix to *L'Avventura di un Povero Cristiano*, p. 257. The chronicler was Stefaneschi.

70. From Silone's Preface to the fourteenth volume of the Touring Club Italiano, *L'Abruzzo e Molise*, p. 10.

71. In his historical notes, Silone says that the evidence about 'this assassination' is very uncertain. Certainly his own followers believed in it, and ancient frescoes (one in the Abbey of S. Spirito in Sulmona, and one in a fresco of an Abruzzese painter of the fourteenth century in the Hermitage of S. Onofrio) show him with the martyr's palm. *L'Avventura di un Povero Cristiano*, op. cit. p. 260.

72. In another of these notes, Silone says that this formula for abdication, which is still valid, was written for Celestino by Cardinal Caetani. Two centuries later, Pope Gregory XII also made use of it. Many of Dante's commentators have tried to explain away the phrase about cowardice, some of them claiming that Dante's accusation was directed against someone else, probably a contemporary of Dante. Others have made such varied suggestions as Esau (who gave away his birthright), Pilate, Diocletian and Julian the Apostate. Petrarch, in his treatise *De Vita Solitaria*, accepts without question that Celestino was intended, but maintains that his gesture was 'more useful than any other both to himself and to the world . . . I consider his work to be that of a very high and free spirit which did not admit orders, a spirit truly divine.' *L'Avventura di un Povero Cristiano*, op. cit. pp. 269–71.

73. Ibid, p. 249.

74. Silone considers the legend as purely 'grotesque,' and makes no use of it in his drama.

75. *L'Avventura di un Povero Cristiano*, op. cit. p. 114.

76. Ibid, p. 199.

77. Ibid, pp. 29–30.

78. Ibid, pp. 202–3.

79. *L'Abruzzo e Molise*, op. cit. pp. 9–10.

80. Father Alessandro Scurani, S.J., in his *Ignazio Silone un amore religioso per la giustizia*, pp. 105–6. In this essay he published, with Silone's permission, his speech at San Fedele.

81. *L'Abruzzo e Molise*, op. cit. pp. 8–9.

82. Monsignor Domenico Grasso, S.J., reviewing *L'Avven-*

tura di un Povero Cristiano, in *Civiltà Cattolica*, 1 June 1965, pp. 464–5.

83. *Una Manciata di More*, Mondadori, 1977, p. 80.

84. Ibid, p. 136.

85. Ibid, p. 95.

86. I owe most of this summary to Geno Pampaloni.

87. Geno Pampaloni, 'Silone Romantico' in *L'Espresso*, 17 March 1952.

88. *Tempo Presente*, March–April 1966, pp. 13–16.

89. Article by Silone in *La Fiera Letteraria* of 22 June 1963, entitled 'Consistenza politica e confronto delle idee,' originally a speech of his at a meeting of The Italian Union for the Progress of Culture.

90. *La Scuola dei Dittatori*, Mondadori, 1978, p. XVI.

91. Ibid, pp. 55–6.

92. Silone, *Severina*, a cura di Darina Silone. Mondadori, September 1981, with a preface by Geno Pampaloni. The name that Silone first gave to Severina was Chiarina, but he changed it when his wife pointed out that no foreigner would be able to pronounce it.

93. Darina Silone, 'History of a Manuscript,' in *Severina*, p. 142.

94. *Severina*, op. cit. pp. 167–82.

95. Ibid, pp. 174–5.

96. Ibid, pp. 163–4.

97. Ibid, p. 187.

98. Silone, *Ai piedi di un mandorlo*. Printed on pp. 191–4 of *Severina*, but originally published in a limited edition, not on the market, by Giuseppe de Luca, as a presentation copy for Silone's seventieth birthday.

99. 'La Scelta dei Compagni' in *Uscita di Sicurezza*, op. cit. pp. 151–2.

Index